Collaboration for the Promotion of Nursing

Collaboration for the Promotion of Nursing

Building Partnerships for the Future

by

LeAlice Briggs, RN, EdD

Sonna Ehrlich Merk, RN, DNS

Barbara Mitchell, RN, MSN, MS

Sigma Theta Tau International
Honor Society of Nursing

Sigma Theta Tau International

Publishing Director: Jeff Burnham
Book Acquisitions Editor: Fay L. Bower, DNSc, FAAN
Graphics Designer: Jason Reuss
Proofreader: Linda Canter

Printed in the United States of America
Composition by Graphic World
Printing and Binding by Edwards Brothers
Cover art by Getty Images, Inc.

Sigma Theta Tau International
550 West North Street
Indianapolis, IN 46202

Visit our Web site at www.nursingsociety.org for more information on our books and other publications.

ISBN: 1-930538-09-X

Library of Congress Cataloging-in-Publication Data

Briggs, LeAlice.
  Collaboration for the promotion of nursing / by LeAlice Briggs, Sonna Ehrlich Merk, Barbara Mitchell.
    p. ; cm.
Includes bibliographical references.
  ISBN 1-930538-09-X (alk. paper)
  1. Nursing. 2. Nursing services. 3. Nursing models.
  [DNLM: 1. Nursing 2000 (Organization) 2. Nursing—organization & administration—Indiana. 3. Community Networks—Indiana. 4. Marketing of Health Services—methods—Indiana. 5. Models, Organizational—Indiana. 6. Organizational Case Studies—Indiana. WY 16 B854c 2003] I. Merk, Sonna Ehrlich. II. Mitchell, Barbara, RN. III. Title.
  RT86.7.B755 2003
  610.73—dc21   2003004528

03 04 05/ 9 8 7 6 5 4 3 2 1

Dedication

To our founders for their vision and
to our volunteers for making that vision a reality

ABOUT THE AUTHORS

LeAlice Briggs, RN, MSN, EdD

LeAlice is dean and professor emerita at the University of Indianapolis. LeAlice provided leadership to the faculty and staff of the School of Nursing for 18 years. In retirement she has served as interim chair of the Department of Nursing, Presentation College, Aberdeen, South Dakota. She is a charter member of Lambda Epsilon and Rho Xi, Sigma Theta Tau International and has served on the board of review for the National League for Nursing Associate Degree Council, the board of directors for Indiana League for Nursing, and Nursing 2000. She currently serves on a part-time basis as the off-campus program coordinator in the School for Adult Learning at the University of Indianapolis. She has been recognized for her commitment to nursing scholarship and mentorship.

Sonna Ehrlich Merk, RN, DNS

Sonna has over 24-years' experience in executive nursing administration at Clarian Health Partners. As senior vice president for nursing and patient care services and chief nurse executive, she led the merger of two large hospital nursing and patient care delivery systems, Indiana University Medical Center and Methodist Hospital. Sonna was responsible for strategic planning and clinical and administrative management for nursing and patient care services. In addition, she served as associate dean for practice, Indiana University School of Nursing. She was co-project director for funded research Strengthening Hospital Nursing: A Program to Improve Patient Care and for Capstone: A Partnership Model of Preceptor Teaching, Innovation Promotion, and Excellence in the Education of Registered Professional Nurses. She is a member of Alpha Chapter, Sigma Theta Tau International. She served as president of the Central Indiana Organization of Nurse Executives, was on the board of the Indiana Organization of Nurse Executives, and on the executive board of Nursing 2000. Sonna completed the Wharton Fellowship program in Management for Nurses and has been recognized for her leadership.

Barbara Mitchell, RN, MSN, MS

Barbara is executive director of Nursing 2000, a central Indiana not-for-profit organization committed to promoting and developing professional nursing careers through nursing service and nursing education collaboration. She manages the operations of the organization including program development, fiscal management, marketing, and communications and directs the volunteer effort in the community. Barbara is responsible for implementation of the organization's strategic plan and served as project manager for replication of the Nursing 2000 model in another region in Indiana. She is a frequent presenter on career decision making and strategies to develop future nursing resources. She is a member of Alpha Chapter, Sigma Theta Tau International and serves on the board of the Central Indiana Organization of Nurse Executives, on the executive advisory board of *NurseWeek*, and on the executive board of Nursing 2000 North Central, Inc.

CONTENTS

Appendices

CONTRIBUTING AUTHORS (CHAPTER 7)

Donna L. Boland, RN, PhD

Donna is associate professor and associate dean for undergraduate programs at Indiana University School of Nursing. Donna consults in the areas of curriculum design and evaluation and in outcome assessment of student learning. She is a presenter at national nursing higher education conferences on faculty evaluation, curriculum and teaching evaluation approaches, and assessment. Donna publishes on issues related to curriculum and program outcomes. She has served as president of Gamma Rho Chapter, Sigma Theta Tau International and on the NLN Council of Baccalaureate and High Degree's Accreditation. Currently she serves as a board member on the Commission on Collegiate Nursing Education. She has been recognized for academic education excellence and leadership.

Pamela Worrell-Carlisle, RN, PhD

Pamela is an educational psychologist early childhood educator and registered nurse. She has extensive experience in recruiting qualified candidates into nursing education as well as working with at-risk college freshmen. Pamela has been involved in curricula and program evaluation both within the university and in community education. She is currently a faculty member with the Department of Teacher Education at the University of Indianapolis.

FOREWORD

Welcome Reader, and be prepared to be delighted! A new era is upon us, one that fosters community, collaboration and expansion of what is possible. Gone is the dark night of competition and control, of divide and conquer. And there is no better example of this enlarging spirit of generosity than Nursing 2000 and the people who give it life and definition.

As you navigate this book you will be treated to the story of Nursing 2000, including examples, models and outcomes that will both inform and enhance your understanding of the complexity of nursing. You will remember why you responded to a call to the discipline when other choices may have been made. In its pages you will experience a creative dance between education and service, between industry and the people being served, between rural and urban areas of a state that has been a dynamic fulcrum for nursing innovation through the years.

Why has such an outcome been achieved in Indiana? Its history is laced with many examples of creativity and collaboration, including the birthing of Sigma Theta Tau, the International Honor Society for Nursing. Intentional partnerships are no stranger to this group of Midwestern pioneers. Approaching the landscape with an "anything is possible" mindset while applying sustained effort towards building and nourishing relationships, its nurses have birthed things others only dream of.

This book is a study of dynamic collaboration; partnership with soul. "Winning partnerships have a purpose, and the partners know it. You have to know your partner's main business challenges, how your partner's success is measured, and what your partner's hopes and dreams are. Meshed with your own, these form the basis of a purposeful partnership, not just a transaction. (Bell & Shea, 1998, p. 91)" Nursing 2000 built its programs as a result of authentic dialogue with area stakeholders: hospitals, schools, governmental agencies, community centers. They listened with a compassionate heart and were astute in "hearing" what the healthcare needs entailed. Such openness and sincere intent brings candor and clarity to the conversation while building trust that sustains such a connection over time.

This book is an expression of generosity. It is a demonstration of the power of noncompetitive relationships where everyone becomes more from the synergy such a context creates. The lessons learned are unconditionally offered, not because the nurse inventors and social scientists involved want something, but simply because it is their nature to "give something back." They are sharing insights with colleagues, hoping that it will seed further work, causing the profession to grow and prosper. This offering creates a legacy of affirmation within a profession that has had difficulty connecting in times past. This book offers a vision of hope and action for nursing along with health and well-being for society.

Finally, this manuscript is a demonstration of nursing "coming of age." As a society we have come to a very special place: the world of the unknown laced with the world of possibility. Out of this void of the unknown will emerge what is really valued by the profession. As a discipline we have endured many challenges to demonstrate our "legitimacy" within the circle of healers in contemporary Western medical terms. We are now moving on the most promising age of all: the age of "authenticity." No longer limited by "conventional" labels and tasks, we are claiming our unique role in offering our guidance and support to a public that is taking a more self-determined stance in the management of its own health journey. As we become increasingly healthy as a group, our role as a guide for others gains legitimacy. The new frontier holds a wonderful partnership dance between people and nurses sharing a journey towards wholeness. And this book is a beacon to lead the way from merely sustained existence to a professional state of vibrancy and life!

"Life is occupied both in perpetuating itself and in surpassing itself; if all it does is maintain itself, then living is only not dying."
—Simone de Beauvoir

JoEllen Goertz Koerner, RN, PhD, FAAN
Sioux Falls, South Dakota

Reference

Bell, C.R., & Shea, H. (1998). Dance lessons: Six steps to great partnerships in business and life. San Francisco: Berrett-Koehler Publishers, Inc.

ACKNOWLEDGMENTS

This book is the story of the development of Nursing 2000 and of the many dedicated volunteers who contributed their expertise and time to Nursing 2000 before it became an entity 13 years ago and during each year it has existed. We thank all the Nursing 2000 volunteers for their service in the past, present, and future. In addition, we are forever indebted to our founders:

- the nurse leaders from service and education who worked at a grass roots level to develop the mission and begin the work of the organization
- the nurse executives and college/university deans and directors who provided the vision to establish the organization and the courage to seek initial funding
- and the chief executive officers of the original member institutions who extended financial support and embraced the long-range goals of Nursing 2000.

We are grateful for the support and encouragement to share, via publication, the emergence of Nursing 2000 during the nursing shortage of the late eighties and early nineties, and the effort to "be in place" and responsive during the new millennium. We thank each executive board member of Nursing 2000 who has been steadfast in holding true to Nursing 2000's mission and vision. We thank members of the advisory board who, through their commitment, have provided the vitality continuously pumped into the programs and the evaluation that has kept the programs strong and relevant. We are thankful for the Helene Fuld Trust grant that supported the replication of the Nursing 2000 model in north central Indiana. A special thanks is extended to the nursing leadership in north central Indiana for their fantastic spirit of camaraderie and for stimulating the need for the book.

We are appreciative of the middle and high school counselors, teachers, students, and parents; non-traditional students; student nurses; and mobility nurses who are consumers of our programs. Their participation is the impetus for Nursing 2000, and their feedback has contributed to the viability of the programs. We are grateful to Nursing 2000 staff members who through the years have carried out their designated responsibilities and, in addition, assumed volunteer roles to assist in meeting the goals of the organization.

A special thanks is conveyed to Lisa Mount for her dedication, time, and indispensable expertise in helping to prepare the manuscript. To our volunteers who willingly gave their time in providing chapter reviews, we ardently state our thanks for your contribution in the development of this book. We gratefully acknowledge the encouragement and professionalism of Dr. Jane Root and Jeff Burnham. For her editing, guidance, and enthusiasm, our sincere thanks are expressed to Dr. Fay Bower. Finally, our utmost appreciation is extended to Dr. JoEllen Koerner for writing a generous and sensitive foreword that captures the richness of Nursing 2000.

INTRODUCTION

Historically nursing has valued the importance and usefulness of collaboration, yet it has been more a discussion than a reality until Nursing 2000, Inc. was formed. This book is the first of its kind. It is a description of a successful model of collaboration between nursing service and nursing education and among nursing organizations, all with the same goal in mind, to promote nursing. While nursing organizations have, in recent years, begun working together for specific reasons and nursing service and nursing education have planned ways to provide clinical education for nursing students for many years, Nursing 2000, Inc. moves collaboration to a broader spectrum with more advanced and global goals. These goals and the strategies for meeting them by Nursing 2000, Inc. are thoroughly described in this book.

This book has ten chapters. In the first chapter the reader is introduced to the organization. It includes a detailed history as to how a group of nurses from service and education came together as volunteers to promote nursing. The initial goal was to increase the number of nurses in the workforce. Organizing, funding, staffing, and the mission and goals are discussed to present an overview of the organization. The chapters that follow present the parts that when put together or used as a model form a *collaborative*.

Chapter 2 contains a discussion of the assessment of external and internal environments and the importance of this process being in place as a *collaborative* works to form an organization. Strategic planning, strategic management, and a systematic approach to assessment are presented as a basic process for successful formation. Determinants used for assessment are listed and discussed.

In Chapter 3 there is a description of each part of the Nursing 2000 model used to form a *collaborative*. The formation of a mission statement and goals as the first step in organizing is presented. The establishment of a funding base, the writing of bylaws, leadership, staffing, and the work of volunteers are described. Housing, services, and equipment needed are discussed. The process that takes place in organizing is woven through the chapter. The model can be used by any size *collaborative* with varying levels of resources to form an organization.

In Chapters 4, 5, and 6, programs are presented to meet goals and carry out the mission of the organization. Procedures for each individual program are given in detail. Announcements, letters, budgets, scripts, evaluation forms, and other items needed for a program are included and may be used as a sample or adjusted for use.

Chapter 7 contains a description of research that has been completed to determine the impact the Nursing 2000 model has had on the promotion of nursing. Research-based evaluation is demonstrated through the use of accumulated evaluation data and surveys of high school participants and student nurses. Results of the research and a comparison to national studies are included.

In Chapter 8 the basis for sustainability of the organization is discussed. The factors that support sustainability of the organization are identified. Each factor, as a process, is described and the rationale for its use is presented. Identified items from the assessment of internal and external environments as well as evaluation that support the processes are described.

The chronological growth of Nursing 2000 is presented in Chapter 9. How the organization has expanded its activities to serve a broader area of central Indiana is included. The visibility of the organization and networking, locally, statewide, and nationally, are discussed. The role the organization has taken in the development of workforce initiatives in Indiana and outcomes of the effort are presented.

Chapter 10 contains a summary of how the model has been developed, what lessons were learned, the strengths of collaboration and the positive outcomes of nurses from service and education working together to promote nursing. The key to success of the organization is shared. Information on the funded project—replication of the Nursing 2000 model adapted to regional uniqueness—is shared.

We would like to add a note about the language used in this book. Today there is as much controversy and change regarding the English language as there is with American healthcare institutions. While some dictionaries do not yet list healthcare as a unique word, the readers for whom this book was written use it extensively. For this reason, we use healthcare instead of health care because the single word best fits the massive change experienced by American health institutions and because literary acknowledgment often follows popular use of a word.

The purpose of writing this book is to offer a model of collaboration of professionals in other regions, with goals similar to those of Nursing 2000, and the opportunity to use procedures that have been developed and effectively implemented over a 12-year period of time. The evaluation process used with each program procedure has brought about revision and refinement as needed. Use of the book will assist an informal group to efficiently organize and to begin to use the program procedures to meet its own goals. Pertinent information is presented that describes details of the organization and the human involvement of dedicated individuals. A book that outlines only procedures would not adequately describe the human investment necessary to create a collaborative organization. The outcome of the use of information provided is the establishment of an effective organization that has been formed in a relatively brief period of time because of clearly stated goals and proven procedures.

1

GETTING STARTED: DEVELOPING A WORKING ALLIANCE

Introduction

Collaboration! What does it mean? It is a word used frequently. Collaboration is people listening and talking to one another. Collaboration is a productive interchange that takes place within a group where several individuals address mutually shared issues. As a result of collaboration, a solution is often the outcome. Nursing 2000 is an example of a collaboration. Nursing 2000 was incorporated in 1990 as a not-for-profit organization. It is a collaborative effort between nursing service and nursing education. It serves an eight-county region of central Indiana. Indianapolis/Marion County is the pivotal center of the region.

Organization and Functions of Nursing 2000

A seven-member board of directors provides direction and vision for the organization. The board includes a chief executive officer and six nurses from the supporting healthcare systems and schools of nursing. A 25-member advisory board, with representatives from affiliated healthcare agencies, schools of nursing, and professional nursing associations, initiates and evaluates programs. The Nursing 2000 volunteers, who are supported by an office staff that consists of the executive director, a part-time program facilitator, an administrative assistant, and a part-time staff assistant, implement specific programs in the community. The staff works together to lead and coordinate more than 200 volunteers in program implementation in central Indiana.

Nursing leaders working to develop an alliance.

The foundation of the organization is the Forum, which is composed of the nurse executives of supporting healthcare systems and the deans/directors of the member schools of nursing, often referred to as the Vice Presidents/Directors and Deans/Directors Forum. This visionary group of individuals meets quarterly to reflect on the mission of the organization, and to determine how the programs of the organization support the mission. It is this collaborative group, representing nursing service and nursing education, that works together to be proactive and to anticipate what the organization can do within the framework of the mission to contribute to the health of individuals within the area by promoting nursing. They are representatives of the professional leadership in the eight-county area the organization serves. This group of leaders understands current trends in the delivery of healthcare and the effects of the changing environment. Together they collaborate to determine how the organization should respond.

The bylaws designate the composition of the board of directors, the advisory board, and the Forum. The members of the Forum serve as members of the board of directors of the organization. By rotating service to the board, each person (nurse executive or dean/director) of the Forum serves on the board at some time. The composition of the board, Forum, and advisory groups reflects the ongoing collaboration of nursing service and nursing education. The functions of the board of directors and advisory board are extensively discussed in Chapter 3 in the section labeled funding and governance.

Mission and Goals

The current mission of the organization is to promote and support the development of careers in registered nursing as a concerted effort to positively impact future healthcare resources. The first mission of the organization was to promote careers in registered nursing to secure an adequate number of nurses in the eight-county area. This original mission statement has been expanded to support the organization, as it has become multi-focused in the promotion and support of registered nursing careers. The organization is a catalyst to more broadly unite nursing service and nursing education to address issues related to workforce development, including image, recruitment, educational access, financial assistance, and quality of work life. Each program presented reflects the mission of Nursing 2000 and is evaluated accordingly.

The goals of Nursing 2000 are:

- Disseminate information about registered nursing as a dynamic profession to elementary school, middle school, and high school students; adult learners; and career mobile nurses;
- Support nurses in educational career mobility to advance nursing practice;
- Impact the education of nurses through collaboration between nursing service and nursing education;
- Recruit a diverse student body reflective of the regional population;
- Attract students into nursing who have demonstrated those potential academic abilities that will lead to a successful career in professional nursing; and
- Reflect a positive image of nursing to the public.

The goals have been met annually through programs based on current educational nursing principles, statistical data from professional and governmental organizations, and trends in healthcare delivery. The vehicle/

The mission of Nursing 2000 is to promote caring in registered nursing.

method of offering these programs to the region has been through presentations, video production, individual career counseling, circulation of printed materials and posters, and the Internet. The programs are assessed using a systematic method of evaluation.

The organization moves forward because of the vision and insight of its leadership. They are sensitive to the needs that prevail in the delivery of care in the eight-county area and have a keen understanding of the current healthcare trends. However, ultimately the success of Nursing 2000 is dependent on the active involvement of all groups within the organization. During orientation of volunteers, special emphasis is placed on the importance of each person's participation and working with others to meet the mission and goals of the organization. The contribution of each volunteer is recognized as supporting the goals of the organization. Without volunteers, the organization could not survive.

Functions of Volunteers

Volunteers are staff nurses, nurse managers, staff development educators, and nursing faculty who have actively participated in the formation and ongoing work of the organization. In the beginning of this joint effort, while carrying an extremely heavy workload because of manpower shortages, they participated on their own time by presenting programs that promoted nursing. As time permitted, they met in groups to discuss how an organization could best serve the community. This dialog enhanced everyone's understanding. Those in healthcare settings believed by organizing a systematic approach to promoting nursing as a profession, they would realize better staffing and a higher caliber of patient care. Nursing faculty, on the other hand, saw a way to increase interest in nursing as a career and ultimately enrollment in nursing programs. Through the collaboration of those from nursing service and nursing education, the volunteer group better understood each other's work goals and what each could bring to the effort.

Membership

The eight-county region served by Nursing 2000 includes those counties sharing boundaries with Indianapolis/Marion County. Each county has acute care facilities/hospitals that serve the area. The schools of nursing holding membership in the organization recruit and serve students in the area, as well as support the goals of Nursing 2000. Originally membership in the organization was held by the major hospitals within Indianapolis/Marion County, and programs were offered in the membership area only. As needs emerged in the healthcare industry and individuals desired information about nursing education in the extended central Indiana area, the nursing leaders of the hospitals in the surrounding counties came forward to participate in the organization. It was their belief a joint effort to promote nursing was much more successful than attempting to recruit and promote nursing alone. Expansion of the organization was a gradual process. As these health facilities became a part of the organization, the opportunity for collaboration between nursing service and nursing education expanded.

Nursing 2000 is an outgrowth of the work of a group of individuals representing their institutions (hospitals and schools of nursing) who came together to address the nursing shortage of the 1980s. When the group had formally served its purpose, the Indianapolis/Marion County members continued to work together to promote nursing and to recruit students. It was entirely a voluntary group with in-kind support from the members' institutions, such as providing a meeting place, fostering release time to participate, supplying paper, and printing handouts to be used by the volunteers when they were invited to present information on nursing as a career. The activities of this group of individuals, representing nursing service and nursing education, reflected the spirit of collaboration.

During the interval before an incorporated organization was formed, the focus of the group broadened and the size of the group expanded. This came about because of the insight and vision of members of the group and the great increase in requests for presentations. Interactions of individuals in the group supported and increased the collaboration between nursing service and nursing education, which continues today as the greatest strength of Nursing 2000. Nursing 2000 members were visionary and saw that through this group an opportunity was available for expansion of recruitment efforts to include, in addition to traditional students, recruitment of mature adults with academic ability and life experiences that potentially could lead to success in a nursing program. They also expanded their efforts by promoting educational mobility for nurses already in the workplace who might want to advance their role.

The number of participants in the group remained stable, with individuals moving in and out as work responsibilities influenced their participation. Other nurses, staff, and faculty joined the group to participate in the presentation of programs. Members of elementary, middle, and high schools, as well as civic groups, began requesting programs on nursing as a career, and representation at educational fairs increased.

Informally the deans/directors of schools of nursing and the vice presidents/directors of nursing services of the institutions represented by volunteer committee members came together as a committee to support the effort, to give direction to the group, and to financially support various activities. It is noted that some deans/directors and vice presidents/directors were members of the original group. It was from this group that the committees became a working alliance. Through the efforts of this alliance, the persistent need to determine how to form a formal organization and ongoing funding was identified.

In 1989, planning for the formation of a formal organization was initiated by the alliance. A nucleus of staff representatives and heads of schools of nursing and nursing service of major hospitals within Indianapolis/Marion County formed the group that laid the groundwork for the organization that would become Nursing 2000. Benefits of collaboration between nursing education and nursing service prevail today as the organization fulfills its mission.

It was the nursing service vice presidents who approached their chief executive officers for a commitment of $30,000 per each institution to fund the organization on an annual basis. This commitment formed the financial sustainability of Nursing 2000. The planning group carefully identified short and long-term goals that gave direction to the organizing effort. Legal counsel from one of the supporting hospitals met regularly with the group that formed the organizing board. The attorney helped the members operate within parameters that prepared for incorporation. It was at this state of planning that the first professional staff and administrative assistant were employed to provide leadership, organize the work to be done, and direct volunteer efforts. Work accomplished by members of the alliance made incorporation a reality. The organization was then formally named Nursing 2000. The name would indicate that the organization was proactive, anticipatory, and a leader in confronting and solving issues affecting the healthcare industry through the promotion of nursing.

Four of the founding members at the second annual Nursing 2000 Scholarship Benefit.

Change has occurred in the membership. Two member hospitals merged but continue their collective support. A fifth hospital joined as a major funding member. Nine hospitals in the eight-county area and four schools of nursing are now contributing members. One school of nursing has closed and a community college nursing program joined the membership. The by-laws can serve as a resource to any collaborative group interested in forming an organization like Nursing 2000.

The work accomplished each year is totally dependent upon the funding by the membership. The total annual budget today covers physical facilities, staff resources, technology, marketing, all forms of communication, and programming. The current organization funding model based on an RN full-time equivalents (FTE) scale will be addressed in Chapter 3 under organizational operations.

Programming

Growth or expansion of programs is ongoing. The board of directors, in collaboration with the executive director, has annually assessed and determined what number and type of programs are reasonable for staff and volunteers to undertake. Such decisions are made only after the mission of the organization has been reviewed and determination is made that the programs are congruent with it. Frequent review of the mission has kept Nursing 2000 on track and able to expand over time. The importance of maintaining a focus on the mission cannot be understated.

Many factors are considered when determining what programming can be managed as long-term planning occurs. The number of participating volunteers, such as staff nurses, nurse managers, staff development educators, and nursing faculty, has determined what the organization is able to accomplish.

The opportunity for growth has occurred because volunteers have represented the organization effectively, which supports the value of a strong orientation program and the collaboration that takes place among volunteers, staff, advisory board, and board of directors. A timetable illustrated in Table 1 shows an increase in the type and number of programs presented each year, the growth of the organization, and how the mission of the organization has been implemented.

Finally, the importance and value of the collaboration that exists in every aspect of the organization cannot be overemphasized. It is collaboration between the representatives of nursing service and nursing education that has made Nursing 2000 a success. It is collaboration that brought vice presidents/directors and deans/directors together in the Forum. It is collaboration that brought together volunteers from nursing education with volunteers from nursing service to present a program to adult learners. It is collaboration that created networking among members of the advisory board and committees of the organization that helped professionals understand the others' situations and to realize that through collaboration they could influence change together. It is collaboration that improved recruitment of students interested in nursing to nursing schools and then into the workforce. It is collaboration that brought programs to agencies throughout an eight-county area. It is a collaboration that made a few dollars go a long way.

The schematic drawing of the Nursing 2000 model in Figure 1 shows the interrelationship between nursing service and nursing education as the

Table 1. Timetable

Nursing 2000 Summary of Programs Year 1 through Year 11

Programs	Year 1	Year 2	Year 3	Year 4	Year 5	Year 6	Year 7	Year 8	Year 9	Year 10	Year 11
A Day in the Life of a Nurse	2	2	2	2	2	2	2	2	2	2	2
# of students accepted	341	401	469	511	517	501	500	471	470	509	533
Presentations	44	61	66	68	71	53	56	66	87	82	64
Number of attendees	1,195	1,740	1,986	1,864	2,556	1,569	2,328	1,975	2,118	2,785	2,069
Career Days/Displays	13	18	32	35	45	48	40	32	33	38	30
Est # of visitors to event	5,805	6,250	9,683	8,095	7,660	7,191	8,506	8,832	8,229	11,893	8,700
Counselor/Teacher Programs											
Seminars	1	3	2	2	1						
Newsletters, # of issues	0	0	3	3	3	3	3	3	3	3	3
# on mailing list	0	0	379	379	379	379	379	380	380	445	445
Career Resource Development											
Adv. Practice Seminars for RNs					1	2	1	1	1	1	
# of attendees					100	220	70	82	80	61	
State of Healthcare in America							1				
# of attendees							102				
Change and You								2			
# of attendees								197			
Spotlight on Re-entry								2	2	1	1
# of registrants								33	41	33	21
Faculty-Student Professional Relations (co-sponsored with ILN)										1	
# of registrants										45	

RN Focus Meetings											5
# of attendees											43
Cross Generational Effectiveness											1
# of attendees											126
Career counseling calls	384	478	506	351	326	280	278	387	333	432	484
Web site hits									67,000	186,984	306,973
Career videotapes											
# distributed						157*	23	26	6	57	114
Nursing is AMAZING poster											
# distributed									1,200	227	293
Nurses Celebration Saturday								1	1	1	1
# of organizations						10	12	11	11	14	22
Est. # of Museum visitors						4,462	5,600	4,420	3,500	2,234	2,803
Adult Learner Seminar	10	10	12	6	0	0	1	3	6	5	4
# of attendees	209	238	207	51	0	0	4	3	7	18	9
Volunteer Program											
# of Active Members			185	200	211	200	204	201	222	213	203
New Member Orientation			35	22	10	17	13	21	21	15	10
Scholarship Benefit Program											
Scholarships amount	$14,114	$16,000	$13,000	$15,000	$12,000	$16,000	$14,000	$19,000	$23,000	$30,000	$32,000**
# of students	21	22	23	29	25	23	26	26	30	30	25

As of Year 3, all public high schools in the 8-county area have participated in the A Day in the Life of a Nurse shadow program.

* Includes 68 high schools and 54 middle schools; 35 public libraries.

** Reached $204,114 in cumulative proceeds; involved 600 individuals – attendees, recipients, contributors, corporate sponsors

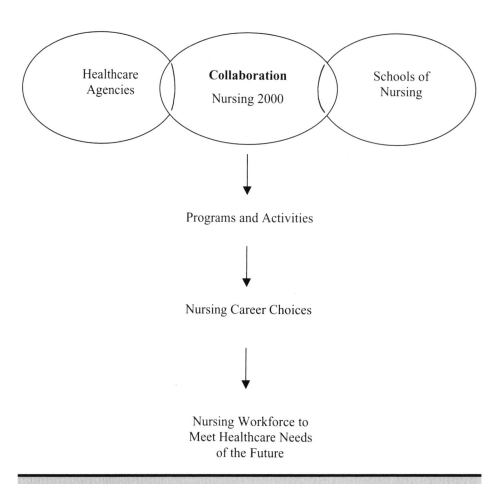

Healthcare
Agencies

Collaboration

Nursing 2000

Schools of
Nursing

Programs and Activities

Nursing Career Choices

Nursing Workforce to
Meet Healthcare Needs
of the Future

Figure 1. The Nursing 2000 Model

basis of Nursing 2000, the *collaborative*. The outcome of the efforts of the *collaborative* is achieved through programs and activities that present nursing career choices that ultimately provide a nursing workforce to meet the healthcare needs of the future.

Collaboration is the essence of the Nursing 2000 model. It is a strategy that was used to resolve a difficult problem encountered in the 1990s. It is a model for other problems or initiatives because it uses the talents of diverse groups with diverse goals that have a natural relationship to solve a problem of greater concern.

This chapter laid the groundwork for the ones to come. It described the model, how it was developed, and why it worked. The history that is the underpinning of the organization has been shared. The next chapter presents a discussion of how an assessment of the external and internal environments can serve as an indicator of the potential strengths and weaknesses of the *collaborative*.

2

ASSESSING THE EXTERNAL AND INTERNAL ENVIRONMENTS

Introduction

Strategic planning provides a set of processes used in many organizations to understand the environment in which an organization is positioned so decision-making guidelines can be developed. Furthermore, it is an effort to achieve a productive and creative fit between the organization's external environment and its internal situation (Duncan, Ginter, & Swayne, 1996). Nursing 2000 has conducted three strategic planning sessions during its 12-year existence to provide future-oriented direction for the organization and responsiveness to the community it serves. The outcomes achieved by the organization are evaluated according to its strategic goals.

Strategic management (Duncan, Ginter, & Swayne, 1996) is essential for a new *collaborative* to pursue in order to determine if the organization's mission and goals are to be met and if the organization is evolving in a productive direction. Four strategic management processes that can be used include:

- Situational analysis
- Strategy formulation
- Strategic implementation
- Strategic control

Strategic management requires the development of an understanding of the forces in the current external and internal environments, formulation of a future-oriented plan, implementation of the programs to meet the plan, and evaluation of the success of the strategies (Duncan, Ginter, & Swayne, 1996).

Situational Analysis

In order to assess the situation, Nursing 2000 implemented focus group sessions. Focus group sessions were held to allow ample opportunity for participation throughout the organization and the community. Participants were invited from the affiliated hospitals and schools of nursing, board of directors, advisory board, volunteer speakers' bureau, community schools, school counselor organizations, nursing organizations, American Association of Retired Persons, home care, and long-term care. Nursing students who were previous Nursing 2000 program participants and current nursing students were also invited to participate. A non-inclusive example of materials, provided prior to the meeting, included the organization's mission, goals, and objectives; program evaluative data; position statements from national nursing and healthcare organizations; school of nursing enrollments and graduation data; and population demographics. The focus group discussions were structured based on a systematic approach in evaluation of program effectiveness and future-oriented (strategic) direction.

Program logic model

A program logic model (W. K. Kellogg Foundation, 2000) was used to illustrate how the work of Nursing 2000 is accomplished and how its program parts are connected. By discussing component relationships within the organization, an examination of resources, activities, and desired results was conducted.

- Resources include the human, financial, organizational, and community resources available to accomplish work. At Nursing 2000, it is a challenge to expand volunteer and staff resources to maintain current programs while simultaneously launching new programs.
- Program activities are the interventions required to achieve program outcomes. It is essential to establish methods for data collection, participant tracking, and program evaluation before the activity is implemented. This has been essential to Nursing 2000's success in reporting to program stakeholders.
- Outputs are the direct products of program implementation and include types, levels, and targets of services to be delivered. Nursing 2000 activities span many age ranges and population groups, such as students, parents, counselors, registered nurses, and consumers.

- Outcomes are the desired changes in target populations based upon a pre-determined time frame of one to six years. Evaluation data in some programs cannot be collected until one to three years after participation. An example is the A Day in the Life of a Nurse shadow program for grades 10 through 12. Participants are not surveyed until they have graduated from high school.
- Impact is a desired or unanticipated change occurring in an organization as a result of program activities within seven to 10 years. In the central Indiana area, a positive impact on nursing school enrollments was observed (reflecting a six-year program investment) at a time when the national enrollment average experienced a decline (American Association of Colleges of Nursing, 1999; W. K. Kellogg Foundation, 2000).

The logic model can be utilized through the life of the program as a tool for systematic program planning, management, and evaluation. It helps to facilitate thinking, planning, and communicating during the development of program objectives and achievement of program outcomes (i.e., focus session meetings). It also provides an effective way to explain and educate about the workings of an organization, which is essential for long-term viability of an organization. By creating a shared understanding of how the organization works, the logic model is an important tool for strategic management.

Analysis of external and internal environments

An assessment of the external environment impacting the organization was followed by an analysis of internal strengths and weaknesses. External forces create a constant state of change for the Nursing 2000 *collaborative*. The response of individuals, organizations, and institutions—the driving influence of the Nursing 2000 program—is impacted by technological advances, the social and healthcare economy, political and legislative issues, higher education initiatives, and regulatory standards. It is imperative to understand the external environment in which the *collaborative* operates and to anticipate and respond to the significant shifts that are taking place. Therefore, it becomes an ongoing challenge for the *collaborative* to assess external forces and analyze their current and potential impact on program outcomes.

An assessment of internal forces requires an analysis of the human resources, individual organizational cultures of the participating institutions, inter-organizational communication, and common goals. The role of the *collaborative* is to tie together commonalties across institutions and educational settings. The goal is to create a synergetic environment in which to cultivate a nursing community compatible with the mission of the organization…the promotion and support of nursing careers at all levels of development.

Strategic Formulation, Implementation, and Control

Data from the external and internal assessment were used to formulate strategies for implementation. These strategies were then taken to the board of directors for finalization and approval. The advisory board set the

Accessibility to school counselors and teachers is essential. Nursing 2000 display at the Math and Science Teacher Conference.

stage for strategic implementation, mobilizing the strategies into specific programs that were carried out by volunteers throughout the organization. Strategic control included a review of goal accomplishment at advisory board meetings throughout the academic year, and the concurrent evaluation of new activities as to their congruency with established goals. As a formal effort at the beginning of the academic year, current goals were evaluated and measured, and new goals identified. The new goals were taken to the board of directors for integration into the strategic plan. The strategic process has served Nursing 2000 well. The *collaborative*, which began as a two-year initiative, is now into its thirteenth year as a viable organization.

Figure 2 illustrates a conceptual model, *Environmental Factors Impacting Nursing 2000*, that was developed as a tool to guide the ongoing process of external and internal assessment.

This conceptual model depicts both external and internal factors imperative to achieving an understanding of the organization. Externally, the *collaborative* interacts with the changing healthcare environments, evolving nursing practice, responsive nursing education, dynamic school systems, catalytic market forces, and higher education policies. Internally, the *collaborative* assesses the strengths of the healthcare systems and affiliated schools of nursing, their interrelationships, and the participation of nursing organizations and volunteers. Each of the internal components is further impacted by the external forces bombarding the *collaborative*. Environs I includes the external forces impacting Nursing 2000 as a part of the healthcare community: the healthcare environment, nursing practice, and nursing education. Environs II illustrates higher education, community school systems, and market forces as public determinants impacting Nursing 2000. The first circle represents the core of the organization—its healthcare agencies, nursing schools, nursing organizations, and nurse volunteers. Nursing 2000 is positioned in the center as the vehicle for the second circle—the programs that reach into the schools, public and healthcare communities, and collaboration between nursing service and education throughout the organization. The desired outcome, a competent nursing workforce to meet the healthcare needs of the future, is mutually shared by the healthcare agencies, nursing schools, nursing organizations, and volunteers that comprise Nursing 2000. The conceptual model provides a framework to re-evaluate, strengthen, and revise the mission and goals of the *collaborative* against the backdrop of the rapidly changing internal and external environments.

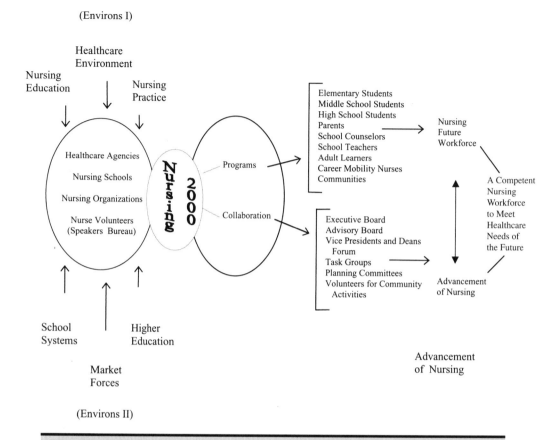

(Environs I)

(Environs II)

Figure 2. Environmental Factors Impacting Nursing 2000

Healthcare environment as a determinant

Using a systematic approach, the assessment begins by analyzing determinants of the healthcare environment in the region of the *collaborative*. The healthcare environment includes organizations that provide healthcare services and organizations that provide healthcare resources, professional organizations, healthcare professionals, and consumers. When assessing the external and internal healthcare environments, the following questions are listed for consideration:

External healthcare environment as a determinant
- Are the major healthcare providers voluntary, for-profit, or government organizations?
- What has been the impact of managed care and third-party reimbursement on the healthcare systems and facilities in the region?
- How will reimbursement influence the ability of healthcare systems and facilities to financially participate in a *collaborative*?
- What are the legislative healthcare priorities?
- What are the issues occurring in healthcare along the care continuum? What scientific and technological innovations are on the horizon that could impact healthcare delivery?
- What are the major information channels for healthcare? What is the most recent information from the Department of Health and Human Services, the Health Care Financial Administration, and the U.S. General Accounting Office?
- What is being published about acute care, intermediate care, and long-term care?
- What are the projected population demographics of those who will be using healthcare services in the future?
- What are the projected population demographics of those who will be the potential labor pool for future healthcare workers?

Internal healthcare environment as a determinant
- What are the relationships among healthcare systems and facilities in the region?
- What is the visibility of each healthcare system and facility in the community? What is the primary message each conveys?
- What is the organizational culture of each institution?
- What are their linkages with the State Department of Health?
- What are the linkages among the healthcare facilities and with physician medical practices?
- What is the role of the State Medical Association in support of nursing?
- Do the healthcare systems and facilities represent the care continuum in the region? How can the *collaborative* increase the public's awareness that healthcare spans the care continuum and that nurses are needed to provide care along the continuum?

- What is the impact of accreditation, across the care continuum, on the *collaborative*? Have new standards been issued that affect nursing practice, nursing students in the care arena, and nursing exploration (health occupations) students?
- What risk management issues are posed in the healthcare environment for caregivers, support personnel, career "shadow" explorers, and visitors?
- Are institutions forming partnerships or merging? Are institutions expanding services or opening new facilities? What will be the demand for nursing resources?
- What are the relationships among the healthcare agencies and nursing educational programs in the region? What clinical affiliations exist and what partnerships are currently in place?
- What resources exist among the healthcare systems and facilities, nursing educational programs, and nursing organizations to support a regional *collaborative*?
- What is the presence of nursing within the regional healthcare community?

Nursing practice as a determinant

Nursing practice is the next determinant to analyze. According to the American Association of Colleges of Nursing, "The essence of a discipline is its body of scientific knowledge, its system of values and ethics, and its societal worth" (AACN, 1999, p. 1). The "essence" of nursing practice is captured below in the American Nurses Association social policy statement (ANA, 1999):
- The focus on the human responses to health and illness
- The integration of objective data based on the patient's or group's experience
- An application of scientific knowledge in care delivery
- A provision for a caring relationship

Clearly, the current and future role of nursing requires critical thinking at the patient's side across care settings and specialties in which nurses practice.

Complex and emerging nursing practice issues will impact the *collaborative*. Pulling information together in a centralized approach that can be easily interpreted by the public is an essential role of the *collaborative*. Preparation and educational mobility, licensure, certification, advanced practice regulations, computerized documentation, and patient record security and confidentiality are a few examples of external issues impacting the interpretation of the role of nursing to the public. Adding to the complexity is the increased demand for nursing services due to a high patient acuity, an aging population, expanding technology, scientific breakthroughs, and the shift to ambulatory services and home care. In addition, a decline in the supply of nurses is accelerating due to an aging nursing workforce, an increase in career opportunities available to men and women of all ages, a decrease in the size of the workforce, and the influence of multi-generational work values. Of significance to future nursing practice is that women graduating from high school in the latter part of the 1990s were 35% less likely to become RNs compared to women in the 1970s (U.S. GAO Report, 2001, p. 6). Men entering the profession have not offset the declining number of women selecting nursing. In essence, the *collaborative* assesses factors occurring externally and internally to disseminate a consistent nursing practice message to the public, stakeholders, and the healthcare community.

External assessment of nursing practice as a determinant

- What data are available that project nursing workforce demands and supply?
- What is the role of the State Board of Nursing? How is it funded and represented? What resources are available?
- What are the local, state, and national messages disseminated by nursing?
- What are the messages about nursing received by the public, the healthcare community, and nurses?
- What are the movements occurring within the nursing specialties, and what new specialties are evolving?
- What nursing organizations can serve as resources for the *collaborative*? What messages can be augmented at the regional level?
- What is the pattern of registered nurse recruitment methods that have been implemented at the local, state, and national levels?
- What nursing images and career campaigns exist at the local, state, and national levels?

Internal assessment of nursing practice as a determinant

- What needs to be incorporated in the strategic plan and goals for the organization related to nursing practice development?
- What needs to be incorporated in career counseling, career materials, and on the Web site for nursing career development?

- What needs to be brought to the board of directors, Vice Presidents/Directors and Deans/Directors Forum, and advisory board related to the promotion of nursing? What needs to be communicated to the Nursing 2000 volunteers regarding the promotion of a consistent, informed, positive message about nursing careers?
- What are the varying philosophies of nursing practice within the *collaborative*?
- What is the nursing profile in the region related to experience, age, diversity, educational preparation, active practice, and active engagement in professional activities?

Nursing education as a determinant

The nursing education environment is the next essential determinant to assess. For purposes of the *collaborative*, nursing education includes the formal programs within the academic settings that lead to an undergraduate or graduate degree in nursing. In addition, continuing education programs are important to the *collaborative* so they can assess the degree of professional development opportunities available as well as opportunities to meet certification requirements in the region. The *collaborative* assesses the nursing educational programs represented in the region that have clinical affiliations with the participating healthcare facilities. The goal is to continually foster nursing service and nursing education collaboration. It is important to recognize the diversity of nursing programs in the region specific to degree options, faculty resources, and public and private institution cost. It is the goal of the *collaborative* to present the prospective nursing students with a variety of options, presented neutrally, to meet their individual needs. A large university in the region may provide less expensive tuition, plentiful classroom resources, an increased number of faculty, and research linkages for the student, whose learning style benefits from the setting. In contrast, a small private college in the region may require higher tuition but offer a smaller student/faculty ratio, offer smaller classroom sizes, and meet the religious or social needs of the student. It is imperative the *collaborative* recognize the contributions of both approaches. The more variety within the *collaborative*, the more enriching are the options for the student.

Agencies that accredit nursing schools in the region are also important to note. Prospective students and parents frequently ask the question, "What is the best nursing program in the state?" The public needs to be informed if state accreditation is required in the region; that the Commission for

Collegiate Nursing Education (CCNE) accredits baccalaureate and advanced degree programs; and that the National League for Nursing Accrediting Commission (NLNAC) accredits associate, baccalaureate, and advanced degree programs.

The availability of nursing faculty presents a growing concern for nursing schools. Long-term, it is important to assess and monitor the supply of faculty to avert an enrollment restriction in the future. If interest in nursing increases, the pool of qualified applicants can exceed the allotted faculty/student ratio. It is important to assess the number of associate, bachelor's, and master's degree enrollments and graduations from each affiliated school of nursing. In addition to determining the supply of graduates from a region, the monitoring of enrollments and graduations provides one indicator to evaluate the long-term impact of a *collaborative* in a region. The following questions are listed for consideration in assessing the external and internal nursing education factors.

External assessment of nursing education as a determinant

- What data are available as a projection of student enrollments and graduations?
- What data are available as a projection of faculty need and supply? For individuals entering the profession, what are the existing and evolving local, state, and national educational pathways? For nurses pursuing educational advancement, what are the matriculation options? Are career mobility options seamless?
- What changes are occurring in the accreditation processes for nursing educational programs? Subsequently, what is the information that should be shared with prospective students, their parents, and significant others?
- What financial assistance is available at the local, state, and national levels for nursing students?

Internal assessment of nursing education as a determinant

- What are the strengths of public and private colleges and universities in the region? What are the strengths that each brings to the *collaborative*? What faculty resources are available in each setting? What advanced degree programs are available in the region to prepare faculty?
- What partnerships are currently in place between education and service settings? Are joint appointments in place to "share and

extend" faculty resources rather than education and service competing for the same advanced degree prepared resources?

- What is the geographic outreach of each of the colleges and universities?
- What is the student population profile in each educational setting?
- What are the commonalties that can be packaged for a "unified" image?
- What is the diversity of the nursing student population in relation to national statistics? How will this affect an outreach to specific target audiences?
- How seamless are the articulation programs for LPN-ADN, RN-BSN, BSN-MSN and individuals with prior degrees in another field in the *collaborative*?

Higher education as a determinant

The impact of higher education (post-secondary education) is also a determinant, as it has a direct impact on academic nursing education in the region. The schools of nursing are a part of higher education just as nursing practice is a part of healthcare. Therefore, the following can be used as a guide when thinking about the impact of higher education on the internal environment of the *collaborative*—in particular, its affiliated schools of nursing:

- What is the role of the Commission for Higher Education (or the entity that manages the fiscal budget for post-secondary education) in the state and its impact on nursing education?
- What are the enrollments in the public four-year and two-year colleges and universities within the state of the *collaborative*?
- What are the enrollments in the independent four-year and two-year colleges and universities within the state of the *collaborative*?
- Are there matriculation agreements between the public and independent colleges and universities?
- What kind of diversity enrollments do colleges and universities have?
- What financial assistance and counseling resources are available from the state?
- Are there strategies within the state for educational mobility between two-year and four-year colleges and universities?
- To what degree is distance learning available within the state?
- What legislative initiatives have been adopted within the state to support student transition from secondary schools to institutions of higher education?

Community school system as a determinant

The community school system is another primary determinant impacting the *collaborative*. The community school system includes elementary, middle, and high school students; teachers; parents; counselors; administrators; and the State Department of Education. Linkages throughout the system are essential to the success of the *collaborative* model. It is important to assess the outreach into the schools from the affiliated hospital systems and schools of nursing as it enhances their visibility and strengthens nursing as a career option.

Nursing 2000 programs are targeted throughout the eight-county area community school systems to reach student populations reflective of the regional population. The largest ethnically diverse populations are represented in the Indianapolis Public Schools and adjacent townships. The surrounding counties, although representative of less ethnic diversity, provide a blend of rural and suburban populations. School size varies widely throughout the eight-county area and impacts the degree of participation in Nursing 2000 programs. Thus, in order to provide representation across individual school populations, ethnicity and school size are critical assessment factors to incorporate in program planning. The following questions are important to include in an assessment of the community school system as a determinant impacting the *collaborative*:

- How supported are school and community partnerships in the region?
- What are the numbers of high schools, middle schools, and elementary schools in the region?
- What network is available to access school counselors, science teachers, health occupation teachers, and school nurses?
- What are the practice and health teaching roles of school nurses in the systems?
- What career development programs are offered in the school systems; who is responsible?
- What are the key career fairs and conferences available in the state and region?
- What are the primary channels of communication used by community school students to access information? Are they school resources and/or the Internet?
- What are the career organizations and/or linkages students use? How do parents obtain career information for their students?

- How do student needs vary, among the school systems, based on standardized testing, pre-college entrance examinations, and percentage of seniors enrolling in college?
- Is there a core program of study expected of students seeking admission to post-secondary institutions?

Market forces as a determinant

Equally as important to assess are the market forces that are impacting the *collaborative*. Information technology has penetrated how the world accesses, processes, and disseminates information. Within a four-year time frame, the majority of the career information shared by Nursing 2000 has converted from a mail system (sending packets of information to individuals) to an electronic system (downloading the career materials via a Web

Information technology is one market force that has impacted Nursing 2000.

site). However, both systems need to remain in place until electronic means is widely available among the target audiences of Nursing 2000. For example, when adult learners telephone Nursing 2000, they may not have access to the Internet in their homes or transportation to the public library to access the Web site.

The *collaborative* also needs to assess how potential nursing students are receiving information from the higher education institutions of learning—both public and private. Middle and high school students are accustomed to receiving feedback to their questions in a matter of seconds by independently accessing a Web site. How do the career materials need to be organized to be a part of the "new" mainstream flow, yet provide a substantive career information tool that can be utilized later as a reference?

In addition, it is important to assess how practicing and inactive nurses are retrieving information. The most successful methods at Nursing 2000 have proven to be the most diverse. The Internet in conjunction with the metropolitan and suburban newspapers, hospital and nursing organization newsletters, and specific mailings from Nursing 2000 have provided an excellent combination for outreach promotion.

The economy is another strong market force impacting the *collaborative*. Assessing the impact of economic forces on potential students is imperative. Buerhaus (1993) has researched the effects of RN wages and economic fluctuations on the complex RN labor market. During economic downturns, high nursing employment has been tracked. While during non-recession periods, RN vacancy rates increased. Equally as strong is the message of the media about traditional students and their parents/guardians. With the increasing costs of higher education, parents are more aware of job and/or career security following graduation. During the downsizing of healthcare facilities in the mid-nineties, Nursing 2000 received concerned calls from parents and high school counselors expressing caution about the investment in a nursing college degree at a time when nursing position reductions were highly publicized (Aiken, Sochalski, & Anderson, 1996). In the early nineties in a time of a nursing shortage, adult learner seminars were offered twice every two months by Nursing 2000 and enjoyed an average attendance of 22 individuals per session. In the mid-nineties, the average attendance dropped to 12. Economics clearly influences not only the employment of nurses but the exploration of nursing as a career and entry into the profession.

Population demographics is another important market force to assess. The size of the college applicant pool determines what realistic share nursing can hope to recruit to the discipline. The pool of traditional students has been declining while competition among career opportunities has increased. As adult learners pursue college and "career changers" return to college, career opportunities among the disciplines have also expanded. According to Peter Buerhaus, nursing has not recruited adequate replacement numbers for the aging "baby boomers." In fact, each five-year cohort since the 1960s has been smaller than any previous one (Buerhaus, Staiger, & Auerbach, 2000; American Hospital Association, 2001).

The forecasting of the working-age population is critical to assess at the national and state levels. For instance, the ratio of the working-age population, 18 to 64, to the population over 85 will decline from 39.5 workers for each person 85 and older in 2000, to 22.1 in 2030 and 14.8 in 2040. The ratio of women age 20 to 54, the cohort most likely to be working in nursing, to the population age 85 and older will decline from 16.1 in 2000 to 8.5 in 2030, and 5.7 in 2040 (U.S. GAO Report, 2001). In Indiana, between the years 2000 and 2025, the number of workers age 18-24 is projected to decline by 2.75%. By contrast, the number of working persons in the middle years of 25-64 will grow slowly. During the same time period, those aged 65 and older will expand by approximately 62% (U.S. Census Bureau, 2000). The population demographics drive the demand for nursing and health professionals across all care delivery settings.

Survey research indicates the public trusts nurses as providers of care delivery. Trust, according to Webster's Dictionary (1998), is to "commit or place in one's care and to rely on truthfulness." It is important to assess the public trust for nursing. If the mission of the *collaborative* is to educate the public about nursing as a profession, it is of ultimate importance to monitor how the public views nursing. According to the annual CNN/USA Today/Gallup poll conducted after September 11, 2001, nurses were ranked second for their honesty and ethical standards by the public. Firefighters displaced nurses in the number one rating. The military, police, pharmacists, medical doctors, and the clergy followed. Nurses were added to the poll in 1999 and received the top ranking for three consecutive years until 2001 (Ulrich, 2001). Clearly this reflects the public's trust of nurses. In a Harris poll on consumer attitudes about nursing, 85% of Americans polled said they would be pleased if their son or daughter chose nursing as a career. Ninety-two percent said they trust information about healthcare provided by nurses (Sigma Theta Tau International and NurseWeek, 1999).

Summary

An assessment of the external and internal environments can serve as an indicator of the potential strengths and weaknesses of the *collaborative*. How strong are internal workings of a new *collaborative* to develop and evolve as a positive force in the community? Does it appear the *collaborative* will have the resources to develop the mission, vision, goals, sources of funding and governance, staff and volunteer resources, physical facilities and technological support, legal and financial assistance, marketing, and receptivity to the organization in the region? Chapter 3 presents the Nursing 2000 model as one example and provides additional direction to assist a new *collaborative*.

3

———◆◆◈◆◆———

THE ORGANIZATIONAL OPERATIONS

Introduction

To this point, background information about Nursing 2000 and the factors that affect the development of a like *collaborative* have been provided. Information pertaining to the beginnings of Nursing 2000, as an organization, has introduced the model. Over and over the collaboration that took place between representatives of nursing service and nursing education has been described. The importance of this collaboration cannot be overemphasized.

The history of the organization has been included so any *collaborative*, using the Nursing 2000 model to develop a formal organization, can understand how it has reached this point. The working alliance that became Nursing 2000 developed the organization and all steps or parts of a procedure for implementing a program that carries out the mission of the organization. Using available information and the model as a guide, a *collaborative* can move quickly to establish a foundation organization and programming. With a sound beginning, expansion of the organization will come gradually and smoothly.

The need to assess the internal and external environments has been discussed extensively. Items and issues to consider have been identified. Clues, "pointers", and suggestions have been given. Nursing resources have been discussed. Again collaboration between nursing service and nursing education is identified as a necessary resource for success. All of the factors discussed in Chapter 2 must be considered as they apply to a *collaborative* when using the model to establish a formal organization. The strengths and weaknesses of the regional *collaborative* have been shared so that a developing *collaborative* can draw on similar strengths and avoid the pitfalls of identified weaknesses.

Developing a Mission and Goals

What is the next step in building a collaborative? Where does the activity begin? What factors must be considered as the *collaborative* faces its task? Basic to all of the work that must be done and before work groups are formed, all individuals in the *collaborative* must work together to develop a mission statement and goals. The different tasks to be accomplished to organize cannot be effectively achieved without a mission statement. A mission statement will come about through discussion, where there is a sharing of thoughts in regard to what each individual believes the mission should be and finally a consensus agreement about what the *collaborative* can do. Individuals will come to realize the mission of the new organization is not an extension of their own views or those of their institutions. All members of the *collaborative* must embrace or buy into the mission statement of the *collaborative*. This buy-in is based on what is best for the whole rather than what one wants from a personal perspective. Agreement about the mission of the *collaborative* must be shared.

The mission statement is the basis of the organization. The mission statement gives purpose to the organization. It is clearly stated and it describes the direction in which the organization will proceed. Often it is difficult to separate the vision for the organization from the mission and to decide if the vision enables a *collaborative* to develop a mission statement or to develop clearly stated goals. Those individual representatives of nursing service and nursing education, who come together to form a *collaborative*, using the Nursing 2000 model for the purpose of forming an organization, hold a common vision. This vision has brought them together. Therefore, the mission statement is a reflection of the vision of the *collaborative*. The goals flow easily from the mission statement when it is clearly written. A word of caution is offered at this time in regard to the development of the statement. The mission statement, if the organization is to be ongoing, should be broad. A narrowly stated mission could bring demise to the organization. If the mission of a *collaborative* is to promote nursing, then goals that flow from the mission statement will provide opportunities for a variety of programs and activities.

Goals must be written in behavioral terms so they are measurable and can provide data for the evaluation of the effectiveness and accomplishments of the organization. Each goal should have a single focus. Compound goals are difficult to meet and to measure. Members of the *collaborative* bring with them the skills and experience to write the mission statement and, in turn, the goals. However, discussion will be necessary to reach consensus.

Mission

To promote and support the development of registered nursing careers to positively impact future healthcare resources

Only after the *collaborative* is formally organized and on firm ground, in terms of financial support, staffing, and volunteer resources, should consideration be given to expanding the mission statement and, therefore, the activities and programs. The mission statement directs the activities of the organization, and only when the mission statement is reviewed and expanded, should new activities be introduced. The mission and goals should be reviewed annually and revised and expanded as appropriate. As a resource, the mission statement and goals of Nursing 2000 are included in Appendix A.

Determining Leadership

It is assumed the members of the *collaborative*, as they come together, will determine how leadership will be decided, whether it will be one person or shared. Likewise, a system of recording the activities of each meeting of the *collaborative* must be determined. Well-taken notes can be a reference for discussions that may take place in future meetings. Note taking is often a thankless task and perhaps should be shared. Groups often rotate the task of recording the activities of meetings. Any subcommittee work group can record the discussions and decisions of the meeting, making certain notes are shared with all members of the *collaborative*.

Funding and Governance

What comes next? Usually people are anxious to move on and to be involved in their communities. However, there are still issues to be discussed and actions to be carried out by the *collaborative* before a representative board is able to take major responsibility for the organization. Dependent upon the size of the membership of the *collaborative*, the work to be done may be accomplished more effectively and efficiently by small work groups that report regularly to *collaborative* members. The work groups need to receive feedback and input, and incorporate, when appropriate, the feedback into the work being done. The final proposal of a work group is presented as a recommendation to the *collaborative* and at that time is modified or revised to the satisfaction of the *collaborative*. Two issues that need to be addressed early on when forming the organization and may be appropriately assigned to work groups are funding and governance. Which one is considered first? How do you develop one without the other or one before the other? The work groups may work simultaneously keeping the *collaborative* informed of progress being made and requesting input or discussion as needed. Again, remember that any work done by work groups is taken to the *collaborative* for discussion, revision or modification and then accepted by the *collaborative* as its work is accomplished.

Two factors need to be introduced as funding and governance are considered. They are important and could influence how successful the *collaborative* is in establishing the organization. First, members of the *collaborative*, vice presidents of nursing service, and deans/directors of nursing education must keep their chief executive officers informed of the progress being made as the organization is formed. The institution that they, the members of the *collaborative*, represent will become the official member of the organization. It is the responsibility of the representative to keep the executive lines of communication open. The institutional representative to the *collaborative* must "bring along" the chief executive officer (CEO) as the *collaborative* members work to form the organization. The representative needs to know how his/her CEO regards the formation of the organization, how well the CEO embraces the concept of the organization, and what input the executive desires to have. It is probable that there will be greater support of the new organization if the executive is aware of the progress.

The second item of importance is legal consultation. Legal assistance can usually be found at a member institution of the organization and should be ongoing. The need will be more intense as funding and governance policies and procedures are developed. It is wise to begin this process of legal consultation early in order to prevent problems. Consultation may be in-kind support from a member and can be rotated among the member institutions. Legal assistance is discussed again later in this chapter under the formation of bylaws and essential services.

Funding and governance are presented as work to be done by the *collaborative*. Decisions in regard to both issues are basic to the formation of the organization and, thereafter, the operation of the organization. Funding does not bear more weight or importance than governance. The organization needs both to survive.

Developing a funding plan or the financial base of the organization must be long range. The *collaborative* members must look beyond the first year of the organization. The members of the *collaborative* need to give thought to the listed issues below, as well as others that will come to mind as the list is reviewed:

- What overall financial backing is needed to carry out the mission of the organization?
- What kind of a facility is needed to house the organization long-term? What expenses in addition to the lease will be involved? What utility and other services must be considered? How much floor space will be needed as programs that carry out the mission are initiated?
- What expenses will be incurred to furnish and keep the facility in good shape?
- What current and future staffing will be needed? Competitive salaries and the benefit package must be considered.
- What kind of insurance is the organization going to need? How is liability to be covered?
- How are the needs for supplies and equipment planned, and how does the plan for the first year differ from subsequent years?

The items listed and others that may be identified must be discussed by the *collaborative* as a whole. There must be a common understanding and identification of the needs before work groups are able to effectively meet their responsibilities. This may be where "dreaming" occurs. Individuals of the *collaborative* need to share their visions of how the organization will function and the contribution the organization will make to the promotion of nursing. Perhaps this will be the beginning of long-range planning and setting of future goals. The recorder, with the help of other members, should list ideas for future reference recognizing that this is not the time to develop long-range plans. Rather, the focus needs to be on immediate priorities. However,

One vision of the organization is to develop a pipeline for future nursing resources.

thoughts and ideas generated at this point may assist the budget work group to see the need to look ahead when planning. Members have undoubtedly been involved in development of budgets in their own work situations and thus have the necessary skills to accomplish the tasks at hand. The issue is for those involved to reach consensus on what is needed to effectively establish this organization through the *collaborative*.

The funding commitment requested of each member institution must be appropriate to the long-term needs of the organization. Therefore, the funding structure for membership must be given serious consideration. To assist the work group in developing a plan, the process used by Nursing 2000 is a good model. Two budgets were developed: a start-up budget and a sustaining budget. Five major hospital healthcare systems in the Indianapolis/Marion County area were the founding members of the organization/corporation and continue to be the voting members of the corporation. Thus the five major hospitals served as the start-up and sustaining funding units of Nursing 2000.

A group coming together for the purpose of forming a *collaborative* needs to have an understanding of the influence of the setting on the development and sustainability of the organization. The organization was developed and operates in a metropolitan area with a population of more than a million and a half. The five major funding hospital systems are teaching and research hospitals. The organization is further supported by nine contributing hospitals and four schools of nursing. The funding structure provides an example for any size *collaborative*. The mission statement and goals of the *collaborative* need to be written based on the resources available in the community and the influence of the same on the organization meeting its goals. Funding structures may be individualized for the *collaborative* based on the source of financial support. Grants, endowments, corporate and public contributions, and government allocations are potential financial resources that can become the basis for the funding structure of the *collaborative*. Thus, it is easy to see that opportunities and limitations vary depending on what resources the *collaborative* can accrue.

Great thought and discussion went into the development of the sustaining budget. The annual membership fees established by dividing the sum equally among the member hospitals/healthcare systems became the total income to support the organization. The question that had to be considered frequently was whether the mission of the organization could be carried out within this budget. For the first two years, Nursing 2000 stayed within the budget by limiting its activities while meeting the mission and goals of the organization. There was no change in the membership fees or increase in the income of the organization until healthcare systems in the adjoining counties and smaller healthcare systems within the city, one by one, joined the organization so they too could participate in and benefit from the activities of the organization. These organizations became contributing members, paying an annual fee of $5,000. It should be noted that these contributions supported the expansion of programs and sustained the quality of the programs offered in the eight-county area including and surrounding Marion County. The operation of the organization continued to be supported by the five major hospitals/healthcare facilities that held membership in the corporation. The schools of nursing that were affiliated with Nursing 2000 did not contribute financially to the organization. In 1997, the board of directors developed a new funding schema after considering changes made in healthcare systems, trends, the healthcare economy, and how the mission had been expanded over the years. A formula was established for all members, funding and contributing, based on RN full-time equivalency staffing. At this time, the four schools of nursing came forward to establish a dollar amount of $500 as their annual contribution.

When a new *collaborative* is organized, the members will need to consider such issues as: Will the mission be expanded or will additional activities/ programs need to be developed to meet the goals of the mission? Is there the potential for additional members? The *collaborative* members must be insightful in their planning and be proactive in determining the potential of the organization. However, as the *collaborative* members determine their funding fees, the sum of the funding support must be enough to meet the budget. Therefore, a dollar amount for membership fees cannot be recommended. The funding structure for Nursing 2000 is included only as a model for a *collaborative* to show how resources available for an organization are influenced by the size and number of healthcare systems in the communities represented in the *collaborative*. Many factors will influence the determination of fees: cost of living, salaries, utilities, location in rural or metropolitan area of the country, space and equipment leasing fees, travel cost, and others that will come to mind as the work group considers its challenge. The Nursing 2000 revenue structure shows the source of income and, for the purpose of giving information, includes the revenue from year one of the organization and the projected forthcoming year. The sliding scale based on RN FTE is included for additional information (see Appendix B).

In addition, Appendix C contains a chart that illustrates the accumulative cost of offering each program activity one or more times in a fiscal year excluding personnel expenses. A copy of the budget for each program activity is included in the appendices. The budgets are included to help a *collaborative* determine the cost of presenting a program similar to ones provided by Nursing 2000 and to make judgments about its program directions. Again, dollar figures included in the discussion are for Nursing 2000, an organization established in a large metropolitan area of the country. A *collaborative* in a rural area may not serve the number of high schools or a general population as large as that served by Nursing 2000; therefore, the total cost for items needed would need to be adapted to the regional area.

A factor that must be considered briefly is the initial funding for the physical establishment of the organization, a start-up budget, or in-kind membership support. The start-up budget should cover all the expenses for establishing a "residence" for the organization. If the *collaborative* accepts in-kind assistance from a member institution, such as housing, clerical support, use of established technology, utilities, etc., then the *collaborative*

Nursing 2000 programs are usually presented at a public facility.

members should consider a funding plan that would allow the organization to be located in an independent setting at an appropriate time.

Nursing 2000 was initially housed in a temporary office before moving to a permanent office with 900 square feet. The organization is now in its fourth site with 1,500 square feet. The second and third moves were in the same geographic area with the last move being down the hall to the larger area. The first permanent housing for the organization was in an office building complex that had parking available for staff and visitors and also had access to a common conference room that could be reserved. Site #4 has a conference room large enough to accommodate a 25-member advisory board. Programs offered for the general public, such as Nursing 2000's seminars, are usually presented at a public library, a member facility, or another public facility.

The organization, once formed, must constantly demonstrate how the goals of the mission are being met. The organization will be recognized by the activities implemented, but support will continue only when the organization is able to demonstrate how the goals have been met. A systematic plan of evaluation must be in place.

Bylaws and Incorporation

Developing a plan of incorporation is a major responsibility of the *collaborative* that must be accomplished before the *collaborative* becomes an organization. The legal counsel of a member institution should take leadership in the development of the bylaws and the articles of incorporation. A copy of the *Amended and Revised Bylaws of Nursing 2000, Inc., Effective October 30, 2001*, is included as Appendix D to be used as a resource.

Upon review of the bylaws, it will become clear to the members of the *collaborative* that their institutions are the members of the organization. The *collaborative*, with the help of legal counsel, should develop bylaws that will serve the organization and describe how the organization will function. The *collaborative* must define what groups within the organization are needed for the organization to be successful. The bylaws must also determine the purpose, responsibilities, and parameters of the roles within the organization. The bylaws provide the framework for the operation of the organization.

The language and format of the bylaws of an organization may be different than those of Nursing 2000 and similar organizations. The bylaws are included to demonstrate how each aspect of this organization is to function and how the roles of its members are to be fulfilled so the members of the board of directors know what they are expected to do. Because the board conducts the ongoing business and provides the strategic planning for the organization, great thought should be given as to how the bylaws of a new *collaborative* can be inclusive and direct the manner in which the organization will function but allow for expansion in order to meet the mission of the organization. Thus the new bylaws must provide direction for:

- How the organization will be managed
- How leadership will be determined
- How volunteers will be used
- Who will be the volunteers
- What qualifications are required of volunteers
- How fiscal management is to take place

It is important to remember that the work group developing the bylaws must take to the *collaborative* as a whole what has been accomplished each step of the way. The response and input from the *collaborative's* members need to be given consideration. It is a similar situation with the budget work group. Each work group must share and consult with the whole *collaborative* as the group makes progress in carrying out the task at hand. The end product will reflect consensus of the entire *collaborative*. Neither work group has an easy task. The members of the *collaborative* must be willing to be fully involved with each phase of developing the organization. The future success of the organization lies in this formation of a sound foundation.

Managing the Collaborative

Staffing

The executive director and an administrative assistant were the initial employee staff. The organization leases its employees from one or more of its affiliated hospitals, thus allowing the organization to offer benefit provisions at competitive prices. During the period of formation of a *collaborative*, thought needs to be given to staffing. What is realistic? What is needed to meet the goals of the organization now? What will be needed later? These issues need to be considered when developing the budget. It is assumed that any *collaborative* that uses the Nursing 2000 model to form an organization will follow the employee staffing model. The staff directs the work of the organization to meet the mission and goals of the organization.

Nursing 2000 is a voluntary organization; thus, the work of the organization is done by volunteers. A new *collaborative* will need to determine the staffing needs for the organization to begin its programming. Once organizing has been completed and additional programs are developed, it is important to demonstrate that the majority of the staff's time must be devoted to the programmatic effort.

Board of directors

The board of directors manages the affairs of the corporation as is stated in the bylaws. The board is composed of two deans/directors of the participating schools of nursing, a chief executive officer of a member institution, three senior nursing executives from supporting member institutions, and one senior nursing executive from a contributing institution. The members serve a two-year term. It should be noted that a board member may serve two consecutive terms. The bylaws describe how positions are to be filled on alternate years to provide an effective transition of the leadership. The directors are elected/approved at the annual meeting, and one member is designated to serve as secretary/treasurer. The executive director presides at all meetings and has the responsibilities of a chief operating officer and program director.

Advisory board

The advisory board is also described in the bylaws. The composition of the advisory board, how member institutions are to be represented on this board, and the functions of the board are all included. In addition to the members, described in the bylaws, the advisory board has a representative from the Indiana League for Nursing, the Indiana State Nurses Association, the Indiana Organization of Nurse Executives, three Sigma Theta Tau chapters, and one chapter of Chi Eta Phi Sorority, the latter providing community and diversity enrichment representation. This work group has the task of meeting the goals of the organization. The advisory board functions under the leadership of the professional staff person, who is directed by the governing board of the organization.

One of the first tasks for the professional staff person is to orient the members of the first board. This orientation should include the number of times the board meets during the year, the purpose of the board, how the board

Advisory board members meet to implement the goals of the organization.

will function, and the expectations of the members for serving the organization and participating in the work to be accomplished. All advisory board members will not be appointed by their institution at the beginning of the organizational year, as it may be necessary for the member institution to fill a vacancy on the board in the middle of the year. The board should develop a plan whereby an orientation is presented for new board members on a schedule, every two to three months as needed to accommodate new members. It is recommended that at the beginning of each year, the professional staff leader review with the entire board the purpose of the board and how the board functions.

The advisory board develops and implements the programs that meet the goals of the organization. Board members recruit volunteers from their institutions to participate in the activities offered by the *collaborative*. After the formation of the organization is complete, the advisory board, under the leadership of the professional staff person, will work together to develop a system to organize volunteers. This system will include determining what the needs of the organization are in the beginning and how volunteers will be oriented. Orientation will include the purpose of the organization, an overview description of the programs to be offered, and the importance of accountability. This broad overview of programs will assist individual volunteers in determining where they may best serve. Programs and the preparation involved are discussed in detail in Chapters 4, 5, and 6.

The advisory board meets on a regular basis at a scheduled time with an agenda prepared in advance. The professional staff person presides. Information is shared, work to be done is identified, and members of the board accept assignments as volunteers. Much of the work of the board occurs during the academic year, as many of the programs involve student populations. The advisory board will form committees to complete major projects as needed. Frequently a volunteer(s) will serve on an advisory committee, providing the manpower needed to meet goals. Advisory board members take the lead.

The professional staff person keeps the focus of the board on meeting the goals of the organization. All discussion and activity of the advisory board must be focused on the mission and goals of the organization.

The advisory board sends recommendations for consideration and action to the executive board through the professional staff person. An example of such a recommendation would be the development of a plan of record keeping of volunteer service. The board will need to determine how records will be kept (by year and if so, is it a calendar year, a budget year, or on the basis of an academic year). The board will also determine and make recommendations on how service is to be acknowledged.

In summary, the advisory board formulates plans for the presentation of programs offered by the organization. Members of the advisory board will recruit volunteers from the institutions or organizations that they represent. All plans developed by the committee are sent to the executive board as recommendations.

Recruitment and orientation of volunteers

Recruitment of volunteers is ongoing. Some individuals need to limit their involvement because of work situations and personal responsibilities, while others are available to help on a regular basis. Individuals are assigned to a program activity only after they have been thoroughly oriented. How often the orientation program is offered depends on when and how many additional programs are developed. The outline of the orientation program is included in Appendix E.

As a part of the orientation of volunteers to the mission and programs of the organization, they should learn about their role in representing the organization. This content should be presented in a positive manner and be non-threatening. However, it should be understood by the volunteers that they are presenting information given to them by the organization. It is not their opinion that is being presented, rather they are representing the organization as an entity. It is similar to any work situation. It is expected that the actions of the volunteer will not place the individual or the organization in a state of liability jeopardy.

Volunteer speakers' bureau

The Nursing 2000 volunteers are considered members of the volunteer speakers' bureau. There are two groups of volunteers within the 200-member speakers' bureau. The first group is composed of the individuals who speak at the various community programs where the volunteer gives information in a formal presentation to a group of individuals organized by age, interest, or focus. There may be five to 10 present in the group or 50-100 depending on such things as the topic, time, day, or weather conditions. The volunteer may represent the organization alone or be accompanied by another volunteer. The professional staff members maximize the strengths of the volunteers through feedback from peers and the evaluations completed by the audience participants. Using this feedback, the professional staff is able to assign volunteers appropriately. A person who represents the organization as a member of the speakers' bureau should have:

- Knowledge of the need for nurses in the workforce
- Understanding of the levels within nursing education
- Awareness of the informational programs available through the organization
- Understanding of the opportunities available for the nurse
- Knowledge of salary ranges and career mobility

The professional staff person keeps volunteers informed through the organization's newsletter and by additional communication as needed. The focus of all volunteers' presentations is to promote and support nursing careers at all levels of development.

Those individuals who prefer to be responsible for representing the organization at career and health fairs form the second group of volunteers. Additionally, in this second group are the individuals who do the behind-the-scenes work of preparing exhibits, planning, assisting with work in the office, etc. There may be volunteers who are comfortable and willing to participate where needed in either group. Wherever individuals choose to serve, there will be a well-planned, informative orientation. A plan must be developed to keep all volunteers informed, especially when the focus of the volunteer program changes.

The staff publishes a comprehensive newsletter for its volunteers two times a year in December and August. Because programs are usually offered based on the academic year, the December newsletter includes the activities that occurred during the first semester of the academic calendar and announces forthcoming events. The August issue covers the second semester and activities planned for the fall. The newsletters include activities that have taken place during the time interval, programs offered, recognition of services rendered by volunteers, any changes in procedures, and other information a volunteer would need to represent the organization effectively.

Volunteer groups are fluid; individuals move in and out of the organization as their time permits or as their expertise is needed. For example, when Nursing 2000 offers its scholarship program, there are individuals who have had experience in fundraising through work in a development office or in another volunteer organization who participate actively in this program yet may not participate in the offering of any other program of the organization during the year. Nursing 2000 maintains an active and inactive list of volunteers. Individuals who do not participate for over a year are moved to the inactive list. An individual can attend an orientation session when ready to return to active status.

Other essential services

Technology

During the formation of an organization, extensive thought should be given to the technology and information support services. The start-up budget will cover the initial purchase of equipment and monies for service providers. However, budgeting needs to include funds for the technical support the staff will need in the future and additional equipment that will be needed as the organization increases its scope of services. The administrative assistant and other support staff will bring with them the skills needed to use technical equipment effectively, but it cannot be expected that they will have the skills to diagnose and correct equipment failures. It is best to establish a link with a service agency that will give the support the organization needs that will permit ongoing production ability. Collaborative members may confer with staff at their institutions and bring to the group recommendations for consideration of a service agency.

Legal assistance

While legal assistance has been discussed earlier, there are a number of issues that must be addressed here. There are initial legal needs, such as the establishment of the organization and the development of the bylaws, incorporation, and membership agreements, etc. The board of directors and the professional staff leader need to have all business contracts reviewed by the legal consultant before signing as representatives of the organization. For example, before signing service contracts, employee contracts, lease agreements, membership agreements, etc., the board of directors should have the documents reviewed by a legal consultant.

The professional staff leader should be able to contact the legal advisor as needed without calling a meeting of the board of directors. The staff leader should be able to have a phone conversation or send a message to a legal advisor to determine if:

- The action to be taken is correct
- Enough information has been obtained to support the action
- No errors are being made
- The action is within legal rights of the organization
- Good judgment has been used

The legal advisor usually attends the meeting of the board of directors as an ex officio member to listen to the discussion and identify areas of concern. While the legal advisor is an important participant in the discussion of the board, the board members make the final decision based on the advice of the legal advisor.

Financial management

The *collaborative* should investigate or request recommendations of an accounting firm to contract for the management of its finances. It is highly recommended the selected accountant be an individual who has had experience with health-related and not-for-profit organizations. This kind of accountant will undoubtedly understand the effect of the healthcare industry on the health of the organization. An accounting service should be in place at the time the agreements for the formation of the organization are orchestrated. The supporting/founding hospitals will send forth the identified amount of financial support when the agreement is signed. It is recommended the accountant be involved at the time the contributions are accepted and initial distributions are made.

Marketing

Marketing needs to be considered so an awareness of the *collaborative's* mission can be known by the public. Part of marketing is developing a plan that announces the existence and purpose of the organization. Because of limited funding, the plan for offering programs must introduce the organization to the communities it serves. First in the development of a marketing plan is to name the organization. The name and the statement of purpose needs to convey to the public what the mission is and how the organization serves the community. As a plan is developed, the *collaborative* member representatives should recognize that the effectiveness of the organization will be dependent upon the volunteers who are recruited. It is reasonable to think it is best to begin with a program that can be offered with few resources, human and financial. As the first program to be offered is determined, other options should be considered. For example, if the program is an offering to adult learners, which radio stations give public service announcements without charge, what coverage will the local newspapers provide without a charge?

Summary

The Nursing 2000 organization has been presented as a model for a *collaborative* to use to form a similar organization. Each part or factor of the model has been discussed separately in a chronological order to indicate the steps taken to form the organization. Detailed information has been given about each factor, what occurred in the beginning, and where the organization is now.

Each program that Nursing 2000 offers to meet its mission is described and discussed in the chapters to follow. Details are included for the use of a *collaborative*. Using the information and details presented, programs that meet the individual mission of a *collaborative* can be developed.

4

NURSING 2000: SCHOOL AND SCHOOL OF NURSING PROGRAMS

Introduction

The development and implementation of Nursing 2000's programs are presented in detail in this chapter and the next two. These programs can be organized into three categories:
- School and school of nursing programs
- Community programs
- Career advancement programs

School and school of nursing programs include the high school A Day in the Life of a Nurse shadow program, classroom presentations, the school counselor newsletter, school career fairs, and the scholarship benefit. Community programs include the Adult Learner Career Seminar, the adult learner shadow a nurse program, community presentations, public library displays, and community career and health fairs. Career advancement programs include career and educational counseling, the re-entry into nursing seminar, and the advanced nursing practice seminar.

School and School of Nursing Programs

School and school of nursing programs provide information to elementary, middle, and high school students and middle and high school counselors about a career in registered nursing. The high school A Day in the Life of a Nurse shadow program describes a one-to-one observational experience designed to introduce sophomores, juniors, and seniors to the role of today's professional registered nurse. Classroom presentations are also offered by the organization to introduce elementary, middle, and high school students to a career in nursing. The school counselor newsletter educates middle and high school counselors regarding current trends in the nursing profession and assists counselors and their students as they explore career options. Participation in middle and high school career fairs that are presented by Nursing 2000 enables students to make informed choices as they consider a career in nursing. There are also programs that assist nursing students with their educational financial commitments, such as the annual scholarship benefit, which provides scholarship dollars while supporting the development of future nursing careers.

Descriptions of the programs, as well as procedures for the development and implementation of the programs offered by Nursing 2000 are available for use. An appendix accompanies each program and provides all written materials utilized by Nursing 2000 to support the program. The appendix also includes a budget for the program.

Nursing 2000 staff members have found the professional staff employed by the *collaborative*, the advisory committee, and the volunteer speakers' bureau excellent people/groups to plan, implement, and evaluate the programs. As a shared activity of the *collaborative*, input from both nursing service and nursing education is provided.

Descriptions and procedures for the development and implementation of the school and school of nursing programs of Nursing 2000 follow. The appendices that support each program are referenced as part of the program. The program descriptions, procedures, and appendices are provided to allow any *collaborative* to develop and implement the programs of Nursing 2000, revising and modifying them to meet their specific needs.

High school shadow a nurse program

The high school shadow a nurse program is titled A Day in the Life of a Nurse and offers a one-to-one observational experience designed to introduce sophomores, juniors, and seniors to the role of today's professional nurse. The program also includes academic counseling for high school students, contact with parents of high school students, rapport-building with high school counselors, subsequent communication with high school students by the schools of nursing, and establishment of a connection between the hospital community and high schools. This program is regarded by Nursing 2000 members as its strongest tool for edu-

Nurse mentor and student during A Day in the Life of a Nurse shadow program.

cating students, parents, and counselors about a career in registered nursing.

The shadow program is offered twice a year in the fall and spring academic semesters. Sixty-eight high schools in the eight counties served by Nursing 2000 and 260 students are offered the opportunity to participate each semester. Senior students are given slightly higher priority in the fall semester to correspond with the college selection process. Junior students are given slightly higher priority in the spring semester, and sophomores are accepted for the program if space is available. Priority is also given to students who have not participated in previous shadow programs offered by Nursing 2000.

Flyers are sent to high school counselors and science teachers prior to the event as an announcement of the program. Shadow program dates are also posted on the Nursing 2000 Web site. Packets, containing the flyers, student application forms, and a letter of instruction for the counselors/teachers, are mailed to high school counselors and science teachers approximately eight weeks before the program. Students interested in the program complete a written application that is submitted four weeks prior to the day of observation. Acceptance is based on the quality of the application, the student's academic preparation (a minimum number of high school courses such as algebra, biology, and chemistry), and parent or guardian, as well as high school counselor, signatures on the application. Information about the high school courses taken, the reasons a student wants to participate and what they hope to learn, plans after graduation, consideration of another healthcare career other than nursing, and the opportunity to identify four hospital preferences for their observation experience can be found in the application.

The Nursing 2000 professional staff review the applications and select the students for participation. Students are then placed in one of their four hospital preferences. Students are rarely placed in a hospital not of their preference. If this occurs, the student and parent are asked for permission to place them in the alternative hospital. The high school counselors are notified in writing of the outcome of their students who have applied to the program. A letter of acceptance including specific program information is sent to the accepted students. The same process occurs with students denied the program or students who are not accepted for the current program, but have been placed on the waiting list for the next program. When there are denials, the students and their high school counselors are told the reasons for denial in their letters. The letters to counselors and students are often used as an incentive for students desiring a career in nursing so they will complete the courses they need to meet the admission criteria.

All high school counselors and science teachers receive a thank you following the program. The thank you may be in the form of a letter or as a mention in Future Focus in Nursing, Nursing 2000's school counselor newsletter.

Over the past five years, an average of 398 students have applied for each program. Of the 398 student applicants, an average of 252 students or 63% have been accepted, 23% have been delayed until the next program, and 13% have been denied entry into the program.

The 14 funding and contributing hospitals of Nursing 2000 participate in the program. Because several of the participating hospitals are multi-hospital systems, 23 acute care clinical site opportunities are provided. Each site determines the number of high school students it can accommodate. Acute care experiences have proven to be the most successful shadow opportunities, and the number of students for each clinical location has varied from two to 30, depending on available opportunities.

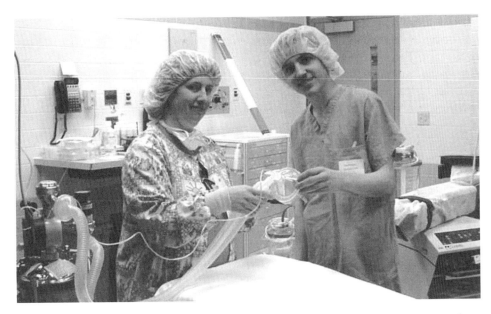

A Day in the Life of a Nurse shadow program participant with nurse mentor at one of the 23 clinical sites.

The program is managed by the professional staff of Nursing 2000 and by volunteer coordinators who represent each clinical site. Clinical sites have one or two coordinators. Volunteer site coordinators are registered nurses selected by their hospitals as representatives. The coordinators are oriented to their roles by Nursing 2000 professional staff, and the organization updates its list of coordinators each semester. Orientation includes a review of the program, a review of the coordinator's role, the day's agenda, the student application process and selection criteria, and the role of the registered nurse preceptor.

Registered nurse preceptors are selected by staff at the clinical sites based on their interest in the program and their previous experience as a preceptor. The registered nurse preceptors are a very critical element of the program. They are the role models for the student observers. They must be skilled caregivers and willing to share their time and expertise with the students. They are expected to dress and interact in a professional manner with their patients, families, and students. Nursing 2000 and the volunteer site coordinators stress the importance of the role when registered nurse preceptors are selected. The impact of the registered nurse preceptor's care for the patient can lead a student to choose nursing as a career. In an expanded research survey conducted in 1998 of graduating high school seniors who had participated in the shadow program, Nursing 2000 found that 84% of the students indicated the shadow experience was influential in their career decisions.

A letter is sent to registered nurse preceptors that includes the following statements:

- Thanks for their participation
- The importance of the day in nursing career selection
- A description of the student application criteria
- The need for patient confidentiality discussions with the student
- The role of the student as an observer only
- The need for the nurse to always accompany the student

A patient confidentiality statement is included with the letter, and the student is asked to sign a statement of patient confidentiality at the end of the experience.

Contracts are established with a public relations representative who sends a press release to media in the eight counties announcing the program. Media coverage of the program occurs frequently and is coordinated by the community relations departments of the participating hospitals. Students or their parents/guardians sign a photograph release statement so that photographs can be used for media coverage of the program or for future events and publications.

The agenda for the day includes a pre- and post-conference with the students led by the volunteer site coordinator(s). The pre-conference allows discussion of expectations for the day and nursing as a career. A hospital tour is also part of the pre-conference. Students are given a packet of materials provided by staff of Nursing 2000 that includes a welcome letter and a name tag, a handout on a career in registered nursing, a list of nursing educational programs in Indiana, a professional nursing and healthcare organizations resource list, volunteer opportunities in affiliated hospitals, financial aid information, and brochures from the affiliated schools of nursing.

The post-conference promotes sharing of the day's experiences and a review of career information. The students also receive a small gift—a duffel bag—that bears the Nursing 2000 logo. The coordinators are asked to show the Nursing 2000 videotape, Nursing Today and Beyond 2000, which highlights the many career tracks available to registered nurses.

Vice president for nursing, at local hospital, welcomes A Day in the Life of a Nurse shadow program participants during pre-conference.

Students are treated as visitors to the clinical sites for purposes of accidents/incidents and infection control. Students are told they have to comply with the dress code of the clinical site, so they change into surgical scrub attire provided by the hospital. The clinical sites cover the expenses of student parking, lunch for the student and registered nurse preceptor, the pre- and post-conference refreshments, and a photograph keepsake of the student with her/his registered nurse preceptor. Some of the clinical sites have found a rotation of the students after the first half of the day provides for a richer experience. Students provide a written evaluation of the program at the end of their day of observation. After the program, ongoing contact is maintained with the students by the affiliated schools of nursing.

When students who were accepted to the program find they cannot attend, they cancel with their high school counselors, who in turn notify Nursing 2000. Students from high schools that have historically higher absence rates receive a reminder phone call prior to the program from Nursing 2000. The no-show rate has been reduced from 10% to 5% during the past five years. If there are students who are absent the day of the program, their high school counselors are notified the same day by Nursing 2000.

The program is evaluated and revised based on high school student evaluations, as well as coordinator and registered nurse feedback, at a meeting one time per year after the spring semester's program. In the early days of the program, it was evaluated after each semester. The dates for the next academic year's programs are also determined at the time of the meeting. In addition, gift suggestions for the registered nurse preceptors are submitted at the evaluation meeting.

Students placed on the wait list for the next semester's program are contacted by letter about the future program. Approximately eight weeks prior to the date, students are asked to confirm their participation in writing for the upcoming program so their space can be assigned to another student if they cannot attend. Student participants in Nursing 2000's A Day in the Life of a Nurse shadow program who reapply and are denied due to space constraints are encouraged to continue to use Nursing 2000 as a resource. For instance, applicants for the fall 2001 program who were denied entrance to the program were offered the opportunity to attend, without cost, the opening day of the Honor Society of Nursing, Sigma Theta Tau International's convention held in Indianapolis, November 2001. Nursing 2000 staff members are continually looking for ways to connect the students with a career in nursing. Previous participants, as well as students accepted into an upcoming program, are invited to attend the Nursing 2000 career seminar, Nursing Now—A First Look at Nursing as a Career.

Nursing 2000's A Day in the Life of a Nurse shadow program is one of the most rewarding programs offered by the organization. It allows high school students contemplating a myriad of career choices the opportunity to experience nursing firsthand in a complex and rich learning environment. The following procedures are offered as a way to develop and implement such a program. A step-by-step process for review of applications for A Day in the Life of a Nurse shadow program is also outlined as part of the procedures.

Program development

The following is a list of the tasks that must be completed to develop a program similar to A Day in the Life of a Nurse shadow program offered by Nursing 2000.

1. Locate clinical sites and recruit one or two volunteer site coordinators from each one.

2. Orient the high school counselors/science teachers to the program concept and request participation.
3. Develop materials for distribution to high schools, such as program announcement flyers, student application forms, and letters of instruction to counselors/teachers.
4. Develop letters to be sent to counselors/teachers informing them of the outcome of their students' applications to the program.
5. Develop letters to be sent to students after their applications to the program are reviewed. These would include acceptance letters, wait list to the next program date letters, and denial letters.
6. Develop the agenda for the program.
7. Determine how many students each clinical location can accommodate.
8. Develop materials for the registered nurse preceptors, which would include letters that explain the program, role descriptions for the preceptor and the student, and thank you letters for their participation.
9. Develop a patient confidentiality statement.
10. Determine a small gift for the registered nurse preceptors.
11. Develop and implement an orientation program for the volunteer site coordinators.
12. Determine a small gift for the volunteer site coordinators.
13. Develop materials for students, including a welcome letter, name tag, and career information materials.
14. Determine a small gift for students, for example, a duffel bag in which to carry their materials.
15. Develop a student evaluation form for the program.
16. Determine how students will be treated in the clinical sites in regard to dress code, parking, infection control, and accidents/incidents.
17. Calculate the expenses for the program, including correspondence, packets, gifts, parking, food, and photographs taken the day of the program. Determine who will bear the costs for the program components.
18. Orient volunteer site coordinators to the program.

Program implementation

The following is a list of the activities that must be accomplished in order to implement a program similar to Nursing 2000's A Day in the Life of a Nurse shadow program.

1. Determine how often the program will be offered each academic year and select a date(s).
2. Send materials to counselors/teachers approximately eight weeks prior to the program date.
3. Expect to receive student applications approximately four weeks prior to the program date, review applications, and select students for participation (see A Day in the Life of a Nurse shadow program application review process).
4. Notify counselors/teachers, in writing, two weeks prior to the program date regarding the outcomes of the applications of their students.
5. Notify students, in writing, two weeks prior to the program date of the outcomes of their applications.
6. Notify volunteer site coordinators, in writing, two weeks prior to the program date of accepted/assigned students.
7. Select and orient registered nurse preceptors in each clinical location.
8. Coordinate communication of student cancellations for the program.
9. Notify media of the program and coordinate media coverage via the hospitals' community relations departments.
10. Deliver student materials to each clinical site within a few days of the program.
11. Coordinate communication about students who are absent from the program.
12. Conduct the program.
13. Evaluate the program with volunteer site coordinators utilizing student evaluations and their feedback.
14. Select date(s) for the next program.
15. Send thank you letters to the counselors/teachers.
16. Maintain an updated list of volunteer site coordinators.
17. Notify students wait-listed for the next program about the selected date approximately eight weeks prior to the date and seek confirmation of their continued interest and participation in writing.

A day in the life of a nurse shadow program application review process
The next list is an outline of the process that can be used to review the applications of students interested in the A Day in the Life of a Nurse shadow program.

1. Administrative assistant checks for application completion, which includes:
   - Signatures of student, parent/guardian, and guidance counselor;
   - Completion of section describing high school coursework; and
   - Completion of narrative section.
2. Administrative assistant enters applicant data into the computer. If the student has previously participated or previously applied and was denied at that time, a notation is made on the application. Priority is given to students who have not previously participated in the program. Strong consideration is given to students who apply a second time who were previously denied, as this often indicates unmet criteria has been addressed or the student is highly motivated.
3. Administrative assistant sorts the applications according to school. Applications are organized into school clusters to ensure a representative number of students from each of the 68 area schools.
4. Professional staff review the applications based on the following criteria:
   - Completion of (or plan to enroll in) algebra, biology, and chemistry;
   - Quality of narrative statements; and
   - Interest in nursing or healthcare career exploration.
5. Professional staff assign a hospital site of choice for the students who were previously accepted to the program and were placed on the waiting list.
6. Professional staff set aside the applications from students who have previously participated in the program. These students are accepted into the program again if clinical assignments of their choice are available after priority is given to new students meeting the application criteria.
7. Professional staff review each remaining application by school. Acceptance is indicated on the applications of those who meet the criteria.
8. Professional staff assign qualified students to a hospital site of their choice. Clinical assignment is based on availability of hospital sites selected by the students on the application. Priority is given to seniors, then juniors, and lastly to sophomores. Qualified students, for whom there is no clinical availability, are placed on the waiting list. These students will be automatically placed during the next program.

9. Professional staff indicate on all applications of students who did not meet the acceptance criteria the reason for non-acceptance, and the reason is included in the individualized notification letter.
10. Professional staff record review outcomes on the individual school log and each hospital roster.
11. Professional staff mail review outcome letters to each high school counselor listing each of their students.
12. Professional staff mail individual notification letters to each student who applied.
13. Professional staff mail the roster of accepted/assigned students to each hospital's volunteer site coordinators.

Materials relevant to Nursing 2000's high school shadow a nurse program can be found in Appendix F. These materials are offered to any *collaborative* for revision and modification as it develops its own high school shadow a nurse program.

Classroom presentations

Nursing 2000 staff and members are frequently invited by the elementary, middle, and high schools in the eight counties it serves to present information about a career in registered nursing. Classroom presentations meet Nursing 2000's goal to disseminate information about nursing as a dynamic profession. To accommodate these invitations and to ensure consistency in content, Nursing 2000 has developed a classroom package that includes an 80-slide presentation with an accompanying script for its registered nurse volunteers and professional staff presenters. The classroom presentation script can be adapted to PowerPoint when equipment is available. Registered nurse volunteer presenters are members of Nursing 2000's volunteer speakers' bureau. Classroom presentations vary in length from 20 to 55 minutes.

The slide presentation helps speakers address the questions of "What is nursing?"and "What do nurses do in providing care for patients?" Speakers also discuss, with support of the slide presentation, the practice settings for nurses, various roles of nurses, diversity of nursing as a career, nurses' salaries, work environment options, college preparation curriculum, types of nursing educational programs, the advantage of a bachelor of science degree in nursing as preparation for an advanced degree, and how to select a college. Content is organized to allow the presenters to incorporate all or

Volunteer presenting nursing as a career to high school students.

part of the scripted presentation to meet specific classroom learning objectives. The Nursing 2000 career videotape, Nursing Today and Beyond 2000, is also used in classroom presentations. In addition, each student receives a packet of information provided by Nursing 2000. The packet contains information regarding the various programs offered by Nursing 2000, a handout on a career in registered nursing, and a list of nursing educational programs in Indiana. The presenters also provide a small gift to the hosting classroom counselor/teacher.

Nursing 2000 markets its ability to provide such classroom presentations in its middle and high school counselor newsletter, Future Focus in Nursing, and annually in a cover letter enclosed with the newsletter. The organization also networks with school counselors and teachers at career fairs and the Indiana Association of College Admission Counselor Conference. Nursing 2000 is invited by counselors/teachers to provide presentations for career days; career exploration classes; and science, growth and development, health, and health occupation classes. The organization has even been invited to provide presentations for English and business classes. Counselors/teachers often invite the organization for return presentations in subsequent years. While the presenters primarily address nursing as a career, they are also able to offer information and answer general questions about other health careers and refer students to additional resources. The presenters are also encouraged to individualize the presentation and integrate their nursing specialty by providing a three- to five-minute biographical sketch.

Classroom presentations allow school-aged students to learn about nursing as a dynamic profession. Many students would have no opportunity to learn about the opportunities of a career in registered nursing without such exposure. The following procedures are suggested as ways to develop and implement classroom presentations.

Program development
1. Orient the school counselors/teachers to the classroom presentation concept and offer services to these schools.
2. Develop or locate presentation material.
3. Develop or locate career information materials for the students.
4. Develop and implement an orientation program for the registered nurse volunteer presenters.
5. Determine a small gift for the counselors/teachers.

Program implementation
1. Market the classroom presentations to counselors/teachers.
2. Schedule classroom presentations.
3. Schedule the registered nurse volunteers to provide the presentations.
4. Provide necessary information to registered nurse volunteers, such as directions for parking and onsite coordination.
5. Prepare career information materials for the students.
6. Provide thank you gifts for the counselors/teachers.
7. Ensure delivery and return of presentation and career information materials.
8. Conduct the presentations.
9. Send thank you letters to registered nurse volunteers who provided the presentation.

Materials relevant to Nursing 2000's classroom presentations are found in Appendix G. These materials are offered to any *collaborative* for revision and modification as it develops its own classroom presentations.

School counselor newsletter

Nursing 2000 staff publishes a newsletter three times annually for the 445 middle and high school counselors in the eight-county service area of the organization. The newsletter is titled Future Focus in Nursing and is distributed in winter, summer, and fall. The newsletter is one tool used by Nursing 2000 to meet its goal to disseminate information about registered nursing as a dynamic profession. The purposes of the newsletter are to educate counselors regarding current trends in the nursing profession and to assist counselors and their students as they explore career options. In addition, the newsletter provides a means of communication with counselors. It allows the staff of Nursing 2000 to highlight programs offered to high school students and local high school alumni who are currently enrolled in a nursing educational program.

The format of Future Focus in Nursing is four 8.5 by 11 inch pages, including text and photographs. Content enables the presentation of diversity in nursing roles by settings, gender and ethnicity, profiles of competent practicing nurses, introduction of future nursing career opportunities, and positive photographic images of nursing practice. The newsletter is published internally and mailed to school counselors. The professional staff serves as the editors of the newsletter and five advisory board/volunteer speakers' bureau members also serve as voluntary editorial board members and contributing writers. Voluntary participation is based on interest and rotation of new members and has occurred by natural attrition. Content for the newsletter is planned and the responsibility for articles and photographs is assigned by the editors and editorial board members annually. The advisory board provides content suggestions for the newsletter.

Future Focus in Nursing has contained information and articles of human interest about varied roles and diversity in the profession of nursing against a backdrop of emerging healthcare choices. The newsletter strengthens Nursing 2000 as a career resource by linking students with the organization's Web site, A Day in the Life of a Nurse shadow program, career fairs, classroom presentations, and counseling resources regarding nursing careers. In addition, the newsletter features local high school students, nursing students, and registered nurses, allowing the newsletter to be individualized to its specific communities. Nursing 2000's network of hospitals, schools of nursing, and professional nursing organizations communicates a positive and supportive environment for prospective students so they can explore career options.

Nursing 2000's newsletter has proven to be an excellent means of communicating with the school counselors and educating them about

Two issues of the School Counselor Newsletter featuring "Men in Nursing" and "Pediatric Nursing."

nursing, thus enabling them to guide students as they explore a career in registered nursing. The following procedures are suggested to develop and implement a school counselor newsletter such as Nursing 2000's Future Focus in Nursing.

Program development

1. Locate and recruit volunteer editorial board members.
2. Determine the format of the newsletters, as well as how frequently they will be published each year.
3. Determine how the newsletters will be published and distributed.
4. Obtain names and mailing addresses of middle and high school counselors.
5. Develop and implement an orientation program for the volunteer editorial board members.

Program implementation
1. Determine content and assign responsibility for articles and photographs.
2. Arrange for on-site interviews and photographs as required. Obtain a signed release form for use of photographs.
3. Edit, publish, and distribute the newsletters.
4. Maintain an ongoing mailing list of middle and high school counselors.
5. Add additional names to the mailing list as requested.

Materials relevant to the newsletter can be found in Appendix H. These materials are offered to any *collaborative* for revision and modification as it develops its own school counselor newsletter.

School career fairs

Members of Nursing 2000 are frequently invited to participate in career fairs for middle and high school students within the eight-county area. School career fair participation allows for dissemination of information about registered nursing as a dynamic profession. Participation enables the members of Nursing 2000 to provide information, as well as counseling, for students who have an interest in a career as a registered nurse. Information sharing might include the practice settings for nurses, the various roles of nurses, diversity of nursing as a career, salaries, and work environment options. Counseling might include guidance regarding college preparation and coursework for a career in registered nursing and information and guidance regarding types of nursing educational programs and how to select a college.

School career fairs are labor intensive, as these events can be scheduled over several hours or even several days. The professional staff of Nursing 2000, as well as registered nurses from the organization's volunteer speakers' bureau, provide the manpower for school career fairs. Volunteers are essential to Nursing 2000's ability to participate in these events. The manpower involved in school career fairs is extensive. Nursing 2000 staff members coordinate all aspects of participation in school career fairs, which includes not only the evaluation of the organization's ability to participate in an event, but the provision of display and career information materials; scheduling of staffing; provision of instructions to staff regarding directions, parking, scheduling, and on-site coordination of the event; and sending thank you letters to the registered nurse volunteer participants.

Volunteer exhibiting at high school career fair.

Career information materials depend on the expected audience for the fair. Middle and high school students receive handouts on a career in registered nursing, while the high school students also receive a list of nursing educational programs in Indiana and financial aid information. One-on-one student counseling is provided by the staff and volunteers whenever feasible. Students are also directed to other relevant programs of Nursing 2000, most frequently A Day in the Life of a Nurse shadow program.

Ensuring an adequate volunteer base is the first step in initiating school career fair participation. Nursing 2000 has a volunteer base of over 200 registered nurses who are members of the organization's volunteer speakers' bureau. These nurses contribute their time for at least one program and usually for multiple programs each year. Each school career fair should be evaluated to determine participation ability as well as congruence of participation with the mission statement of the *collaborative*. Coordination of school career fairs also requires the resources to be able to recruit and schedule the volunteers, provide them with the necessary information, and find back-up coverage if necessary. The credibility of the *collaborative* rests with its ability to provide knowledgeable staff coverage for the fairs. The time required to develop display and handout materials is another important consideration.

School career fairs are a positive way to interact with middle and high school students and to provide them with information and one-on-one counseling regarding the choice of nursing as a career. The following procedures are suggested to develop and implement participation in school career fairs.

Program development

1. Ensure an adequate number of registered nurse volunteers to support participation in school career fairs.
2. Orient the counselors to the school career fair participation concept and determine participating schools.
3. Develop and implement an orientation program for the registered nurse volunteers.
4. Determine how the coordination for the school career fairs will be handled.
5. Develop display materials.
6. Develop career information materials geared to the student audience.

Program implementation

1. Market the ability to participate in school career fairs to the counselor.
2. Schedule the school career fair.
3. Schedule the registered nurse volunteers to staff the school career fair.
4. Provide necessary information to registered nurse volunteers, such as directions for parking, scheduling, and on-site coordination.
5. Determine and prepare appropriate career information materials for the students.
6. Ensure delivery, set-up, and return of display and career information materials.
7. Arrange for backup staff coverage, if necessary.
8. Conduct the school career fairs.
9. Send thank you letters to registered nurse volunteers who participated.

Materials relevant to Nursing 2000's participation in school career fairs are found in Appendix I. These materials are offered to any *collaborative* for re-

Scholarship recipients recognized on stage at the Benefit.

vision and modification as it develops its own ability to participate in school career fairs.

Scholarship benefit

Nursing 2000's scholarship benefit is held annually and provides scholarship dollars for nursing students attending the four schools of nursing that are affiliated with the organization. Scholarship proceeds are divided equally among the schools of nursing. The purpose of the scholarship benefit is to support development of future nursing careers by assisting nursing students with their financial commitments. The benefit meets the Nursing 2000 goal to attract students into nursing who have demonstrated those potential academic abilities that will lead to a successful career in registered nursing. Through the 11th anniversary of the benefit, $204,000 in cumulative proceeds were awarded by Nursing 2000 to 279 students. An additional $54,000 in scholarship proceeds were raised with the complement of a walk/run for nursing within the Indianapolis community.

Approximately 500 individuals attend the benefit that includes an elegant social hour and sit-down dinner with a keynote speaker. The keynote speaker, an individual of national prominence and name recognition, is frequently a registered nurse. The main objective in selection of a keynote speaker is the ability of the individual to elevate and enhance the evening, thus engaging the audience, which often helps with fundraising and an interest in programs offered by Nursing 2000. The speaker is provided with an honorarium and is compensated for all travel expenses.

Scholarship dollars are raised in many different ways, such as underwriting of specific expenses, in-kind donations, individual attendees, individual sponsorships, sponsored tables, individual patrons, patron tables, and sponsorship packages. Underwriting opportunities are offered for the patron reception ($1,000), written program brochure advertising ($500 for a full-page and $300 for a half-page advertisement), patron dinner reservations for two guests ($250 each), dinner reservations for a scholarship recipient and guest ($100 each), contributions directly to the scholarship fund ($100), and other miscellaneous expenses. In-kind donations are services offered for reduced or no fees. Individual sponsorships ($60) and sponsored tables ($480) allow others to attend the benefit for the same costs as individual attendees. Patrons ($90) and patron-sponsored tables ($720) provide additional scholarship dollars. Sponsorship packages include diamond sponsors ($5,000), platinum sponsors ($3,000), gold sponsors ($1,500), silver sponsors ($1,000), bronze sponsors ($500), friend sponsors ($250), and nursing scholarship fund sponsors ($100). Many of those providing sponsorship packages are corporations that have been cultivated by Nursing 2000 via its network. Corporate sponsorships have doubled the dollars available for scholarships in recent years. Recognition is provided for:

- Underwriters
- Those who contribute in-kind donations
- Individual sponsors
- Table sponsors
- Individual patrons
- Patron table sponsors
- Those who contribute sponsorship packages
- Individual contributors

Recognition is commensurate with the level of support and includes recognition in the written program brochure; dinner reservations for a number of guests at the benefit; invitation to the patron reception; a half-page to full-page advertisement in the written program brochure; special recognition during the program with a crystal award, plaque, or certificate; mention in affiliate-produced news releases; and signage recognition during the benefit.

The annual scholarship benefit starts with a welcome luncheon for the keynote speaker and the co-chair planning committee members the day of the event. The social hour and patron reception begin the festivities of the evening starting at 6:00 p.m. Dinner is served from 7:00 p.m. to 8:00 p.m. The evening's program starts promptly at 8:00 p.m. The honorary chair welcomes all attendees to the event and then introduces the master of ceremonies. The master of ceremonies presents the proclamations from the governor and mayor and coordinates the rest of the program. The executive director of Nursing 2000 is introduced for remarks. She also announces the scholarship dollars raised by the event, recognizes any special guests, and recognizes and presents the awards for those providing sponsorship packages valued at $250 or greater. One of the current year's scholarship recipients presents remarks on behalf of all awardees after the other current year's scholarship recipients are recognized and gathered on stage as a group. The opportunity for a recipient to present remarks is rotated among the four schools of nursing. Each scholarship recipient also receives a certificate and a group photograph. The master of ceremonies then introduces the keynote speaker for the evening. The program ends at approximately 9:30 p.m.

Local news co-anchor as emcee for annual Scholarship Benefit.

Several committees, comprised of members of Nursing 2000's advisory board and volunteer speakers' bureau, plan the scholarship benefit. There are seven planning committees, which include the following:

- Patron reception committee
- Invitation/program committee
- Publicity committee
- Registration committee
- Seating committee
- Dining/decorations/entertainment committee
- Development committee

Two co-chairs lead each of the planning committees, and committees meet as often as necessary during the year to accomplish their work. In addition, the co-chairs comprise an overall planning committee that includes the professional staff of Nursing 2000. This co-chair planning committee meets four times a year to coordinate the scholarship benefit and once a year following the benefit to evaluate its success. The co-chair planning committee also selects the keynote speaker and the location for the event, and recruits volunteers to staff each planning committee. In

Keynote speaker, JoEllen Koerner, addressing Scholarship Benefit attendees.

addition, the co-chair planning committee develops and approves the budget for the benefit. Planning and implementing an event such as the scholarship benefit takes a full 12 months, even though the event has been held many times.

Patron reception committee

The patron reception committee manages the patron reception, which includes determining room layout, selecting beverages and hors d'oeuvres, greeting and hosting guests, obtaining and coordinating the photographer's activities for the reception as well as the rest of the evening, and obtaining a musician for the reception. The patron reception occurs simultaneously with the evening's social hour, but it is held in a separate location from the social hour. The reception is for invited guests only and includes those sponsoring patron tables; individual patrons; underwriters of the patron reception and event speaker; and those contributing at the bronze, silver, gold, platinum, and diamond sponsorship package level. Written invitations are sent to those invited to the reception. The patron reception offers those attending the opportunity to meet and mingle with the evening's keynote speaker and with each other.

Invitation/program committee

The invitation/program committee develops and coordinates all printed materials for the scholarship benefit. This responsibility includes preparing invitations and written program brochures, and proofing and ordering materials. Invitations announce the event and are distributed, when possible, by advisory board members to people within their institutions and organizations. The majority of invitations are mailed. A cumulative three-year attendance list from previous scholarship benefits is maintained and serves as the invitation roster. All former and current scholarship recipients are invited to the scholarship benefit. For the most recent annual events, each of the current scholarship recipients had his/her attendance sponsored. The program brochure is multifaceted and contains the program, photographs of key individuals, recognition, and advertising. Each attendee at the scholarship benefit receives a program brochure.

Publicity committee

The publicity committee works with a public relations consultant contracted by Nursing 2000. The committee manages publicity to heighten public awareness of the scholarship benefit in order to increase reservations by the community, hospitals, and schools of nursing. Committee members develop a promotional flyer and a promotional packet that are used by Nursing 2000 volunteers. With the assistance of the public relations consultant, the committee coordinates distribution of press releases to magazines and newspapers, preparation of public service announcements, development of a calendar of events, and procurement of proclamations from the governor of Indiana and the mayor of Indianapolis for use during the scholarship benefit. To recognize nursing as a profession and proclaim Indiana Nursing Scholarship Day, both proclamations are read the evening of the benefit. The date of the annual scholarship benefit is also posted on the Nursing 2000 Web site calendar. The scholarship benefit has an honorary chair who is a prominent and recognizable individual from the Indianapolis community. The public relations consultant coordinates activities of the honorary chair. The committee also distributes a program brochure to any media person who attends the event.

Registration committee

The registration committee recruits volunteers and coordinates the registration and greeting process the evening of the scholarship benefit. Greeters are familiar with special guests, such as the scholarship recipients and their guests and corporate sponsors, and are responsible for seeing that guests feel welcome and know the sequence of events for the benefit. Greeters are also available to escort guests who need assistance in locating their tables.

Seating committee

The seating committee determines table assignments and seating arrangements for all in attendance at the scholarship benefit. Since the committee members are responsible for strategically and appropriately seating approximately 500 attendees, the expected attendance must be known before the event so planning can occur. This task is usually coordinated and completed during the week before the benefit.

Dining/decorations/entertainment committee

The dining/decorations/entertainment committee selects the location for the scholarship benefit. Although Nursing 2000 has selected the same location for all of its benefits, the committee conducts a comparative evaluation of the usual location with other facilities, including site visits, every three years. The committee also does the following:

- Determines the room layout
- Selects the menu for the evening
- Provides appropriate decorations (flowers and table centerpieces)
- Coordinates signage, lighting, stage placement and setup, and audio-visual requirements
- Coordinates the agenda for the evening's program that occurs after dinner is served
- Arranges for background music by a pianist during dinner
- Locates a person(s) for external traffic control for attendees who arrive and leave the event

The committee also arranges for a master of ceremonies for the scholarship event. A television news anchor has historically been selected as the master of ceremonies and has been provided with a gift of appreciation.

Development committee

Lastly, the development committee seeks scholarship proceeds and/or support for the scholarship event by identifying and building relationships with underwriters, patrons, sponsors, and contributors. The committee also develops all materials used to support development activities, such as the sponsorship/advertising brochure that identifies sponsorship and advertising opportunities for the scholarship benefit. They also coordinate preparation of development packets that are sent to previous and potential corporate sponsors.

The scholarship benefit is Nursing 2000's only program that directly raises scholarship dollars for nursing students. Careful and comprehensive planning has made the benefit a very successful event. Two factors have been essential for this success: (1) a minimum of 12 months planning time, and (2) a significant volunteer force.

The following procedures are suggested for development of a program like the scholarship benefit. Nursing 2000 and the co-chair planning committee use the scholarship benefit timeline overview as a tool to track planning activities and planning progress. This timeline overview is found in Appendix J with other materials relevant to the scholarship benefit. These materials are offered to any collaborative for revision and modification as it develops its own scholarship benefit.

Program development
1. Determine a committee structure for planning.
2. Enlist registered nurse volunteers.

3. Determine the format for the scholarship benefit including reception(s), meals, and program.
4. Develop and approve a budget including projected expenses (keynote speaker, printing, entertainment, photographer, audiovisuals, public relations, facility rentals, reception(s), meals, service charges), projected revenues (underwriting, in-kind and sponsorship opportunities, individual and table revenues), and projected scholarship proceeds.
5. Determine how scholarship proceeds will be distributed, including the criteria for distribution and the expectations for follow-up communication.
6. Prepare materials including recognition for each level of support if offering underwriting, in-kind, and sponsorship opportunities. Develop a contact list of those who might provide such support.
7. Determine public relations activities and prepare materials including flyers, packets, press releases, public service announcements, and calendars of events.
8. Determine invitation list.

Program implementation
1. Determine a date and confirm a keynote speaker and a facility location.
2. Determine facility layout, reception beverages and hors d'oeuvres, if applicable, and the meal menu.
3. Arrange for facility decorations, signage, lighting, stage placement and setup, audiovisual requirements, and traffic control, as applicable.
4. Arrange for entertainment during the reception(s) and meal, if applicable.
5. Arrange for a photographer to take pictures during the reception(s), meal, and program, if applicable.
6. Invite and confirm an honorary chair, if applicable, and a master of ceremonies for the scholarship benefit program.
7. Mail underwriting, in-kind, and sponsorship opportunities materials.
8. Initiate follow-up contact with those who received mailed packets for underwriting, in-kind, and sponsorship opportunities.
9. Initiate public relations activities.
10. Make travel arrangements for the keynote speaker.
11. Order invitations and response cards.
12. Mail and deliver invitations.

13. Determine the registration process and solicit registered nurse volunteers.
14. Determine the number of greeters needed and solicit registered nurse volunteers.
15. Request proclamations and frame for presentation, if applicable.
16. Order any needed recognition materials such as banners, posters, crystal awards, plaques, and certificates.
17. Mail invitations to those providing underwriting, in-kind, and sponsorship opportunities.
18. Finalize the written program brochure format and generic content.
19. Collect any artwork or photographs for the written program brochure.
20. Finalize the written program brochure and send to printer.
21. Confirm attendance of all persons to be introduced during the program.
22. Finalize the program agenda and script.
23. Send invitations for any special reception, if applicable.
24. Arrange seating at each table. Consider placement of each table within the facility.
25. Prepare honorarium for keynote speaker and any payments due during the event. Select any gifts to be distributed during the event.
26. Welcome the keynote speaker.
27. Register and greet guests.
28. Conduct the scholarship benefit.
29. Schedule and hold a post-event evaluation meeting and incorporate suggested planning for next year's scholarship benefit.
30. Determine proceeds to go to scholarship and distribute. Include criteria for distribution and expectations for follow-up communication.
31. Determine the role of scholarship recipients for future scholarship benefits.
32. Maintain a cumulative attendance list to serve as the future invitation roster.

Summary

This chapter has provided descriptions and procedures for development and implementation of Nursing 2000's school and nursing school programs. These programs include A Day in the Life of a Nurse shadow program, classroom presentations, the school counselor newsletter, school career fairs, and the scholarship benefit. The program descriptions and procedures are offered to any *collaborative* as tools for its own use in developing similar programs. School and nursing school programs provide a framework for Nursing 2000 staff and members provide information to elementary, middle, and high school students and middle and high school counselors about a career in registered nursing.

5

NURSING 2000: COMMUNITY PROGRAMS

Introduction

The previous chapter focused on the school and school of nursing programs of Nursing 2000. This chapter contains discussions about community programs of the organization. Community programs include:

- Adult Learner Career Seminar
- Adult learner shadow a nurse program
- Community presentations
- Public library displays
- Community career and health fairs

The purposes of community programs of Nursing 2000 are to expand the visibility of registered nursing in the community, provide education to the public about a career in registered nursing, and address current issues and future opportunities for the nursing profession. The Adult Learner Career Seminar introduces adult learners to a career in registered nursing. Adult learners are defined as potential or existing non-traditional college students and those who are interested in a second college degree. Non-traditional college students are students who have not pursued a college education immediately following high school. The adult learner shadow a nurse program provides adult learners considering nursing as a career the opportunity to observe the role of the professional nurse in a clinical setting. Community presentations are programs that provide information about a career in nursing, as well as current issues and future implications for the profession. Public library displays allow Nursing 2000 to expand the visibility of nursing and disseminate information about nursing in the community. Community career and health fairs serve as additional vehicles for Nursing 2000 to provide education about registered nursing to the public.

Community Programs

Adult learner career seminar

Nursing 2000's Adult Learner Career Seminar is offered one time per month at a community location within the eight-county area served by the organization. The seminar meets Nursing 2000's goal to disseminate information about nursing as a dynamic profession and introduces adult learners to a career in registered nursing. The adult learner who has an interest in nursing as a career contacts the Nursing 2000 office and is informed about the next scheduled Adult Learner Career Seminar. The professional staff of Nursing 2000 or a registered nurse member of the volunteer speakers' bureau conducts the seminar. Presenters are aided in their 1 1/2-hour seminar by a 68-slide presentation with an accompanying script. The seminar presentation can be adapted to PowerPoint when equipment is available.

The slide presentation helps the speaker address the questions about nursing and what nurses do when providing care for patients. The speakers also discuss, with the support of the slide presentation, the current job market for nurses, the practice settings for nurses, the various roles of nurses, the diversity of nursing as a career, current salaries, and work environment options. The Nursing 2000 career videotape, Nursing Today and Beyond 2000, is also available for use during the seminar presentations, incorporating the content with an alternate methodology. In addition, each adult learner receives a packet of information. The packet contains information regarding the various programs of Nursing 2000, an agenda and evaluation forms for the seminar, a welcome letter, a handout on a career in registered nursing, a list of nursing educational programs in Indiana, a professional nursing and health-care organizations resource list, financial aid information, a list of supporting hospitals of Nursing 2000 including human resource department contacts and volunteer opportunities, and brochures from the affiliated schools of nursing. Attendees complete an evaluation form after the seminar. The roster of those who registered for the program is sent to the four affiliated schools of nursing after the seminar for follow-up.

The Adult Learner Career Seminar is marketed to the community by library displays and the organization's Web site. In addition, an ongoing list of interested individuals, who have called or made e-mail inquiries, is maintained at the Nursing 2000 office. The seminar is now a pre-requisite for adult learners who also want to participate in the adult learner shadow a nurse program. Over the years of experience in offering the program, attendance at the Adult Learner Career Seminar has been positively correlated with the individually scheduled shadow experience. In contrast, the organization found that poor attendance for shadow experiences was correlated with no attendance at the Adult Learner Career Seminar.

Program development

The following procedures are suggested as strategies for the development and implementation of an Adult Learner Career Seminar.
1. Develop the presentation materials for the seminars.
2. Develop career information materials.
3. Develop and implement an orientation program for the registered nurse volunteer presenters.
4. Determine how often the seminars will be offered.

Program implementation

1. Determine a location and schedule the seminars.
2. Market the seminars.
3. Send letters of invitation to adult individuals who have made inquiries regarding career counseling. Include directions to the locations of the seminars.
4. Schedule attendance of those interested in the seminars.
5. Schedule the registered nurse volunteers to provide the seminars.
6. Provide necessary information to registered nurse volunteers, such as directions, parking, and on-site coordination.
7. Prepare career information materials for the adult learners.
8. Ensure delivery and return of presentation and career information materials.
9. Conduct the seminars.
10. Determine which adult learner attendees are interested in the shadow a nurse program.
11. Send roster of those who registered for the seminars to the schools of nursing.
12. Send thank you letters to registered nurse volunteers who provided the seminars.

Materials relevant to Nursing 2000's Adult Learner Career Seminar are found in Appendix K. These materials are offered to any *collaborative* for revision and modification as it develops its own Adult Learner Career Seminar.

Adult learner shadow a nurse program

Nursing 2000 offers a program based on its high school shadow a nurse program titled A Day in the Life of a Nurse for adult learners. The adult learner shadow experience provides individuals considering nursing as a career the unique opportunity to observe the role of the professional nurse in a clinical setting. The purpose of the observational experience is to assist individuals in making a career choice.

The program is coordinated by the professional staff of Nursing 2000 and by volunteer coordinators who represent each clinical site. The 14 supporting hospitals of Nursing 2000 participate in the program. The adult learner shadow experience was initiated following the development of the high school student shadow a nurse program, thus enabling Nursing 2000 to take advantage of the existing program elements. Adult learners desiring information about nursing as a career may contact the Nursing 2000 office or the hospitals directly. The adult learners are guided to the Adult Learner Career Seminar if they have not yet attended, because the seminar is a prerequisite to the shadow experience.

The hospital volunteer site coordinator for the high school shadow a nurse program also coordinates the adult learner shadow experiences. Once a shadow experience is scheduled, the hospital volunteer site coordinator arranges the shadow experience for the adult learner with a registered nurse preceptor in the clinical setting, obtains a signed patient confidentiality statement, leads a pre- and post-shadow conference with the adult learner, coordinates the shadow experience, provides the adult learner with a program evaluation form and a small gift, and sends a copy of the completed evaluation form to Nursing 2000. A small gift is given to the registered nurse for sharing his/her time and experience with the adult learner. The adult learner's name is entered into the computer database for future follow-up.

The development and implementation of two programs, the high school shadow a nurse program and the Adult Learner Career Seminar, have been instrumental to Nursing 2000's ability to offer the adult learner shadow a nurse program. The adult learner shadow experience is based on the high school shadow a nurse program and, therefore, benefits from the high school program's successes. The following procedures for program development and implementation of an adult learner shadow a nurse program assumes such a high school program is in place.

Program development
  1. Develop an adult learner evaluation form for the program.

Program implementation
  1. Arrange the date and time of the shadow experience with the adult learner.
  2. Select and orient the registered nurse preceptor.
  3. Obtain a signed patient confidentiality form, and conduct the program incorporating a pre- and post-shadow experience conference.
  4. Provide a small gift for the registered nurse preceptor.
  5. Send a copy of the completed evaluation form to Nursing 2000.
  6. Enter the adult learner's name in Nursing 2000's computer database for future follow-up.

Materials relevant to Nursing 2000's adult learner shadow a nurse program are found in Appendix L. These materials are offered to any *collaborative* for revision and modification as it develops its own adult learner shadow a nurse program.

Community presentations

Nursing 2000 has often presented other programs related to the profession of nursing within its eight-county service area and beyond as the organization evolved its network development. The organization serves as a resource that responds to various nursing organizations, as well as to Nursing 2000's affiliated hospitals and schools of nursing, to address topics of relevance to the nursing profession. Topics of relevance to nursing might include the programs of Nursing 2000, the evolving demand for nursing, registered nurse mobility, and future implications for the profession. The professional staff of Nursing 2000 usually present these programs. In addition, registered nurse members of the volunteer speakers' bureau present programs about registered nursing to scout groups, church groups, and members of boys' and girls' clubs.

One such program that Nursing 2000 presents is a seminar titled Nursing Now—A First Look at Nursing as a Career. This seminar was piloted in

Individual contact with a nurse is important for career decision making.

early 2001 as a restructured version of the Adult Learner Career Seminar. The purpose of the seminar is to present nursing as a challenging, diverse profession that makes a difference in the lives of others. The target audience is both traditional students and adult learners considering nursing as a first or second career. The seminar location is rotated among the four affiliated schools of nursing. Publicity for the seminar is promoted by flyers sent to the vice presidents and deans of the affiliated hospitals and schools of nursing, members of the advisory board and volunteer speakers' bureau, and high school counselors in the eight-county service area for posting in their organizations. Additional publicity for the seminar occurs via newspaper advertisements, Nursing 2000's Web site, affiliated hospital newsletters, and flyers sent to public libraries in the service area for posting, as well as exhibition in any library display. In addition, individuals who have contacted Nursing 2000 by telephone and/or e-mail for career counseling are informed by mail about the seminar. Seminar registration is required and is coordinated through the Nursing 2000 office.

Seminars last for 1 1/2 hours and include a welcome and introduction; viewing and discussion of Nursing 2000's videotape, Nursing Today and Beyond 2000; a presentation of opportunities, rewards, and advancements in nursing; an overview of career information materials; and a presentation of the evolving demand for nursing. The highlights of the seminar are a panel presentation by four practicing nurses and a presentation by a nurse educator regarding academic and life experience preparation needed to enter nursing. The four practicing nurses include a clinical nurse with a traditional entry into nursing, a clinical nurse with a non-traditional entry into nursing, an advanced practice nurse who discusses the various advanced practice nursing roles, and an experienced nurse who discusses expanded career opportunities in nursing. Presenters are guided in their presentations by a script of questions they are asked to address. Representatives from the four affiliated schools of nursing are available after the seminar to provide information and answer questions for seminar participants. The seminar is an excellent example of collaboration between nursing service and nursing education with broad representation from both.

Each attendee receives a packet of information. The packet contains information regarding the various programs of Nursing 2000, an agenda and evaluation form for the seminar, a welcome letter, a handout on careers in registered nursing, a list of nursing educational programs in Indiana, a professional nursing and healthcare organizations resource list, financial aid information, a list of supporting hospitals of Nursing 2000, including their human resource department contacts and volunteer opportunities, and brochures from the affiliated schools of nursing. Attendees complete the evaluation form after the seminar. The roster of those who registered for the program is sent to the four affiliated schools of nursing after the seminar for follow-up. Adult learners attending the seminar are offered the opportunity to participate in the adult learner shadow a nurse program. All presenters and the school of nursing representatives receive a small gift and a thank you letter.

The success of the pilot restructured version of the Adult Learner Career Seminar, Nursing Now—A First Look at Nursing as a Career, prompted Nursing 2000 to expand the audience for future seminars. All high school juniors who have participated in A Day in the Life of a Nurse shadow program during the previous academic year and their parents are now sent a letter of invitation to the seminars. Attendance for subsequent seminars increased by 50% and included some parents. It is anticipated the seminar will continue to be offered in each academic semester. The Adult Learner Career Seminar also continues to be offered monthly.

Seminars such as Nursing Now—A First Look at Nursing as a Career allow traditional students as well as non-traditional adult learners to learn about nursing as a dynamic profession and to be made aware of the many career opportunities available for registered nurses. The following procedures are suggested to develop and implement a seminar such as Nursing 2000's Nursing Now—A First Look at Nursing as a Career. Other community presentations would require many of the same procedural elements.

Program development
1. Develop presentation materials.
2. Develop career information materials.
3. Develop an orientation program for the registered nurse volunteer presenters.
4. Determine how often the seminars will be offered.
5. Determine a small gift for the registered nurse volunteer presenters and school of nursing representatives.

Program implementation
1. Determine a location and schedule the seminars.
2. Market the seminars.
3. Send letters of invitation to adult learners who have made inquiries regarding career counseling and high school juniors who have participated in the shadow a nurse program during the previous academic year and their parents/guardians.
4. Schedule the attendees for the seminars.
5. Send letters of confirmation to attendees and provide directions and parking instructions.
6. Schedule the registered nurse volunteer presenters and school of nursing representatives to provide the seminars and orient them to their roles in the seminars.
7. Provide necessary information to the registered nurse volunteer presenters and school of nursing representatives, such as directions, parking, and on-site coordination.
8. Prepare career information materials.

9. Ensure delivery and return of presentation and career information materials.
10. Conduct the seminars.
11. Arrange individual shadow a nurse program experiences for adult learners as requested.
12. Send roster of those who registered for the seminars to the schools of nursing.
13. Provide a thank you letter and a small gift for the registered nurse volunteer presenters and the school of nursing representatives who participated in the seminars.

Materials relevant to Nursing 2000's community presentations, including its seminar titled Nursing Now—A First Look at Nursing as a Career, can be found in Appendix M. These materials are offered to any collaborative for revision and modification as it develops its own community presentations.

Library displays

Nursing 2000 provides window displays for public libraries within its eight-county area in order to expand the visibility of nursing in the community and to disseminate information about registered nursing as a dynamic profession. The displays are in each library for approximately one month, and the organization attempts to display materials in at least three libraries per year. Every May, Nursing 2000 has a display in the Indianapolis-Marion County Public Library to correspond with National Nurses' Week and the festivities associated with the Indianapolis 500 auto race. The professional staff of Nursing 2000 and registered nurse members of the volunteer speakers' bureau coordinate the delivery, set-up, and return of the display materials.

Displays consist of a variety of materials, such as poster boards depicting nursing as a career which describe the programs of Nursing 2000, the organization's poster titled Nursing Is AMAZING, and various nursing handouts that are also used during career and health fairs. The displays also provide information regarding Nursing 2000, including ways to contact the organization. Library display dates are posted on the Nursing 2000 Web site calendar.

Library displays expand the visibility of nursing in the community and link the community with resources to learn more about registered nursing. The following procedures are suggested to develop and implement library displays.

Volunteer after setting up community library display.

Program development
1. Contact public libraries and orient them to the concept of window displays.
2. Determine participating libraries.
3. Develop materials for the displays.

Program implementation
1. Schedule public library displays. Determine the time frames for the displays.
2. Schedule the registered nurse volunteers to deliver and set up the displays.
3. Incorporate announcements of upcoming programs in materials for displays when appropriate.
4. Provide necessary information to registered nurse volunteers, such as directions, parking, scheduling, and on-site coordination.

5. Schedule registered nurse volunteers to disassemble and return the displays.

6. Send thank you letters to registered nurse volunteers who participated. Materials relevant to Nursing 2000's library displays are found in Appendix N. These materials are offered to any *collaborative* for revision and modification as it develops its own library displays.

Community career and health fairs

Nursing 2000 is frequently invited to participate in career and health fairs in the community within its eight-county area. Career and health fairs are usually sponsored by affiliated healthcare organizations and are held in a variety of community locations. A special event that Nursing 2000 hosts annually is Nurses' Celebration Saturday at The Children's Museum of Indianapolis. The event serves as a National Nurses' Day celebration and coincides with National Nurses' Week. Nursing 2000 coordinates the Saturday event with 22 Indiana professional nursing organizations, schools of nursing, and healthcare facilities. Each annual event has a theme about nursing, and the event is posted on the Nursing 2000 Web site calendar. Children and their families participating in the event have an opportunity to interact with registered nurses who are demonstrating equipment and talking about the role of the registered nurse in health promotion and healthcare. The event provides an ideal method for registered nurses to interact with elementary and middle school students and their parents from the tri-state area. Participation in career and health fairs in the community serves the purposes of reflecting a positive image of nursing to the public and disseminating information about registered nursing as a dynamic profession. While the organization may receive requests to provide hands-on healthcare screening, it is important to emphasize that the organization is insured to provide education to the public about nursing careers; it is not insured to provide patient care.

Community career and health fairs are very labor intensive because the events can be scheduled over several hours and even several days. The professional staff of Nursing 2000, as well as registered nurses from the organization's volunteer speakers' bureau, provide the manpower for community career and health fairs. Volunteers are essential if Nursing 2000 is to participate in these events. Labor for career and health fairs includes delivery and return of displays and career information materials, set-up of displays, and staffing of the event. Nursing 2000 coordinates all aspects of participation in

"Hands-on" and more at Nurses' Celebration Saturday.

career and health fairs including evaluation of the organization's ability to participate in an event; provision of display and career information materials; scheduling of staffing; provision of instructions to staff regarding directions, parking, scheduling, and on-site coordination of the event; and sending thank you letters to the registered nurse volunteer participants.

While community career and health fairs are mostly focused on exhibiting information regarding the role of the registered nurse in health promotion and healthcare, career information materials are also available. Materials available for distribution depend on the expected audience for the fair. Depending on their ages, elementary school students receive nursing-related coloring books or word puzzles. Middle and high school students and adults in the community receive handouts on a career in registered nursing, and high school students also receive a list of nursing educational programs in Indiana. Licensed practical nurses receive a mobility guide to registered nursing. Registered nurses in the community receive an educational mobility guide, information regarding advanced practice roles in nursing, a guide to specialty certification in nursing, a professional nursing and healthcare organizations resource sheet, and a fact sheet regarding Nursing 2000.

Ensuring an adequate number of volunteers is the first step in initiating community career and health fair participation. Nursing 2000 has over 200 volunteer registered nurses who are members of the organization's volunteer speakers' bureau. These nurses contribute their time each year for at least one program and usually for multiple programs. Each community career and health fair is evaluated to determine Nursing 2000's ability to participate, as well as the congruence of the fair's purpose with the mission statement of Nursing 2000. Coordination of community career and health fairs also requires the resources to be able to recruit and schedule the volunteers, provide them with necessary information, and find back-up coverage if necessary. The credibility of Nursing 2000 rests with its ability to provide knowledgeable staff coverage for the fairs.

Community career and health fairs enable interaction with a broad community audience to provide education about registered nursing and to provide information regarding the choice of nursing as a career. The following procedures are suggested as ways to develop and implement participation in community career and health fairs.

Program development
1. Ensure an adequate number of registered nurse volunteers to support participation in community career and health fairs.
2. Orient the affiliated healthcare organizations to the community career and health fair participation concept.
3. Develop and implement an orientation program for the registered nurse volunteers.
4. Determine how the coordination for the community career and health fairs will be handled.
5. Develop display materials.
6. Develop career information materials geared to the community audience.

Program implementation
1. Market the ability to participate in community career and health fairs to the affiliated healthcare organizations.
2. Schedule the community career and health fairs.
3. Schedule registered nurse volunteers to staff the community career and health fairs.
4. Provide necessary information to registered nurse volunteers, such as directions to the site, parking, scheduling, and on-site coordination.
5. Determine and prepare appropriate career information materials for the community audience.
6. Ensure delivery, set-up, and return of display and career information materials.
7. Arrange for back-up staff coverage if necessary.
8. Conduct the community career and health fairs.
9. Send thank you letters to registered nurse volunteers who participate.

Materials relevant to Nursing 2000's participation in community career and health fairs are found in Appendix O. These materials are offered to any *collaborative* for revision and modification as it develops its own ability to participate in community career and health fairs.

Summary

Nursing 2000's community programs have been described in this chapter. Procedures for development and implementation of the programs have been offered to any *collaborative* as tools for its own use in developing similar programs. These programs include the Adult Learner Career Seminar, the adult learner shadow a nurse program, community presentations such as the organization's seminar titled Nursing Now—A First Look at Nursing as a Career, library displays, and community career and health fairs. The community programs provide opportunities for Nursing 2000 to expand the visibility of registered nursing in the community, provide education to the public about a career in registered nursing, and address current issues and future prospects for the nursing profession.

6

NURSING 2000: CAREER ADVANCEMENT PROGRAMS

Introduction

While the previous two chapters focused on the school and nursing school programs and the community programs of Nursing 2000, this chapter contains discussions on the career advancement programs of the organization. Career advancement programs include career and educational counseling, the re-entry into nursing seminar, and the advanced nursing practice seminar.

Career advancement programs of Nursing 2000 disseminate information about nursing as a career and about the educational requirements and opportunities available within the nursing profession. They also provide support for registered nurses returning to the workplace and information about advanced practice roles in nursing. The membership of Nursing 2000 offers career and educational counseling to individuals who contact the organization and as part of the many programs of Nursing 2000. Materials that support career and educational counseling include career and educational information handouts, Nursing 2000's Web site, and a videotape and poster developed by the organization. Nursing 2000's re-entry into nursing seminar is offered to support registered nurses who desire to re-enter nursing and return to the workplace after a period of clinical inactivity. The advanced nursing practice seminar provides information to registered nurses about advanced nursing practice roles and opportunities and graduate program requirements and expectations.

Career Advancement Programs

Career and educational counseling

Since its incorporation, Nursing 2000 has developed as a resource for both nursing career and educational counseling. Nursing 2000 has developed several handout materials to support career and educational counseling. These materials are used as part of many of the programs offered by the organization, as well as distributed to individuals who contact the Nursing 2000 office by telephone, by e-mail, or in person for information and counseling. A Web site, a nursing videotape, and a nursing poster have also been developed. The videotape and poster are often used in many of the programs offered by the organization.

Handouts

For career counseling, several career information handouts have been developed, including two brochures that present information about a career as a registered nurse. The longer of the two handouts is a four-page brochure that includes:

- An overview of a career as a registered nurse
- A discussion on the foci of nursing, as well as the profile of today's nurses
- A description of nursing career paths
- A discussion on career diversity
- A review of the job market
- A discussion on nursing salaries
- An overview of the current work environment
- A discussion on the required academic preparation for each nurse role
- Profiles of entry level and advanced nursing education programs

This brochure is used with high school students, traditional nursing students, and adult learners exploring registered nursing as a first or second career. A shortened two-page version of the handout is used with middle school students. An information sheet that provides contact information for all undergraduate nursing educational programs in Indiana has also been developed by the staff of Nursing 2000.

A third handout offers information about specialty careers available to registered nurses and post registered nursing specialty certification and advanced nursing practice education. Nursing 2000 staff members have also produced a professional nursing organization resource list with contact information. Lastly, the staff has developed a four-page handout that presents

Volunteer providing career mobility counseling.

an overview of financial aid resources for nursing students. This handout also includes a discussion of scholarships, tuition assistance/reimbursement, loans, and student nurse employment offered by affiliated healthcare institutions.

Nursing 2000 staff members have also developed several educational information handouts. An educational mobility guide serves as a resource for the registered nurse exploring educational mobility and includes the RN-BSN, BSN, RN-MSN, MSN, and PhD nursing educational programs in Indiana. A second handout serves as a guide for those interested in nursing specialty certification. A resource list of state and national organizations has also been developed that may be used to receive information about advanced nursing practice roles. Lastly, the organization staff has developed an LPN-RN mobility guide for the licensed practical nurse exploring a career as a registered nurse.

Web site

The Web site developed for Nursing 2000 was a collaborative community project of nursing service and nursing education to disseminate information to the public and to the profession to advance nursing careers. Funding for the Web site was provided by Nursing 2000. All of the handouts described above are available on the Web site. Target populations for the Web site include middle and high school students and counselors, parents of prospective nursing students, adult learners exploring registered nursing as a first or second career, nursing students, and registered nurses pursuing professional development. The Web site provides hyperlinks with Indiana nursing educational programs, professional nursing organizations, and affiliated hospitals to facilitate a broader promotion of nursing career information. To date, Nursing 2000's Web site has received nearly 307,000 "hits" and has extended the impact of the organization well beyond the central eight counties of Indiana to all 50 states and internationally.

Videotape

The seven-minute career videotape, Nursing Today and Beyond 2000, was also developed as a collaborative community project of nursing service and nursing education. The fast-paced videotape was created as an information source to introduce high school students and their counselors to contemporary and emerging role expectations of nursing as knowledgeable caregivers, leaders, and researchers. The message is clear that nursing responds to the healthcare needs of people worldwide. The videotape contrasts traditional and contemporary views of nursing in a variety of clinical settings. Although acute care roles are presented, emphasis is also given to preventive and community-focused care. Beginning, experienced, and advanced nursing practice roles are highlighted in the videotape, and student nurses appear in several clinical scenes. The videotape is narrated using a dual-gender approach. By sharing resources, healthcare organizations and nursing educational programs were able to collaborate on the common goal of enhancing traditional views of nursing with contemporary perspectives that are shaping the profession. Based on positive responses to the videotape, copies have been distributed to 68 high schools and 49 middle schools for their media centers. The videotape was also sent to public libraries in the service area for their career shelf as a tool for adult learners considering nursing as a profession. In addition, nursing educational programs and clinical leaders have utilized the videotape for recruitment purposes and to educate both the public and professionals about nursing into the 21st century. Brochures accompany the videotape highlighting key points of the script to serve as a learning resource. Development of the videotape was fully funded by Nursing 2000.

Poster

Nursing 2000's poster project was also a collaborative community project of nursing service and nursing education. Twenty-five Indiana nursing educational programs, healthcare organizations, and professional nursing organizations joined Nursing 2000 in funding the project. The Honor Society of Nursing, Sigma Theta Tau International, provided in-kind support for the project. The poster serves as an informative tool for future students as they explore career choices. The poster, titled Nursing Is AMAZING, depicts a contemporary positive image of registered nursing reflective of the diverse roles in the profession. Generic nursing roles, represented by diverse photographs, appear against a backdrop of the practice setting's image. Opportunities, rewards, and advancements in nursing also appear on the poster. Information about Nursing 2000's Web site appears at the bottom of the poster as a resource for more information. The poster was sent to 860 school nurses throughout Indiana to be displayed in their offices as a way for middle and high school students to access nursing career information. The following procedures are suggested as ways to develop and implement career and educational counseling.

Program development

1. Decide what career and educational information handouts and other materials (videotapes, posters, displays, etc.) are necessary to support programs as they are developed.
2. Develop handouts and other materials.
3. Determine the communication mechanisms to provide career and educational counseling (including telephone, e-mail, in person, Web site, etc.).
4. Develop the communication mechanisms.

Program implementation

1. Distribute handouts and other materials to support programs and career and educational counseling.
2. Revise handouts and other materials as necessary.
3. Market communication mechanisms to provide career and educational counseling to the intended audiences.
4. Provide career and educational counseling.
5. Revise communication mechanisms as needed.

Materials relevant to Nursing 2000's career and educational counseling are found in Appendix P. These materials are offered to any collaborative as it develops its own resources for career and educational counseling.

Re-entry into nursing seminar

The membership of Nursing 2000 offers a seminar annually for registered nurses who want to re-enter nursing and return to the workplace. The seminar, titled Spotlight on Re-Entry: A Program for Inactive Registered Nurses, is offered in a community location to registered nurses who have not practiced nursing for five or more years. The 1 1/2-hour program includes a welcome and overview and a discussion of the role of nursing in today's changing healthcare environment. A panel presentation follows and features registered nurses who discuss their own career paths as re-entry nurses. These nurses have completed refresher courses and have successfully re-entered the workplace. The panel presentation is followed by a discussion of registered nurse refresher course descriptions and opportunities within the hospitals affiliated with Nursing 2000. Lastly, a representative from the Indiana Association of Healthcare Recruiters provides guidance to the attendees regarding accessing opportunities for employment.

The attendees also receive a packet of career information materials that includes an agenda and evaluation form for the program, a professional nursing organization resource list, a state and national advanced nursing practice organization resource list, a list of supporting hospitals of Nursing 2000 including their human resource department contacts, a registered nurse educational mobility guide, a guide to registered nursing specialty certification, a handout focusing on the future of nursing, and information regarding the nursing shortage. Attendees complete an evaluation form at the end of the seminar.

Marketing of the seminar occurs by newspaper advertising, press releases to the public relations departments of affiliated hospitals, flyers sent to public libraries within the eight-county area served by Nursing 2000, and the organization's Web site. In addition, letters of announcement are sent to members of the Indiana Association of Healthcare Recruiters and vice presidents/deans of the hospitals/schools of nursing affiliated with Nursing 2000. Letters of invitation are sent to registered nurses who have inquired by contacting Nursing 2000 or the affiliated hospitals about their registered nurse refresher courses. Registration for the seminar, by contacting Nursing 2000, is required.

Members of Nursing 2000 also conduct a post-seminar evaluation of the program. Approximately one year after the seminar, attendees receive an evaluation form in the mail. They are asked to assess their experience in a registered nurse refresher course and their employment or future employment plans in nursing. The evaluation also requests an assessment of the value of the seminar as a facilitator of career decision making and requests feedback on other seminars or information that would be helpful in ongoing career development. The post-seminar evaluations are being used to assess the effectiveness of the seminar in meeting its objectives.

The following procedures are suggested as ways to develop and implement a re-entry into nursing seminar.

Program development
1. Prepare the presentation materials for the seminars.
2. Prepare career information materials.
3. Determine how often the seminars will be offered.

Program implementation
1. Determine a location and schedule the seminars.
2. Locate and schedule the registered nurse volunteer presenters to provide the seminars.
3. Orient registered nurse volunteers to their role in the seminars.
4. Market the seminars.
5. Send letters of invitation to registered nurses who have made inquiries regarding entering nursing. Include directions to the locations of the seminars.
6. Schedule the registered nurses to attend the seminars.
7. Provide necessary information to registered nurse volunteers, such as directions to the site, parking, and on-site coordination.
8. Prepare career information materials for the attendees.
9. Ensure delivery and return of presentation and career information materials.
10. Conduct the seminars.
11. Send thank you letters to registered nurse volunteers who provided the seminars.
12. Send post-seminar evaluation forms to attendees approximately one year after the seminars.

Materials relevant to Nursing 2000's re-entry into nursing seminar are found in Appendix Q. These materials are offered to any *collaborative* for revision and modification as it develops its own seminar to support registered nurses who desire to re-enter nursing and return to the workplace.

Advanced nursing practice seminar

Members of Nursing 2000 offer a seminar to promote advanced nursing practice in order to meet the goal of supporting nurses with educational career mobility to advance nursing practice. The message of the seminar is that professional nursing offers opportunities for advanced roles, educational mobility, and career diversity. The four-hour seminar, titled Advanced Roles in Nursing…Opportunities and Challenges, provides an opportunity for collegial exchange regarding advanced roles in nursing and shares career mobility information for those interested in pursuing advanced practice. The program includes a welcome, discussion of advanced practice roles and opportunities within nursing, and a presentation regarding graduate nursing educational programs and expectations. The highlight of the seminar is a panel presentation featuring a variety of advanced practice nurses discussing expectations and responsibilities of various advanced nursing practice roles. Interactive breakout sessions allow participants individual contact with nurses in advanced nursing practice roles. Representatives from the graduate educational programs of nursing in Indiana exhibit during the seminar, facilitating the sharing of information regarding specific programs. Initially, the seminar was offered semi-annually. It is now offered on a demand basis in a community location.

Panelists presenting at the Advanced Nursing Practice Seminar.

Seminar participants receive a packet of career information materials that includes Indiana State Board of Nursing information on advanced nursing practice; a position statement on advanced nursing practice from the American Association of Colleges in Nursing; a state and national advanced nursing practice organization resource list; sample role responsibilities of advanced practice nurses; a handout that contrasts the role of a nurse practitioner and a physician's assistant; a professional nursing journal resource list; and a handout of agreed upon competencies developed by nursing service and nursing education leaders within Indiana for ASN, BSN, and MSN graduates.

Marketing of the seminar occurs by newspaper advertising and press releases sent to the public relations departments of Nursing 2000 affiliated hospitals. In addition, letters of announcement are sent to the vice presidents/deans of the hospitals/schools of nursing throughout the state of Indiana, and the seminar date is posted on Nursing 2000's Web site. Letters of invitation to the seminar are also sent to registered nurses who have contacted Nursing 2000 to inquire about advanced nursing practice. Registration for the seminar is required at a cost of $15. The registration fee covers the basic costs of providing the seminar.

The following procedures are suggested as ways to develop and implement an advanced nursing practice seminar.

Program development
1. Develop the presentation materials for the seminars.
2. Develop career information materials.
3. Determine how often the seminars will be offered.

Program implementation
1. Determine a location and schedule the seminars.
2. Schedule the registered nurse volunteer presenters, breakout session facilitators, and graduate educational programs of nursing exhibitors who will provide the seminars.
3. Orient registered nurse volunteers, facilitators, and exhibitors to their role in the seminars.
4. Market the seminars.
5. Send letters of invitation to registered nurses who have made inquiries regarding advanced nursing practice. Include directions to the locations of the seminars.
6. Register the nurses for the seminars.

7. Provide necessary information to registered nurse volunteers, facilitators, and exhibitors, such as directions to the locations, parking, and on-site coordination.
8. Prepare career information materials for the attendees.
9. Ensure delivery and return of presentation and career information materials.
10. Conduct the seminars.
11. Send thank you letters to registered nurse volunteers, facilitators, and exhibitors who provided the seminars.
12. Send roster of attendees to the graduate educational programs of nursing that provided exhibits at the seminars for follow-up.

Materials relevant to Nursing 2000's advanced nursing practice seminar are found in Appendix R. These materials are offered to any *collaborative* for revision and modification as ways to develop its own seminar to support registered nurses who desire to pursue advanced nursing practice.

Summary

This chapter has provided descriptions and procedures for development and implementation of Nursing 2000's career advancement programs. These programs include career and educational counseling, the re-entry into nursing seminar, and the advanced nursing practice seminar. Career advancement programs disseminate information about nursing as a career and about the educational requirements and opportunities available within the nursing profession. The program descriptions and procedures are offered to any *collaborative* as ways to develop similar programs.

7

IMPACT OF THE NURSING 2000 MODEL

Introduction

Nursing 2000 was established with specific goals that promote, educate, and advance a regional nursing workforce, and, as such, accountability is fundamental to the continued existence of this organization. Unlike many organizations that work toward the accomplishment of both internal and external organizational goals, the inception and continued existence of this specific non-profit organization is largely based on the organization's ability to demonstrate program outcomes consistent with the mission and goals established by the stakeholders. To fully understand the impact that Nursing 2000 programs were having on the promotion of a nursing workforce, the leadership identified the need to engage in program evaluation activities as programs were being implemented.

Program evaluation must be part of the planning and design process in the development of any program. This is especially so when instituting a model similar to the Nursing 2000 model. Successful evaluation is a circular process that takes root in the planning phase of any model development; produces blooms in the implementation phase through the identification and clarification of the how, when, where, and who of evaluation; and bears fruit during the assessment, or "how well are we doing," phase of the program. Program evaluation cannot be a casual sidebar to organizational events but must be perceived as a sustainable core activity within the organization. Resources need to be made available and commitment must be evident to maximize the utility of evaluation to ensure the continued success and quality improvement of any organization.

Throughout the presentation of the Nursing 2000 model, reference has been made to evaluation and the importance of evaluation feedback in demonstrating organizational effectiveness. The programs presented in each of the previous chapters have included discussions on how the program has been evaluated and the measures used to collect information regarding program effectiveness. This chapter will focus on the process and outcomes of some of the major evaluative actions undertaken to date.

The leadership of Nursing 2000 was committed to program evaluation. The desire was to create a research-based collaborative approach to evaluation. This approach would support the maximization of resources through the building of collaborative evaluation teams and generate valid and reliable data that would drive future program decisions. These data would also be used in addressing accountability to the organization's stakeholders through annual reporting mechanisms. Unanticipated but valuable uses of evaluation outcome data included the incorporation of these data in public presentations to those interested in nursing or those in positions to affect career choices of those potentially interested in nursing, as well as the incorporation of data into grant proposals. It is through the evaluation process that Nursing 2000 has made quality improvement decisions in refining its activities and designing new program activities. These data also drive the annual process of review and reaffirmation of the mission and goals by Nursing 2000's executive and advisory boards. The following discussion will reflect the evaluation activities undertaken for some of the larger and more resource-intensive program activities designed to promote a career in nursing.

Nursing as a Career Decision

As the leadership of Nursing 2000 developed program activities to promote the themes of nursing as "dynamic, diverse, and rewarding" and that nurses were amazing people who through their education and abilities changed the lives of others, three main questions emerged from their experience and were validated by the professional nursing literature. The first question dealt with information processing in relation to decisions made. As informational materials were being developed and distributed to high school students and young adults, it became apparent that there was a need to know from these target groups what information was important, when the information had the most impact on career choices, and when these groups began to consider career choices. The second question related to what, if any, information tended to discourage target groups from seriously considering nursing as a career choice. The third and most important question posed to the participants in Nursing 2000 activities was what informational factors could be changed given all the data gathered from high school students and young adults.

A review of the literature was undertaken to determine what was known about the three questions being posed. Kersten, Bakewell, and Meyer (1991) surveyed nursing students in associate and baccalaureate programs and found 38% named a nurse as the most influential person in their career decision. Interviewing the same population, Williams, Wertenberger, and Gushuliak (1997) rank ordered the following factors as most important in nursing students' career decision making: "(1) job opportunity and security; (2) working with or helping others; (3) interest in science; (4) family influence; (5) previous job experience; (6) always wanting to be a nurse; (7) financial benefits; (8) personal attributes; and (9) illness experience" (pp. 346-347).

The literature was less clear on when children make career decisions. A study conducted in the United Kingdom by Borrill (1989) found that 75% of the children chose nursing as a career after the age of 16. These results are consistent with a study conducted in the United States by Grossman and Northrop (1993), who reported that approximately 25% of 493 10th and 11th graders considered nursing. Of those, only seven percent pursued nursing. The effect high school counselors have on decision making in this study population is unclear. A survey of high school counselors in the Midwest found 96% of counselors report that they recommend nursing as a career choice; however, the basis on which they make these recommendations is uncertain (Hendrix & Finke, 1994).

There appears to be a number of misconceptions about nursing that have a negative impact on children when they consider career options. The perception that nurses are submissive, powerless, and underpaid persists among this age group (Grossman & Northrop, 1993; Reiskin & Haussler, 1994; Marriner-Tomey, Schwier, Marticke, & Austin, 1990). These negative perceptions are shaped or influenced by racial values and beliefs, gender expectations and stereotyping, socio-economic status, and the public media that connotes demeaning images of nursing and nurses. However, exposure to a "real" nurse through family ties or personal healthcare experiences appears to be a positive balancing factor.

Based on an analysis of the literature, the leadership of Nursing 2000 proposed two research evaluative efforts to substantiate the findings in the literature as well as generate information to determine the effectiveness of their current program activities. In 1999, Wilson and Mitchell set about assessing awareness of, participation in, and influence over career decision making of Nursing 2000 program activities among nursing students enrolled in the four local contributing partner educational institutions. The Nursing 2000 program elements being assessed for effectiveness were the A Day in the Life of a Nurse shadow program, the high school counselor newsletter, high school career day/fair programs, literature (print and nonprint) designed for information-giving, community presentations, telephone contacts, and scholarship awards. A 23-item survey was distributed to 1,598 nursing students enrolled in the four local partnership schools. The return rate was 40% among the sample representing associate, baccalaureate, and master's students. The majority of the respondents were white females under the age of 35 and pursuing a bachelor's degree. Adjusting for respondents who lived outside the Nursing 2000 target area, 92% indicated an awareness of Nursing 2000 with 30% of this population having participated in one or more Nursing 2000 program activities (Wilson & Mitchell, 1999).

Of the respondents having participated in Nursing 2000 activities, 37% cited the A Day in the Life of a Nurse shadow program as influencing their career choice decision process at a probability level of .001 (Wilson & Mitchell, 1999). Other influencing factors included classroom (37%) and community (46%) presentations, and telephone contacts (54%) (Wilson & Mitchell). The most influential impact on career decision making for these respondents that were outside Nursing 2000 sphere of influence came from knowing a family member who was a nurse or having contact with nurses who were identified as their personal or family healthcare provider (Wilson & Mitchell).

It appeared that the A Day in the Life of a Nurse shadow program was perceived as having a dramatic effect on the decision to choose nursing as a career. As this program activity appeared to be so influential, the leadership of Nursing 2000 sought to better understand how this shadowing experience affected the career decision mechanics for high school students. Consistent with the literature, the shadowing program activity was designed for sophomore, junior, and senior high school students who were entertaining a career in the healthcare field. For students to participate in the A Day in the Life of a Nurse shadow program, students need to have successfully completed courses (or be enrolled) in algebra, biology, and chemistry. Academic counselors verified the completion of this course work for the participants of the A Day in the Life of a Nurse shadowing experience. This criterion was established to help program participants understand the academic expectations of a nursing program. It was also believed to be important background for students in filtering and interpreting their observations during the shadowing experience.

Survey instrument and procedure

The leadership of Nursing 2000 partnered with faculty at the Indiana University School of Nursing to conduct a survey study of recent A Day in the Life of a Nurse shadow program participants to understand more about the process they used in making their career choice regarding nursing. Three aims for this evaluation research project were identified. Based on these aims, the researchers developed a survey instrument that would identify factors affecting participants' decision making in choosing a nursing career; assess the impact of the A Day in the Life of a Nurse shadow program; and evaluate the impact of other Nursing 2000 program activities on providing information that is perceived as facilitating their choice of nursing as a career.

A convenience sample of six hundred and twenty-five 1997 and 1998 graduating seniors from 68 Indiana high schools who had participated in the Nursing 2000 A Day in the Life of a Nurse shadow program were invited to participate in this research study. These students had participated in the shadowing program as sophomores, juniors, or seniors. All research participants were 18 years of age or older and had voluntarily agreed to participate after being informed of their human rights.

The researchers developed a survey titled "Choosing a career in nursing" (Mitchell, Carlisle, & Boland, 1999). This survey included 22 multiple-choice items that were drawn from a review of the literature on career decision making. Construct validity was established through an expert critique by nurse faculty dealing with student recruitment and retention. Baccalaureate students, who were then ineligible to participate, also critiqued the survey tool for clarity. The survey was mailed at two different time intervals. Time one was fall of 1997 to those who had participated in the shadowing experience during the 1996 to 1997 cycle. The second mailing was sent in the spring of 1998 to those participating in the shadowing experience during the 1997-1998 cycle. The 1997 mailing went to 292 shadow participants with an additional 333 shadow participants receiving the survey in spring 1998. A follow-up postcard was mailed two weeks after the initial mailing as a reminder to the participants. This follow-up was designed to increase participation.

Survey response and findings

The response rate was 30% for the 1997 mailing and 23% for the 1998 mailing. Although this rate is lower than desired, it is consistent with generally expected response rates for mailed surveys and consistent with other surveys mailed by the Nursing 2000 staff. The respondents represented 36 different Indiana high schools spread across the eight-county Nursing 2000 service area. The descriptive data from each mailing were analyzed separately. The results between the two years showed no statistical difference among groups so the data were collapsed and summarized around key categories consistent with the stated purposes of this project.

The first category examined factors that affected participants' decision to pursue nursing as a career. Consistent with Borrill's (1989) findings, participants actually made the decision to pursue nursing sometime between the 10th and 12th grades (sophomore, junior, and senior years). However, participants noted that they first thought about a career in nursing as early as the first grade. The majority first entertained the idea of a nursing career between eighth and 12th grades. This is evident in the following figure.

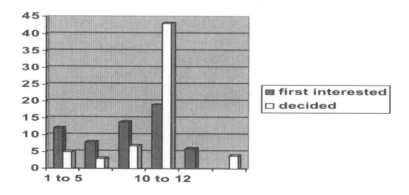

Figure 3. Timing of career decisions (n = 165)

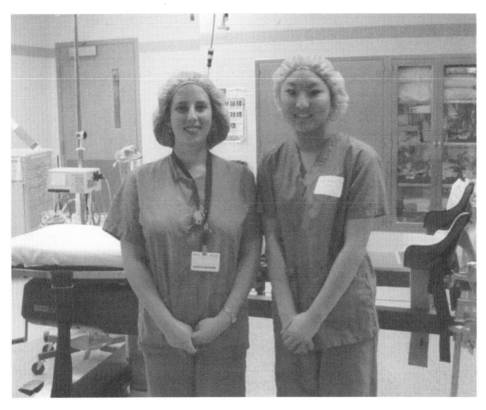

In a survey conducted by Nursing 2000, the majority of respondents made the decision to pursue nursing between the 10th and 12th grades.

Participants' decision to pursue nursing was influenced by others as well as by some personal knowledge of nursing. When asked to indicate "others" who influenced their career choice, participants reported friends and family members in the nursing profession most often influenced them. High school teachers and the participants' personal experience with a nurse or other healthcare worker also had some influence over the decision to pursue a career in nursing. As indicated in the literature, high school counselors and higher education recruiters were less likely to be an influencing factor in the decision to pursue nursing (Hendrix & Finke, 1994). This distribution of influence is summarized in Table 2.

Table 2: People of Influence (n = 165)

Categories	Percentage of respondents
Friend/neighbor pursing nursing as a career	24%
Family member a nurse	22%
High school teacher	15%
Nurse who cared for me	15%
Other: Non-nurse family members	11%
High school counselor	10%
Recruiter/counselor from a nursing program	5%
Other: experience observing nursing care	3%
College/university recruiter	2%

Factors influencing career decision making

There are other factors that affected respondents' decision making process. Fifty-three percent of the respondents believe observing a nurse at work influenced their actual decision to pursue nursing. This experience was followed by observing a sick family member or friend (32%); working or volunteering in a healthcare setting (28%); watching TV or movies that featured nurses (26%); personal experiences as a patient (22%); reading books or stories about nurses or nursing (10%); and being a member in a career club that stressed science, math, or health (8%). An impressive 57% of the respondents expressed the intent to enroll or were already enrolled in a college or university to pursue an educational degree in nursing. It appears the experience of seeing a nurse in action is the strongest influencing factor when it comes to affecting a nursing career choice. It is important to note that this experience also helped those who thought they might be interested in nursing to make a clearer choice to either seek or not seek a career in nursing. Of the 57% (1997) and 63% (1998) who participated in the A Day in the Life of a Nurse shadow program, the majority intended to obtain a bachelor's degree in nursing.

The results of the assessment to determine the compelling factors among respondents to choose a career in nursing yielded the following information. Collectively, 50% of the population selected "nursing allows me to work with people" from among the choices given. The second most frequently selected response (32/165) was "there will always be a job in nursing." Still, few respondents chose a career in nursing to gain respect, make decisions independently, or obtain financial security. This finding supports the traditional idea of nursing being a vocation or calling (Mitchell, Carlisle, & Boland, 1999).

The opposing side of this assessment was the exploration of indices that influenced thinking about a career other than nursing. The most common reason noted by respondents was the finding that nursing was not what they thought it was (30/165). The second most frequently chosen answer was "nursing does not seem to be as prestigious as other careers" (17/165). Other telling responses included "I have not taken the required science and math courses needed," "nursing does not pay as well as many other professions," and "nurses do not seem to have much independence in their job as I am looking for in a career" (Mitchell, Carlisle, & Boland, 1999).

Implications for career decision making

The results of this research evaluation project have multiple implications for the A Day in the Life of a Nurse shadow program. Clearly this is a highly effective program in influencing participants' decision to seek a career in nursing with 75% seeing this experience as moderately to highly influential in their choice of nursing as a career. The outcomes of the shadowing experience are consistent with the goals of Nursing 2000, and the results validate the investment of resources. The results indicate the individuals participating in this experience are seriously considering a career in nursing and this experience facilitates a resolve or affirmation of their decision. The research data also confirmed the appropriateness of targeting sophomore, junior, and senior high school students with the A Day in the Life of a Nurse shadow program, as this is reported to be the time when career decisions are being made (Mitchell, Carlisle, & Boland, 1999).

Additional attention has been given to those nurses who volunteer for the A Day in the Life of a Nurse shadow program given the potential impact these nurses have in the decision processes of high school students. The leadership of Nursing 2000 makes every effort to pair participants with nurses who are able to present nursing as a dynamic, diverse, and rewarding career. This attention to detail appears to have positive results among program participants. Not only have participants seen the A Day in the Life of a Nurse shadow program as excellent, the reported enrollment or application of these participants in nursing programs has increased from 57% in 1999 to 65% in 2001 (Nursing 2000, 2001). The A Day in the Life of a

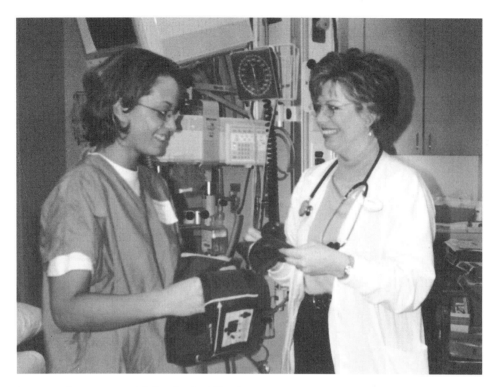

Seventy-nine percent of A Day in the Life of a Nurse shadow program students state the experience is highly influential in their career choice.

Nurse shadow program has also targeted the need to increase minority participation. Gender and minority representation are monitored via data obtained on the individual evaluation tool completed by each participant at the end of the A Day in the Life of a Nurse shadow experience.

As noted in this study, respondents cited teachers (15%) and counselors (10%) as influencing their decision to choose nursing as a career; this combined 25% sphere of influence reaffirms the importance of providing teachers and counselors with age-specific materials that help explain nursing as a career. Surveys have been conducted to determine the impact of the newsletter as an informational tool for high school counselors and high school students. Both groups have responded positively to the newsletter indicating that the information in the newsletter and the newsletter itself is shared with those interested in knowing more about a career in nursing (Nursing 2000, 2001). Additionally, specific issues of the high school counselor newsletter focus on minority students, including men, who often do not see nursing as a career opportunity that encourages diversity among its workforce. As the newsletter gives high school students information on the shadowing program, it is also seen as a way of increasing program enrollments. A Day in the Life of a Nurse shadow program participants have increased from 470 participants in 1999 to 533 participants in 2001. Nineteen percent of the 2001 participants declared they represented a minority group. It appears that this communication tool is a contributing factor in boosting enrollment in A Day in the Life of a Nurse shadow program.

The leadership of Nursing 2000 has also focused on identifying a diverse panel of nurse experts to participate in classroom and community presentation activities for school-aged children. As these "live" interactions reach over 2,000 people each year, 37% to 47% of the participants self-report that the information gained from these interactions influenced their career decision making (Nursing 2000, 2001). As these interactive activities are so influential, it is extremely important to capitalize on opportunities that bring audience and presenters together in dialogue.

Impact on organization effectiveness

Program evaluation is critical to the success of any organization, especially organizations like Nursing 2000 whose clear mission is to serve its constituency. By posing questions related to the effectiveness and efficiency of Nursing 2000's organizational model and the collection and interpretation of program evaluation data, results have been continually fed back into the organizational structure to promote continuous quality improvement and increased productivity for resources extended. This evaluation process has influenced decisions made regarding the mix of program activities, the modifications made to program activities, and the addition or deletion of program activities. Data are also used to determine the degree to which program goals are being met and how to allocate resources to sustain those program activities that are most effective in promoting and supporting professional nursing career decision making. The process of program evaluation has been one more successful collaborative effort between nursing education and Nursing 2000 as the organization continues to make significant contributions to the profession and practice of nursing.

8

····✦·※·✦·····

SUSTAINABILITY

Introduction

Incorporated in 1990, Nursing 2000 has become and remained a highly successful and viable organization over the years. As an organization, it has experienced significant growth, having expanded the vision, mission, goals, funding, community relationships, programs, human resources, and systems and infrastructure during its tenure as an entity. What factors have contributed to the success and sustainability of the organization? Four key factors have been identified that have enabled the organization to sustain its work during times of nursing shortage as well as during times of adequate nursing supply. These four factors include: (1) regular evaluation of the organization, (2) leadership and management, (3) community relationship building and management, and (4) the interdependency of Nursing 2000's programs. Each of these factors is described in detail in terms of how they support and facilitate the organization's long-term future.

Regular Evaluation of the Organization

The process of regular evaluation of the organization has been a key factor that has enabled Nursing 2000 to sustain and thrive. Regular evaluation of the organization includes long-range strategic planning as well as annual renewal. Strategic planning involves decisions that are vital to the organization's future and success, commits resources, and affects the entire organizational system. Strategic planning and strategic management require development of an understanding of the forces in the current external and internal environments, formulation of a future-oriented plan, implementation of the actions and programs to accomplish the plan, and evaluation of the actions and programs to measure the success of the strategies (Duncan, Ginter, & Swayne, 1996). Strategic management also requires that the strategic plan be updated and adjusted annually based on regular monitoring of the plan, a process referred to as annual renewal. This annual renewal process, conducted at the beginning of each academic year, helps the organization summarize the activities that have taken place during the year, as well as assess how the goals for the organization were met. The board of directors reviews new goals, identified during the annual renewal process, for integration into the strategic plan. Nursing 2000's current goals and strategic initiatives are found in Appendix S and are offered to any *collaborative* as an example of a plan resulting from the regular evaluation of the organization.

There are various methods for regular evaluation of the organization. A *collaborative* may decide to search the literature and use a model that is found to be appropriate. The members of the *collaborative* may decide, because of experience with such a process, to develop their own model. The plan need not be complicated or burdensome. A simple plan with evaluative data can be effective in demonstrating that the *collaborative* has been successful in achieving its desired outcomes. Whatever model the *collaborative* members choose or develop, the plan will include an assessment of the external environment impacting the organization and analysis of internal strengths and weaknesses, including the vision, mission, goals, programs, community relationships, funding, human resources, and systems and infrastructure. It is through this process of regular evaluation that the members will determine if the mission of the *collaborative* is being met. Any major change that comes about as a result of this regular evaluation process will be brought to the total *collaborative* for consideration and acceptance. Total organizational input during the regular evaluation process has been a key factor in the long-term sustainability of Nursing 2000.

Leadership and Management

A second key factor that has enabled Nursing 2000 to sustain as an organization is leadership and management. Visionary and collaborative nursing service and nursing education leadership were essential to the early success and viability of Nursing 2000. The organizational structure of Nursing 2000 has continued to build on this model from the board of directors to the volunteer speakers' bureau. The board of directors has senior leader representatives from nursing service and nursing education, as well as a chief executive officer of a funding hospital who willingly serve a two-year term on a rotating basis and provide strategic direction for the organization. The Vice Presidents/Directors and Deans/Directors Forum, comprised of nursing service and nursing education senior leader representatives from supporting hospitals and affiliated schools of nursing, serves as the think tank for the organization. The Forum has guided Nursing 2000 to serve as a catalyst for addressing such issues as planning for nursing education and workforce development. The Forum also guided the organization to pursue a grant to document and replicate the Nursing 2000 model.

The heart and soul of the organization rests with the advisory board and the 200+ registered nurses in the volunteer speakers' bureau. The strong performance characteristics and commitment of advisory board members, who represent supporting hospitals, affiliated schools of nursing, and professional nursing organizations, cannot be overstated. The advisory board assumes responsibility for developing and implementing the actions

Speakers' bureau volunteers preparing for a community program.

and programs that meet the goals of the organization. A volunteer speakers' bureau, whose registered nurse members donate 3,950+ hours per year, works with the Nursing 2000 staff to implement the organization's programs. These volunteers are selectively assigned and oriented to their roles as organizational representatives. Nursing 2000 is an organization that is owned by the participants and is well served by their collective strengths, commitment, and generosity of time. In turn, the organization knows the value of these participants and recognizes, rewards, and includes the participants in planning for the organization at every opportunity. As previously indicated, representatives from each of these groups were included in the organization's strategic planning sessions and are included in the process of annual renewal.

The executive director of Nursing 2000 is a master's level prepared registered nurse who brought strong leadership and management skills to the organization. The board of directors has provided visionary leadership for Nursing 2000. They have approved additional resources for the organization so that the executive director can be freed enough from daily respon-

Remarks from the first executive director during the Tenth Anniversary Scholarship Benefit.

sibilities to also focus on regular evaluation of the organization, leadership and management development, and community relationship building and maintenance. The leadership and management of Nursing 2000 have been key factors in the viability and success of the organization.

Community Relationship Building and Maintenance

Community relationship building and maintenance is a third key factor that has enabled Nursing 2000 to sustain and grow as a viable organization. From its inception, Nursing 2000 has been viewed as a vehicle for strong nursing service and nursing education collaboration. In developing and nurturing partnerships and alliances, the members of Nursing 2000 have added nine supporting hospitals and one affiliated school of nursing to its membership since its early beginnings and now has five professional nursing organizations as members of its advisory board. There are many reasons for this confidence in Nursing 2000 as an organization.

It has been a priority of the leadership of Nursing 2000 to know and understand its internal and external environments, enabling the organization to build and maintain strong relationships within the nursing and healthcare community. With very limited staff resources, the leadership and the participants of Nursing 2000 have maintained a local presence and involvement within the communities it serves. Its volunteer speakers' bureau members have been effectively assigned and oriented to their roles as organizational representatives to Nursing 2000's constituencies as well as the general public. The leadership of Nursing 2000 has also communicated a clear organizational image and mission to its constituencies as well as to the public. To its constituencies, Nursing 2000 is viewed as the vehicle for its hospitals and schools of nursing to link with the public and private school systems in the community. To the broader public, it serves as a consistent, dependable nursing career resource with mechanisms in place to handle and direct public queries. As discussed in the previous chapter, a recent study by the leadership of Nursing 2000 showed that in a survey of 1,598 nursing students enrolled in the four schools of nursing affiliated with Nursing 2000, 79% reported an awareness of the organization's school and school of nursing programs, and 65% reported an awareness of the organization's community programs and career advancement programs. This level of awareness is a result of community relationship building and maintenance, a key viability factor for Nursing 2000.

Interdependency of Nursing 2000's Programs

The interdependency of Nursing 2000's programs is an additional factor that has contributed to Nursing 2000's success and long-term sustainability. The nature and design of the organization's school and school of nursing programs, community programs, and career advancement programs create cycles of visibility, accessibility, education, and referral for Nursing 2000 that are self-sustaining and multipurpose. The shadow a nurse programs, classroom and community presentations, school and community career and health fairs, nursing seminars, public library displays, and career counseling queries generate a cycle of visibility, education, and ongoing referral. The school counselor newsletter, poster, videotape, and Web site of the organization create a cycle of career information accessibility. The scholarship benefit assists students with financial responsibilities through the generation of nursing scholarships, but also serves a dual purpose of creating an opportunity to recognize and thank its constituencies and celebrate nursing as a career. For the

The Walk & Run promotes health and raises scholarship proceeds for nursing students.

most recent scholarship benefit, a community-based corporate sponsor organized a walk/run with 627 participants generating nearly $20,000 in additional scholarships. The walk/run is a promising, ongoing event tied to the scholarship benefit that will generate more monies for nursing scholarships, but will also encourage the broader community to celebrate nursing as a career. Next year's walk/run event anticipates 1,500 participants. The interdependency of Nursing 2000's programs creates cycles of visibility, accessibility, education, and referral for the organization and has been another important factor in ongoing sustainability.

Summary

Four factors have contributed to the success and sustainability of Nursing 2000. The four factors include regular evaluation of the organization, leadership and management, community relationship building and maintenance, and the interdependency of the organization's programs. These processes have kept Nursing 2000 current, relevant, and in concert with its internal and external environments. The organization has adapted and grown over the years from a new organization focused on collaboration, cohesiveness, and community visibility to a thriving organization that has broadened its perspective to include a statewide and national focus. The growth and broadened perspective of Nursing 2000 will be discussed in depth in Chapter 9.

Nursing 2000's current mission, goals, and strategic initiatives are also very much in concert with *Nursing's Agenda for the Future* (American Nurses Association, 2002), established as the profession's strategic plan for change. *Nursing's Agenda for the Future* is intended to stimulate the nursing community to find the match between their own entity and the profession's strategic plan in order to realize the desired future state of nursing. Nursing 2000, as an organization and as a model for other *collaboratives*, exemplifies what can be achieved through nursing collaboration, commitment, and dedication.

9

---◆◆✕◆◆---

GROWTH OF NURSING 2000

Introduction

Nursing 2000 has grown with broadened perspectives as it has developed as an organization. The growth and broadened perspective of Nursing 2000 is described in this chapter and focuses on the organization's involvement in state and national networking, workforce development initiatives, and grant funding to replicate and share its collaborative model.

During Nursing 2000's early years as an organization, the focus was collaboration between nursing service and nursing education, building cohesiveness, and gaining visibility in the Indianapolis and Marion County community. More hospitals added their support to fund Nursing 2000 and its programs. The registered nurse volunteer speakers' bureau was established, and the organization strived for increased penetration of targeted audiences with its initial offering of programs. During the middle years of the organization's existence, programs were expanded and the area of service grew from Marion County to also include the seven surrounding Indiana counties. Nursing 2000 became established as a consistent, dependable career resource to the public and to healthcare and nursing communities. The focus of the organization expanded to include career mobility and demand for nurses at all levels of educational preparation. The later years of Nursing 2000 have seen growth and increased outreach to the state and national communities. As Nursing 2000's visibility and reputation grew, the organization became a statewide and national resource known for developing and promoting careers in registered nursing. Nursing 2000 served as a catalyst for nursing service and nursing education to collaborate and expand local and statewide workforce development initiatives. Increased

Poster presentation presented at Nursing Conference.

demand for its resources prompted Nursing 2000 to seek grant funding to develop tools to replicate the organization and its programs.

State and National Networking

The collaboration between nursing service and nursing education that has made Nursing 2000 a strong and viable organization has also attracted statewide and national attention. The executive director is frequently asked to speak at local and state conferences about the organization and issues impacting the profession of nursing. Nursing 2000 staff members have generously shared, when requested, copies of brochures, plans, and outcomes of successful organizational programs. The executive director has served as a resource, representing Nursing 2000 to various groups and other organizations in Connecticut, Florida, Kentucky, Ohio, Oklahoma, Pennsylvania, Tennessee, and Wisconsin. The organization has also published and shared its impact on nursing resources in the nursing literature.

Nursing 2000, through the executive director, participates as an independently funded organization in the Colleagues in Caring program funded by the Robert Wood Johnson Foundation. Colleagues in Caring is a program to support regional *collaboratives* in building systems of nursing workforce development with the capacity to adapt to the rapid and continual changes in the nation's healthcare system. There are 35 Colleagues in Caring sites nationally. Nursing 2000 serves as a conduit for the state of Indiana in providing information to the Colleagues in Caring network. The executive director participates as a member of the program's recruitment taskforce. She has shared the Nursing 2000 model as a part of a panel presentation at the Colleagues in Caring annual meeting and in the program's newsletter.

Nursing 2000 was also recognized in the American Hospital Association's (2002) report *AHA Commission on Workforce for Hospitals and Health Systems*. The organization was cited as an example of collaboration with other hospitals to change the image of healthcare careers and to influence youth and others toward healthcare careers within the community.

Workforce Development Initiatives

Nursing 2000 has served as a catalyst for nursing service and nursing education, under the direction of the Vice Presidents/Directors and Deans/Directors Forum, to collaborate and expand local and statewide workforce development initiatives. Nursing workforce development focused on five areas along a continuum that includes image, recruitment, educational access, financial assistance, and quality of work life. Image, recruitment, and educational access are recurrent themes incorporated into Nursing 2000's career materials, Web site, videotape, and poster. These themes are also a major focus of Nursing 2000's programs. The organization's resource materials and proceeds from the scholarship benefit address the theme of financial assistance. Quality of work life is supported through the identification of registered nurse retention and satisfaction factors.

As the most current nursing shortage emerged in Indiana, the Vice Presidents/Directors and Deans/Directors Forum expressed the need to address registered nurse retention. Nursing 2000 served as the coordinator for registered nurse focus meetings to meet this need. Forty-three nurses from 12 hospitals affiliated with Nursing 2000 participated in the 2-hour focus group meetings. The purposes of the focus group project were: (1) to provide a constructive, structured medium in which new and experienced staff nurses could identify factors that contribute to a positive work environment in a trans-institutional discussion setting and (2) to identify the drivers related to retention and satisfaction of staff nurses in hospital-based care. A professional facilitator was engaged for the process. Fourteen themes emerged as factors that positively influence nurse retention. The factors included:

- Adequate staffing
- Career advancement and rewards for clinical expertise and leadership
- Collegial relationships with physicians and other disciplines
- Communication with co-workers
- Communication with leadership and management
- Flexible staffing
- Intrinsic rewards derived from satisfaction with patient care
- Participation in decision making
- Professional development program including orientation and continuing education
- Rapport with leadership and management
- Recognition and celebration of accomplishments
- Salary and benefits
- Self-scheduling
- Teamwork among co-workers

The project report was shared with the affiliated hospitals and schools of nursing for their internal review, sharing of results, and use. The project led to creation of an RN exit tool used by the affiliated hospitals to continue to collect data for retention analysis specific to the eight-county area. The 14 retention factors identified in the focus meetings are included as part of the survey. The exiting registered nurse is asked to identify and to rank order the five most important retention factors to her/him. The exit survey is voluntary and anonymous and is returned by the exiting registered nurse in a pre-addressed, stamped envelope to Nursing 2000. The initial response rate was low, but the Vice Presidents/Directors and Deans/Directors Forum viewed the data that was collected as valuable. The commitment was made to continue to collect the surveys. It was determined that the process for survey collection could be improved by doing follow-up with the exit interviewers in each of the affiliated hospitals. This follow-up is in progress.

In 2001, the leadership of Nursing 2000, under the direction of a statewide steering committee, coordinated the planning of the Nursing Workforce Summit. The forum was to promote statewide collaboration to evaluate the scope of the nursing shortage and to strategize about solutions to address the shortage issues in Indiana. The purpose of the summit was to initiate a systematic planning approach to address the demand for registered nurses across all types of settings and the continuum of care in order to meet healthcare needs in Indiana. The organizers intended the summit to serve as a vehicle to develop a collaborative vision for nursing that establishes Indiana as a workplace of choice. The desired outcomes for the day were to provide:

- An exchange of information among stakeholders resulting in a shared background about the nursing shortage
- A statement of the nursing shortage in Indiana
- An identification of next steps to guide Indiana in responding to the nursing shortage

Planning participants for the September 2001 summit included representatives from Nursing 2000, the Indiana Hospital and Health Association, the Indiana Association of Homes and Services for the Aging, the Indiana Health Care Association, VHA Central, the Indiana Organization of Nurse Executives, the Indiana State Nurses Association, and Indiana nursing educational programs.

There were approximately 150 statewide representatives from nursing, healthcare provider organizations, and educational institutions, as well as policymakers and interested stakeholders, in attendance. The summit agenda included presentations about the nursing state of the nation. One presentation, provided by the deputy director of the Colleagues in Caring program, shared the goals and progress of the program. The chief executive officer of the Honor Society of Nursing, Sigma Theta Tau International, spoke about the Nurses for a Healthier Tomorrow initiative. The state of nursing in the state was described by a panel presentation. Representatives from the Indiana Hospital and Health Association and Indiana Association of Homes and Services for the Aging discussed public policy to support development of nursing resources to meet healthcare needs. Data workforce analysis to assist in workforce projections was presented by a representative from the Indiana State Board of Nursing. Initiatives to strengthen collaborative opportunities were described by a university school of nursing dean. A hospital system chief nurse executive and the executive director of Nursing 2000 discussed development of a statewide network to build a mutual sharing process. For the afternoon session, the audience was divided into work groups to address questions related to public policy initiatives, data workforce analysis, collaborative initiatives, and development of a statewide network for communication. The work groups reported group recommendations and strategies, and next steps were identified.

A steering committee was established to guide the ongoing work identified by the summit participants. The steering committee held a post-summit retreat to develop an action plan from recommended strategies identified at the summit, prioritize next steps, and establish a framework for goal progression. Four priorities emerged from the work of the summit and include:

- Establish the nursing shortage as a workforce economic development issue for Indiana
- Promote nursing as a career of choice for college-bound and second-degree audiences
- Develop collaborative relationships between nursing education and nursing service in preparing future nurses
- Develop a statewide communication infrastructure for disseminating developments in the aforementioned areas

Specific goals were developed by the steering committee based on the strategic foci of public policy, data workforce analysis, collaborative initiatives, and communications infrastructure. Five independent work groups were established consisting of steering committee members and other interested stakeholders who attended the summit. The five work groups were to focus on the following:

1. Provide evidence that the nursing shortage is a workforce economic development issue for the state.
2. Assure the "Indiana Nursing" message is consistent and available to all interested individuals.
3. Maximize existing mechanisms to fund, serve, and promote educational partnerships.
4. Locate, compile, organize, and disseminate information related to the image of nursing, quality of nursing work life, and public policy as it relates to the nursing workforce.
5. Continue the work of the summit in a formalized structure with sustained funding.

The accomplishments of the steering committee and work groups to date are significant. The steering committee has developed a "white paper" titled *The Nursing Workforce Shortage in Indiana—Current Status and Future Trends*. Multiple alliances are being explored with city, state, and regional groups, in both public and private sectors, interested in the relationship between economic and workforce development. Because the nursing shortage has regional variations, additional summits have been held in the northwest and southwest areas of Indiana. These summits have served to share the work of the original summit, to gain regional input and guidance, and to enlist increased participation in the state. A *Guide to Nursing in Indiana* is being developed for the Web site to depict Indiana as a workplace of choice. Nursing profile data is being compiled including baseline data on Indiana nursing educational program faculty. Best practices for nursing educational programs and clinical partnerships are being articulated. A formal Web site has been launched and the "white paper" is available on the site. Corporate partnerships and governmental support are being sought to build an infrastructure for sustainability. Factors driving the ongoing work of this initiative include development of a statewide coordinating center, insurance of coordinated efforts with local and statewide activities, and enlistment of community and statewide support to assure adequate nursing resources.

Grant Funding

In response to increasing inquiries regarding the Nursing 2000 model as a long-established and successful local initiative, the organization's leadership applied for and received a grant from the Helene Fuld Health Trust. The Helene Fuld Health Trust is the nation's largest private fund devoted to nursing students and nursing education. A $150,000 grant was awarded to Nursing 2000 from the Fuld Trust to address the nursing shortage. The one-year grant was awarded to develop a plan for the replication of the Nursing 2000 model in another geographical region. The plan had two phases: (1) to develop, in publication format, the procedures for establishing an organization such as Nursing 2000, including the programs and activities that have been effective in meeting the goals of the organization and (2) to use the procedures to establish an organization similar to Nursing 2000 in another region in Indiana. The first phase of the plan resulted in the publication of this book to serve as a resource for any *collaborative* seeking to develop an organization similar to Nursing 2000. The second phase of the plan resulted in the Nursing 2000 North Central project, a regional *collaborative* established in 2002.

Nursing 2000 North Central has been legally incorporated and serves four Indiana counties (Elkhart, LaPorte, Marshall, and St. Joseph) located in the northern part of the state. The newly formed organization is funded by five area hospitals and has six nursing educational programs as contributing sponsors. The board of directors has been organized and an executive director serves as the operating officer for the corporation. The election of officers, adoption of bylaws, designation of a fiscal depository,

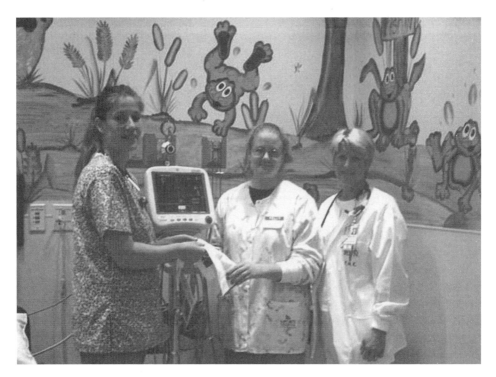

Nurse mentors welcome shadow student during Nursing 2000 North Central's first A Day in the Life of a Nurse shadow program.

approval for filing of applications for recognition of exemption from federal and state taxation, ratification of the acts of incorporation, and election of the first board of directors for the corporation was accomplished at the first meeting. The new organization's membership has implemented a high school student shadow a nurse program and two nursing seminars. The leadership of Nursing 2000 North Central used the procedures provided in this book and have provided useful evaluative feedback to program implementation. The lessons learned from regional adaptation of the Nursing 2000 model are discussed in Chapter 10.

Summary

Nursing 2000 continues to grow, mature, and develop as an organization. Efforts related to state and national networking, workforce development initiatives, and grant funding are examples of this growth.

10

LESSONS LEARNED

Introduction

Throughout this book, a collaborative organization (Nursing 2000) has been described as a model that could be replicated by anyone interested in forming a similar organization. Chapter 1 contained a discussion about how the collaborative developed as a working alliance. In Chapter 2, a model was presented on how to assess the internal and external environments and how the data were used for change. Chapter 3 contained a discussion about the operations of the organization, and in chapters 4, 5, and 6, detailed discussions of the programs offered that meet the mission of the organization were described. In Chapter 7, the impact of Nursing 2000 was discussed, and in chapters 8 and 9, a discussion of the growth of Nursing 2000 and its sustainability, which demonstrates the success factors needed for an organization's future, were described.

This chapter (10) contains a discussion of what has been learned from all of the activities of Nursing 2000. The purpose of the discussion is to help others develop a *collaborative* by sharing the successes of Nursing 2000 and the problems to avoid that are inherent in the development of something new.

Lessons have been learned from positive and negative situations, spontaneous situations, one-time happenings, and quick decisions. An action or the results of an activity of a *collaborative* may be determined as a lesson learned. For example, the Nursing 2000 staff and volunteers have learned that attempting to fill all requests for program presentations is unwise and virtually impossible and that limits must be established on what is reasonable for the organization to provide. The number of offerings of identified programs that can be presented effectively must be determined when planning for the program year is accomplished. The advisory board of Nursing 2000 discovered volunteers were over-extended and that the organization could be more effective setting limits. The longer an organization is in place, the more challenging it is to set limits. For example, for a number of years, the staff and advisory board members of Nursing 2000 developed and staffed a display at a public fair for 15 hours a day for 10 days each year. An assessment of this activity revealed the process exhausted the human and financial resources of the organization limiting what could be accomplished in other areas. As a result of this assessment, the program/project was discontinued.

Many lessons were learned from this assessment and others that were conducted by the Nursing 2000 staff and advisory board members. A modified version of Warshawski's (n.d.) model, *Organizational Self-Assessment Checklist,* has been used to assess the mission and goals, programming, governance, marketing, community relations, financing, and planning for Nursing 2000. Following is a discussion of these assessments and how they led to "lessons learned."

One lesson learned by Nursing 2000 is to utilize volunteer resources and programs with the most impact.

Mission and Goals

A broad statement provides the opportunity for the organization to:
- Expand the programming
- Serve an increased number of people
- Be involved with state and national initiatives

Since the goals fulfill the mission statement, they provide direction for how the operations and programming are implemented. The first lesson learned was that periodic review of the mission and goals of Nursing 2000, at scheduled times, has kept the organization on track and the activities in line with the mission.

Programs

The types and numbers of programs offered have gradually been increased only after it had been determined that staff and volunteers were available to develop and offer the programs congruent with the mission of the organization. Together, the staff and advisory board members learned another lesson. For budgeting, programs needed to be scheduled in advance for the program year. For example, even though schools and civic groups were encouraged to submit requests for programs early in the budgeting process, in order to address late requests for programs, a line item was included in the budget that was designated for these late submissions. Also, when a display was placed in a public library, the staff had to determine that the printed material served the public and could be supplied without exceeding the budget line.

Governance

The membership of the board of directors evolved to reflect representation of the major funding institutions as well as supporting institutions. This composition of the board, the third lesson learned, was essential in order to meet the mission and purpose and sustainability of the organization.

Marketing

Another lesson learned had to do with marketing. Successful marketing was accomplished by using internal resources such as advisory board members, who promoted program offerings; recruitment volunteer participation in the work of the organization; and sharing information about the work of the organization within the larger community. The relationship formed with individuals in the high school counselor network was identified as a source to acquire student program participation. The quality programs offered by the organization were identified as the optimal marketing strategy. Individuals frequently indicated on an evaluation form that they learned of the program or the organization through a friend who attended an offering.

Community Relations

The organization has established a relationship within the community and is recognized for the contributions its members have made to central Indiana. This relationship was formed through students, their parents, and adults who have attended a program; the advisory board members and the institutions they represent; nursing organizations that have joined forces with the organization to support initiatives that promote nursing; and hospital staff and faculty of schools of nursing who work with the organization to promote nursing. An important lesson learned is that community linkages are important and vital ways to meet the mission and goals of the organization.

Fundraising

Early on, the staff of Nursing 2000 learned one major event for nursing scholarships is more effective than multiple small efforts. Volunteer and staff resources were channeled and more effectively used when there was one event.

Financial Management

The board of directors set the direction for the fiscal management of the organization. In addition, the accountant provides consultation to the executive director and the board of directors in the management of the budget of the organization. His expertise and skill in finances is an asset to the organization. Clearly, it was learned that longevity of the relationship with an accountant supports continuity and sustainability for the organization.

Planning

An important lesson learned is that planning conducted in an organized and long-range manner promotes nursing. For example, for the expansion of programs, there must be adequate funding. The planning must cover development of the programs, cultivation in the community, staffing, and coordination of other needed resources in order to effectively implement the programs.

A Pilot Project

The Nursing 2000 model has been successfully implemented in another geographical region. The Nursing 2000 North Central project was launched within the limited time frame of the Helene Fuld Trust grant. The success of the project was due to the determination, leadership, and involvement of nursing leaders in the designated region. These nurse leaders recognized the

Nursing 2000 North Central successfully launched its pilot A Day in the Life of a Nurse shadow program. In this picture, a nurse mentor and student interpret patient monitoring data.

need to promote nursing within their region and understood the immediate and long-term benefits of such an organization. The nurse leaders included the chief executive officers of their institutions.

The nurse leaders kept nurses of all levels of employment informed and recognized their potential for immediate involvement in the work of the organization. The *collaborative* that came together to test the model and form the organization under the direction of the project manager has been successful and is now offering the following program activities: A Day in the Life of a Nurse shadow program, Nursing Now–First Look at Nursing as a Career, program presentations, career fairs, and publishing and distributing a high school counselors newsletter. Lessons learned from this project are identified as:

1. The Nursing 2000 model can be adapted to "fit" another geographical region.
2. *Collaboratives* in rural or less-populated geographical regions can use the model by decreasing the number of programs offered based on need, number of volunteers, and participating institutions.
3. A *collaborative* can increase the size of the involved region to include additional institutions and the potential pool of volunteers and resources.
4. Legal counsel needs to be located within the first phase of organizing to guide the process of incorporation.
5. The number of institutions participating in the *collaborative* determines the number of human resources available to form volunteer pools, advisory boards, and various committees. For example, in order to maximize resources, the Day in the Life of a Nurse committee has now evolved into the advisory committee of the newly formed organization.
6. Project nurse leaders state use of the plan/guide of the Nursing 2000 model saved 3-5 years of time for the development of a new organization, especially with limited resources.
7. Resources (human, financial, and environmental) vary from one region to another and influence how a *collaborative* implements its mission statement.
8. The approved budget in place determines the number and types of programs and activities that can be initiated.
9. As a result of the project and the organization formed using the Nursing 2000 model, collaborative relationships have been built among schools of nursing, supporting healthcare institutions, and public/private school communities.

10. As the project concludes, the organization is operating as an independent entity with the official title, Nursing 2000 North Central, Inc.

The broader community

1. The model can be used by other non-profit organizations, as well as professional organizations that function to promote a cause or meet a need.
2. The mechanics for forming an organization of this kind can be effectively used as a guide for a collaborative with another focus.
3. The organizational procedures for offering programs can be used as a guide for developing programs that meet the mission statement of another type of *collaborative*.
4. The procedures for planning and implementing a program included with the model can be adapted to serve the purpose of various types of *collaboratives*.
5. The region may be limited as to the number of individuals who volunteer to carry out the work of the organization. Educational preparation of individuals in the region may limit the number of individuals available for leadership.
6. The group of individuals that comes together to form an organization using the *collaborative* model are individuals who are willing to extend themselves and volunteer their time and who have a passion for the promotion of a cause. Through their sharing of the work and a common focus, the group has become a *collaborative* and in turn has formed an organization.
7. The geographical size of a region served influences the services that can be provided.

Summary

Any group interested in establishing a *collaborative* should look at the lessons learned by the members of Nursing 2000. The lessons learned that have been identified in this book can assist others in the development, implementation, and assessment of a *collaborative*.

Individuals that are a part of the Nursing 2000 organization have willingly and openly shared all there is to know about the organization. These individuals are like other nurses who form a *collaborative* because they, too, are eager to promote nursing. They want the best healthcare for those people residing within their region. To accomplish this, as volunteers, they have joined together to promote nursing. Through their efforts, nurses are providing information to individuals of all ages regarding the educational process and opportunities available for nurses. The contributions these nurses make to the delivery of healthcare and the growing demand for individuals to enter the nursing workforce are critical for survival of the public's health and the profession.

> May the contents of the book give direction to a collaborative. Might the pages be worn thin from use as a reference and the cover tattered from handling. Perhaps those members of a collaborative who use the Nursing 2000 model will be encouraged to meet their own goals of organizing to achieve collaboration for the development of nursing careers.

References

Aiken, L. H., Sochalski, J., & Anderson, G. F. (1996). Downsizing the hospital nursing workforce. *Health Affairs, 15*(4), 91.

American Association of Colleges of Nursing. (1999, April). *Faculty shortages intensify nation's nursing deficit.* Retrieved on December 16, 2002, from http://www.aacn.nche.edu/Publications/issues/IB499WB.htm

American Hospital Association. (2001, January) Workforce supply for hospitals and health systems issues and recommendations. *AHA Policy Forum.* Retrieved on February 5, 2001, from http://www.ahapolicyforum.org/policyresources/WorkforceB0123.asp

American Hospital Association. (2002, April). *AHA commission on workforce for hospitals and health systems.* Chicago, IL: Author.

American Nurses Association. (1999). *Nursing's social policy statement.* Washington, DC: Author.

American Nurses Association. (2002). *Nursing's agenda for the future.* Washington, DC: Author.

Borrill, C. (1989). Nursing an ambition. *Nursing Times, 85*(34), 30, 32.

Buerhaus, P. I. (1993, May-June). Effects of RN wages and non-wage income on the performance of the hospital RN labor market. *Nursing Economics, 11*(3), 133-134.

Buerhaus, P. I., Staiger, D. O., & Auerbach, D. I. (2000, June). Implications of an aging registered nurse workforce. *The Journal of the American Medical Association, 283*(22), 2948-2954.

Duncan, W. J., Ginter, P. M., & Swayne, L. E. (1996). *Strategic management of health care organizations,* (pp 18, 20-22; 33-34). (2nd ed.) Cambridge, MA: Blackwell Publishers.

Grossman, D. G., & Northrop, C. (1993). What high school students think of a nursing career: A survey of Dade county senior high schools. *Journal of Nursing Education, 32*(4), 157-162.

Hendricx, L., & Finke, L. (1994). High school guidance counselors' attitudes toward nursing as a career. *Journal of Nursing Education, 33*(2), 87-88.

Kersten, J., Bakewell, K., & Meyer, D. (1991). Motivating factors in a student's choice of nursing as a career. *Journal of Nursing Education, 30*(1), 30-33.

Marriner-Tomey, A., Schwier, B., Marticke, N., & Austin, J. (1990). Sophomore high school students' perceptions of ideal and nursing career choices. *Nursing Forum, 25*(2), 27-32.

Mitchell, B., Carlisle, P., & Boland, D. (1999). [The influence of a shadow experience on career decision making]. Unpublished raw data. Nursing 2000. (2000). Annual report. Indianapolis, IN: Authors.

Nursing 2000. (2001). Annual report. Indianapolis, IN: Author.

Random house Webster's unabridged dictionary (2nd ed.) (1998). New York, NY: Random House.

Reiskin, H., & Haussler, S. (1994). Multicultural students' perceptions of nursing as a career. *IMAGE: Journal of Nursing Scholarship, 26*(1), 61-64.

Sigma Theta Tau International. (1999, August) [Executive Summary]. Harris Poll on consumer attitudes about nursing. Indianapolis, IN: NurseWeek.

Ulrich, B. (2001, December 17). A matter of trust. Public continues to regard nurses highly in honesty and ethics [Electronic version]. *NurseWeek,* Editor's Note, p. 4. Retrieved on May 11, 2002, from http://www.nurseweek.com/ednote/01/121701a.html

United States Census Bureau. (2000). *Population projections for states by selected age groups and sex: 1995 to 2025 Indiana.* Retrieved on December 17, 2002 from http://www.census.gov/population/www/projections/stproj.html

United States GAO Report. (2001). *Nursing workforce, emerging nurse shortages due to multiple factors,* July 2001, (No. GAO-01-944). United States: Author.

Warshawski, M., (Ed.). (n.d.). *Organizational Self-Assessment Checklist.* Retrieved on June 26, 2002, from http://www.nea.gov/pub/Lessons/index.html

Williams, B., Wertenberger, D. H., & Gushuliak, T. (1997). Why students choose nursing. *Journal of Nursing Education, 36*(7), 346-347.

Wilson, C. S., & Mitchell, B. S. (1999). Nursing 2000: Collaboration to promote careers in registered nursing. *Nursing Outlook, 47*(2), 56-61.

W.K. Kellogg Foundation. (2000). *Logic model development guide.* Battle Creek, MI: Author.

Appendix A. Nursing 2000 Mission Statement and Goals

FACT SHEET

MISSION
Nursing 2000 is an educational organization designed to promote and support careers in registered nursing. The organization's nursing membership includes practicing nurses from healthcare agencies, universities, professional nursing associations, and communities who work together to promote the positive image of professional nursing.

PURPOSE
By communicating the challenges, rewards and diversity of the profession, Nursing 2000 positively promotes nursing careers through education, counseling and public presentations in eight central Indiana counties (Marion, Boone, Hamilton, Hancock, Shelby, Johnson, Morgan, Hendricks).

GOALS
- To disseminate information about registered nursing as a dynamic profession to the following groups: elementary school age; middle school age; high school age; adult learners; and career mobility nurses.
- To support nurses in educational career mobility and clinical practice to advance nursing careers.
- To impact the education of nurses through collaboration between nursing service and education.
- To recruit a diverse student body reflective of the regional population.
- To attract students into nursing who have demonstrated those potential academic abilities that will lead to a successful career in registered nursing.
- To reflect a positive image of nursing to the public.

PROGRAMS
"Day in the Life of a Nurse" (shadow experience) • Classroom Presentations • Career Days/Displays • School Counselor/Science Teacher Program • School Counselor Newsletter • Career Mobility Seminars • Career Counseling • Nursing Scholarships to area universities

SPONSORSHIP
Nursing 2000 is funded by five Indianapolis area hospitals: Clarian Health Partners, Inc.—Methodist · IU · Riley • Community Health Network • St. Francis Hospital and Health Centers • St. Vincent Hospitals & Health Services • Wishard Health Services

The following hospitals are contributing sponsors for Nursing 2000: Hancock Memorial Hospital and Health Services • Hendricks Community Hospital • Johnson Memorial Hospital • Major Hospital • The Rehabilitation Hospital of Indiana • Riverview Hospital • St. Elizabeth Ann Seton Hospital of Central Indiana • Westview Hospital • Women's Hospital of Indianapolis

Appendix B. Nursing 2000 Revenue Structure

Revenue Structure		
Revenue Source	**Year #1**	**Year #12**
Funding Hospitals	$150,000	$160,000
Contributing Hospitals	0	40,000
Schools of Nursing	0	2,000
Materials & Miscellaneous	567	2,900
Interest	8,000	9,000
	$158,567	$213,900

Sliding Scale Based on RN Full-Time Equivalents		
Number of RN Full-Time Equivalents		**Contribution Level**
1,800 and above	=	$50,000
1,000 – 1,799	=	$35,000
400 – 999	=	$25,000
200 – 399	=	$15,000
21 – 199	=	$5,000
20 and under	=	$2,500

Appendix C. Accumulative Cost of Offering Each Program Activity

Year #12 BUDGET

INDIVIDUAL PROGRAM EXPENSES:	Year #12 Budgeted
Travel:	
est. 5,000 miles/yr @$.32/mile & parking	$1,657.00
Postage:	5,722.00
A Day in the Life of a Nurse Shadow Program:	8,000.00
Classroom Presentations:	8,204.00
School Career Fairs/Days/Displays:	4,487.70
Counselor/Teacher Program:	
Newsletter, Seminars, IACAC Conference	4,273.50
Career Resource Development:	
Adult Learner Seminar	1,290.00
Adult Learner Shadow Program	1,015.00
Community Presentations – Nursing Now	2,074.00
Library Displays	423.00
Community Health Fairs	3,430.00
Career and Educational Counseling	3,623.00
Re-Entry Seminar	1,815.00
Speakers' Bureau Volunteer Program:	
Orientation Costs, Volunteer Recognition, Newsletter	3,660.00
Total:	$49,674.20

Appendix D. Amended and Revised Bylaws of Nursing 2000, Inc. Effective October 30, 2001

ARTICLE I
Membership

Section 1.1. <u>Qualifications for Membership</u>. Each member shall at all times be a hospital as that term is defined in Section 501(e) of the Internal Revenue Code of 1986, (the "Code") or any corresponding provision of subsequent federal tax laws, and any regulations promulgated thereunder.

Section 1.2. <u>Membership Certificates</u>. As provided by law, each member of the Corporation shall be entitled to a certificate signed by the President and attested by the Secretary certifying the membership held by him and such other information as may be required by law. The form of such certificate shall be prescribed by the Board of Directors. Such certificate shall not be transferable.

Section 1.3. <u>Duration of Membership; Resignation</u>. Membership in the Corporation may terminate by voluntary withdrawal as herein provided, or as otherwise provided in these Bylaws. All rights and privileges of a member in the Corporation shall cease on the termination of membership. Any member may voluntarily withdraw from membership by giving written notice of such intention to the President of the Board of Directors. Such notice shall be presented to the Board of Directors at the next succeeding meeting of the Board of Directors. Withdrawal of a member shall be effective upon fulfillment of all obligations of such member to the date of such meeting.

Section 1.4. <u>Suspension and Termination of Voting Membership</u>. Any voting membership may be suspended or terminated, for cause. Sufficient cause for suspension or termination of voting membership shall be loss of qualification status described in Section 1.1 hereof, violation of these Bylaws, nonpayment of dues, if any, violation of any lawful rule or practice duly adopted by the Corporation, or any other conduct prejudicial to the interests of the Corporation. In the event that a member no longer meets the qualifications described in Section 1.1 hereof, such member's membership shall be immediately terminated. In all other cases, proceedings for suspension or expulsion of a voting member may be instituted by a petition to the Board of Directors in writing signed by any three (3) members, or by the Board of Directors on its own motion. The affirmative vote of three-fourths (3/4) of the entire membership of the Board of Directors shall be required in order for a voting member to be suspended or expelled. A statement of the charges on which such action is based shall be mailed by registered mail to the last recorded address of the member at least fifteen (15) days before final action is taken thereon. This statement shall be accompanied by a notice of the time and place of the meeting of the Board of Directors at which the charges shall be considered and the member shall have the opportunity to appear in person or by its representative and present any defense to such charges before action is taken thereon.

Section 1.5. <u>Dues, Fees, and Assessments</u>. The amount of any membership fees, dues, and assessments applicable to membership in the Corporation or to any class of such membership and the time and manner of payment thereof shall be determined by the Board of Directors.

ARTICLE II
Meetings of Members

Section 2.1. <u>Annual Meetings</u>. The annual meeting of the members of the Corporation shall be held within six (6) months of the close of each fiscal year on such date and in such location as may be designated by the Board of Directors.

Section 2.2. <u>Special Meetings</u>. Special meetings of the members may be called by the President, the Chief Operating Officer, a majority of the Board of Directors, or a petition in writing of at least three (3) of the voting members.

Section 2.3. <u>Notice of Meetings</u>. Written notice stating the place, day and hour of any meeting of members and, in the case of special meetings or when otherwise required by law, the purpose of which any such meeting is called, shall be delivered or mailed by the Secretary of the Corporation to each voting member of record, at such address as appears upon the records of the Corporation, and at least ten (10) days before the date of such meeting.

Section 2.4. <u>Waiver of Notice</u>. Notice of any meeting may be waived by any voting member in writing filed with the Secretary of the Corporation. Attendance at any meeting in person or by proxy shall constitute a waiver of notice of such meeting.

Section 2.5. <u>Voting Rights</u>. Each member of the Corporation shall have the voting rights specified in the Articles of Incorporation of the Corporation.

Section 2.6. <u>Voting by Proxy</u>. A member entitled to vote at any meeting of members may vote either in person or by proxy executed in writing by the member or a duly authorized attorney-in-fact of such member. (For purposes of this section, a proxy granted facsimile by a member shall be deemed "executed in writing by the member.") No proxy shall be voted at any meeting of members unless the same shall be filed with the Secretary of the meeting at the commencement thereof.

Section 2.7. <u>Quorum</u>. At any meeting of members, a majority of the members qualified to vote as members by the Articles of Incorporation, represented at the meeting in person or by proxy, shall constitute a quorum. A majority vote of such quorum shall be necessary for the transaction of any business by the meeting, unless a greater number is required by law, the Articles of Incorporation or these Bylaws.

Section 2.8. <u>Voting List</u>. The Secretary or Assistant Secretary of the Corporation shall at all times keep at the principal office of the Corporation a complete and accurate list of all members entitled to vote by the Articles of Incorporation. Such list may be inspected by any member for any proper purpose at any reasonable time.

Section 2.9. <u>Conduct of Meetings</u>. Meetings of members, including the order of business, shall be conducted in accordance with <u>Roberts' Rules of Order, Revised</u>, except insofar as the Articles of Incorporation, these Bylaws, or any rule adopted by the Board of Directors or members may otherwise provide. The members may, by unanimous consent, waive the requirements of this section, but such waiver shall not preclude any member from invoking the requirements of this section at any subsequent meeting.

Section 2.10. <u>Action by Consent</u>. Any action required to be taken at a meeting of members, or any action which may be taken at a meeting of members, may be taken without a meeting but with the same effect as a unanimous vote at a meeting, if, prior to such action, a consent in writing, setting forth the action so taken, shall be signed by all members entitled to vote with respect thereto, and such consent is filed with the minutes of the proceedings of the members.

ARTICLE III

Board of Directors

Section 3.1. <u>Duties and Qualifications</u>. The business and affairs of the Corporation shall be managed by the Board of Directors. At least two directors shall be persons employed as a dean/director of a school of nursing and at least one director shall be a chief executive officer of a member and the remaining directors shall each be Registered Nurses employed in a senior nursing executive position, three from a funding member, and one from a contributing institution. Each director's term will be two years. No more than two consecutive terms may be served by each director except as recommended by the Board of Directors to maintain continuity of leadership. Terms of office will alternate with one dean/director and senior nurse executive elected in even years; one dean/director and senior nurse executive elected in odd years.

Section 3.2. <u>Number and Election</u>. There shall be seven (7) directors of the Corporation who shall be elected by the members at the annual meeting of the members. If the annual meeting of the members is not held at the time designated in these Bylaws, the directors then in office shall hold over until their successors shall be elected and qualified, or until their resignation, removal or death.

Section 3.3. <u>Vacancies</u>. Any vacancy among the directors caused by death, resignation, removal or otherwise may be filled by a majority vote of the remaining members of the Board of Directors. In the event the vacancy is created by an increase in the number of directors by amendment of the Bylaws, the election of the additional director or directors shall be by a vote of the members of the Board of Directors. The term of office of a director chosen to fill a vacancy shall expire at the next annual meeting of the members.

Section 3.4 <u>Removal</u>. Any director may be removed, with or without cause, by the Board of Directors whenever a majority of such Board shall vote in favor of such removal. Further, any director qualified to be a director because they are employed by a member or employed in a particular field or position shall be removed (i) upon termination of that employment or (ii) upon the alteration of that employment, if the alteration results in a loss of qualification.

Section 3.5. <u>Annual Meetings</u>. In preparation for the annual meeting of the members, the Board of Directors shall propose a slate for the Directors of the Corporation for submission to the members for vote of approval at the annual meeting.

Section 3.6. <u>Other Meetings</u>. Regular meetings of the Board of Directors may be held pursuant to a resolution of the Board to such effect, and shall be held as necessary for the Board of Directors. No notice shall be necessary for any regular meeting. Special meetings of the Board of Directors may be held upon the call of the President, Chief Operating Officer or of any three (3) members of the Board and upon twenty-four (24) hours' notice specifying the time, place and general purposes of the meeting, given to each director either personally or by mail, facsimile or telephone. Notice of a special meeting may be waived in writing or by facsimile before the time of the meeting, at the time of the meeting, or after the time of the meeting. Attendance at any special meeting shall constitute waiver of notice of such meeting.

Section 3.7. <u>Quorum</u>. A majority of the entire Board of Directors shall be necessary to constitute a quorum for the transaction of any business except the filling of vacancies, and the act of the majority of the directors present at a meeting at which a quorum is present shall be the act of the Board of Directors unless the act of a greater number is required by law, the Articles of Incorporation, or these Bylaws. In the event a quorum is not present, Section 3.8 may be invoked. When filling vacancies, a majority of the existing directors shall be required for a quorum.

Section 3.8. Action by Consent. Any action required or permitted to be taken at any meeting of the Board of Directors may be taken without a meeting, if prior to such action being implemented, a written consent to such action is voted upon or signed by all members of the Board and such approval or disapproval is filed with the minutes of proceedings of the Board of Directors.

Section 3.9. Advisory Committee. An advisory committee shall be established that shall consist of leaders in healthcare. The advisory committee shall serve as a resource for the Corporation to draw upon in fulfilling its purposes. Each member hospital of Nursing 2000 shall be entitled to two advisory committee representatives as appointed by the senior nursing executive. Each supporting institution contributor shall be entitled to one advisory committee representative as appointed by the senior nursing executive. Each affiliated school of nursing will be entitled to two advisory committee representatives as appointed by the dean/director. Each affiliated nursing organization will be entitled to one advisory committee representative as appointed by the respective organization's Board of Directors or President. An affiliated organization is defined as an educational and/or service organization, based in the target area, that provides state, regional, or national leadership to organized nursing, and can therefore serve as a resource on trends in healthcare. Affiliation will be determined by the Board of Directors of Nursing 2000. If advisory board representation does not include representation from Nursing's minority population (ethnic diversity and male) then a member-at-large will be appointed by the Board of Directors. Each representative's term shall be two years and is subject to renewal.

Section 3.10. Other Committees. The Executive Director or the Board of Directors may from time to time create and appoint standing and special committees to undertake studies, make recommendations and carry on functions for the purpose of efficiently accomplishing the purposes of the Corporation.

Section 3.11. Conflicts of Interest. No contract or other transaction between the Corporation and one or more of its directors, or between the Corporation and any other corporation, partnership, trust, firm, association or entity in which one or more of the directors of the Corporation is a director, officer, partner, shareholder, member, employee, or agent or is financially interested, shall be either void or voidable because of such relationship or interest or because such director or directors are present at the meeting of the Board of Directors or a committee thereof which authorizes, approves or ratifies such contract or transaction or because the vote(s) or such director or directors is or are counted for such purposes, if:

(a) The fact of such relationship or interest is disclosed or known to the Board of Directors or committee which authorizes, approves, or ratifies the contract or transaction by a vote or consent sufficient for the purpose without counting the votes or consents of such interested director or directors; or

(b) The fact of such relationship or interest is disclosed or known to the members entitled to vote and they authorize, approve or ratify such contract or transaction by vote or written consent sufficient for the purpose; or

(c) The contract or transaction is fair and reasonable to the Corporation.

Such interested directors may be counted in determining the presence of a quorum at a meeting of the Board of Directors or a committee thereof which authorizes, approves or ratifies such contract or transaction. This section shall not be construed to invalidate any contract or other transaction which would otherwise be valid under the common and statutory laws applicable thereto.

ARTICLE IV

Offices

Section 4.1. <u>Offices and Qualifications Therefor</u>. The officers of the Corporation shall consist of an Executive Director and a Secretary/Treasurer. The officers shall be selected by the Board of Directors. The duties of the Executive Director and the duties of Secretary/Treasurer shall not be performed by the same person.

Section 4.2. <u>Terms of Office</u>. The Executive Director shall hold office from the time of selection by the Board of Directors until resignation, removal or death. Any remaining officers of the Corporation shall be submitted by the Board of Directors for the annual meeting of the members and each shall hold office for a term of two (2) years (with option of two year renewal) or until a successor shall be duly elected and qualified, or until resignation, removal or death.

Section 4.3. <u>Vacancies</u>. Whenever any vacancies shall occur in any of the offices of the Corporation for any reason, the same may be filled by the Board of Directors at any meeting thereof, and any officer so elected shall hold office until the expiration of the term of the officer causing the vacancy and until a successor shall be duly elected and qualified.

Section 4.4. <u>Removal</u>. Any officer of the Corporation may be removed, with or without cause, by the Board of Directors whenever a majority of such Board shall vote in favor of such removal.

ARTICLE V

Powers and Duties of Officers

Section 5.1. <u>Executive Director</u>. The Executive Director, subject to the general control and direction of the Board of Directors, shall preside at all meetings, shall discharge all the usual functions of a program director and chief operating officer of a corporation and shall have such power and duties as these bylaws or the Board of Directors may prescribe. The Executive Director may participate in financial related activities as designated by the Secretary/Treasurer of the Corporation.

Section 5.2. <u>Secretary/Treasurer</u>. The Secretary/Treasurer shall attend all meetings of the members and of the Board of Directors, and keep, or cause to be kept, a true and complete record of the proceedings of such meetings, and shall perform a like duty, when required, for all committees appointed by the Board of Directors. If required, the Secretary/Treasurer shall attest the execution by the Corporation of deeds, leases, agreements and other official documents, shall attend to the giving and serving of all notices of the Corporation required by these Bylaws, and shall have custody of the books (except books of account) and records of the Corporation.

The Secretary/Treasurer and the Executive Director shall keep correct and complete records of account, showing accurately at all times the financial condition of the Corporation. The

Secretary/Treasurer shall have charge and custody of, and be responsible for, all funds, notes, securities and other valuables which may from time to time come into the possession of the Corporation and shall deposit, or cause to be deposited, all funds of the Corporation with such depositories as the Board of Directors shall designate. The Secretary/Treasurer shall furnish at meetings of the Board of Directors, or whenever requested, a statement of the financial condition of the Corporation, and in general shall perform all duties pertaining to the office of secretary or treasurer and such other duties as the bylaws or the Board of Directors may prescribe.

Section 5.3. Assistant Officers. The Board of Directors may from time to time designate and elect assistant officers who shall have such powers and duties as the officers whom they are elected to assist and shall specify and delegate to them, and such other powers and duties as these Bylaws or the Board of Directors may prescribe. An Assistant Secretary/Treasurer may, in the absence or disability of the Secretary/Treasurer, attest the execution of all documents by the Corporation.

ARTICLE VI

Miscellaneous

Section 6.1. Corporate Seal. The Corporation shall have no seal.

Section 6.2. Execution of Contracts and Other Documents. Unless otherwise ordered by the Board of Directors, all written contracts and other documents entered into by the Corporation shall be executed on behalf of the Corporation by the President and/or Chief Operating Officer, and, if required, attested by the Secretary/Treasurer.

Section 6.3. Fiscal Year. The fiscal year of the Corporation shall begin on September 1 of each year and end on the immediately following August 31.

Section 6.4. Compliance with Section 501(e). The Corporation shall at all times comply with the requirements of Section 501(e) of the Code, or any subsequent federal tax law, and any regulation promulgated by the Internal Revenue Service thereunder, including, specifically, the requirements that (i) all net earnings of the Corporation be allocated or paid to the patron hospitals of the Corporation within eight and one-half (8 1/2) months after the close of the taxable year of the Corporation on the basis of the percentage of the Corporation's services performed for each such patron, and (ii) to the extent the Corporation provides services to patron hospitals which do not have voting rights, at least 50% of the Corporation's services are to patron-hospitals which do have voting rights in the Corporation.

Section 6.5. Operation. The operations of the Corporation shall be to provide the patron hospitals a portion of personnel services necessary to the provision of healthcare, including, in particular, the education of the public regarding nursing careers, the recruitment of individuals into nursing, and the educational mobility and retention of practicing nurses.

ARTICLE VII

Amendments

Subject to law and the Articles of Incorporation, the power to make, alter, amend or repeal all or any part of these Bylaws is vested in the Board of Directors. The affirmative vote of a majority of the entire Board of Directors shall be necessary to effect any such changes in these Bylaws.

ARTICLE VIII

Approval

IN WITNESS WHEREOF the undersigned members of the Board of Directors, by their signatures below, affirm that a meeting of the Board of Directors was held on October 30, 2001, for the purpose, among others, of consideration and revision of the Bylaws of the Corporation; that at said meeting of the Board of Directors, the Bylaws attached hereto were revised by the unanimous vote of the Board of Directors and that the Secretary of the Corporation was thereafter directed to initial and date a copy of the Bylaws and place such copy in the minute book of the Corporation.

_____
Name
Institution

_____
Name
Institution

_____
Name
Institution

_____
Name
Institution

_____
Name
Institution

_____
Name
Institution

_____
Name
Institution

I hereby certify by my signature below that the above signatures are the true and correct signatures of the members of the Board of Directors of the Corporation and that the Bylaws attached hereto are true and correct copies of the Bylaws revised by the unanimous vote of the Board of Directors on October 30, 2001.

_____
SECRETARY TO THE CORPORATION

Appendix E. Speakers' Bureau Orientation

Slide #	Narrative	Slide Content
1	Nursing 2000... Promoting Careers in Registered Nursing Through Counseling, Education, and Public Presentations	Nursing 2000 logo
2	Purpose Nursing 2000 is an educational organization designed to promote and support careers in Registered Nursing	Purpose
3	• History Nursing 2000 is a 12-year-old success story at a local level. What started out as a joint effort of area hospitals to meet the nursing shortage of a few years ago has evolved into a rich collaboration between nursing service and nursing education.	• History Nursing 2000 = local success story Nursing shortage in 1980s to Rich collaboration today
4	• Vision Due to the vision of the vice presidents for nursing from the funding hospitals and the four deans from the schools of nursing, a proposal was presented to the CEOs. Thanks to the support of the CEOs, Nursing 2000 was incorporated as a not-for-profit organization in 1990.	• Founders' Vision VPs of nursing and deans' proposal CEO support Incorporation of Nursing 2000 in 1990
5	• Evolution Nursing 2000 has evolved from a single-purpose focus—recruit more individuals into nursing—to a multi-purpose focus—ensure a stable nursing workforce at all educational levels no matter what the market forces.	• Evolution Single-purpose focus of recruitment in 1990 to Multi-purpose focus of stabilizing workforce at all educational levels
6	FUNDING HOSPITALS • Clarian Health Partners, Inc. Methodist · IU · Riley • Community Health Network • St. Francis Hospital and Health Centers • St. Vincent Hospitals & Health Services • Wishard Health Services	FUNDING HOSPITALS • Clarian Health Partners, Inc. Methodist · IU · Riley • Community Health Network • St. Francis Hospital and Health Centers • St. Vincent Hospitals & Health Services • Wishard Health Services
7	CONTRIBUTING HOSPITALS • Hancock Memorial Hospital & Health Services • Hendricks Community Hospital • Johnson Memorial Hospital • Major Hospital • The Rehabilitation Hospital of Indiana • Riverview Hospital • St. Elizabeth Ann Seton Hospital of Central Indiana • Westview Hospital • Women's Hospital of Indianapolis	CONTRIBUTING HOSPITALS • Hancock Memorial Hospital & Health Services • Hendricks Community Hospital • Johnson Memorial Hospital • Major Hospital • The Rehabilitation Hospital of Indiana • Riverview Hospital • St. Elizabeth Ann Seton Hospital of Central Indiana • Westview Hospital • Women's Hospital of Indianapolis

Slide #	*Narrative*	*Slide Content*
8	SCHOOLS OF NURSING • Indiana University • Ivy Tech State College • Marian College • University of Indianapolis	SCHOOLS OF NURSING • Indiana University • Ivy Tech State College • Marian College • University of Indianapolis

9	PROFESSIONAL NURSING ORGANIZATIONS
	• Eta Chi Chapter, Chi Eta Phi Sorority, Inc.
	• Indiana League for Nursing
	• Indiana Organization of Nurse Executives
	• Indiana State Nurses Association
	• Sigma Theta Tau,
	   Alpha Chapter
	   Lambda Epsilon Chapter
	   Omega Chapter-at-Large
		PROFESSIONAL NURSING ORGANIZATIONS
		• Eta Chi Chapter, Chi Eta Phi Sorority, Inc.
		• Indiana League for Nursing
		• Indiana Organization of Nurse Executives
		• Indiana State Nurses Association
		• Sigma Theta Tau,
		   Alpha Chapter
		   Lambda Epsilon Chapter
		   Omega-at-Large Chapter

10	Nursing 2000—Organizational Structure	Nursing 2000—Organizational Structure
11	Staff • Executive Director • Program Facilitator • Administrative Assistant • Resource Assistant • Resource Facilitator during Helene Fuld Grant	Staff • Executive Director • RN Facilitator • Administrative Assistant • Resource Assistant • Resource Facilitator during Helene Fuld Grant
12	Executive Board • CEO • Nurse Executive • Nurse Executive • Nurse Executive • Dean • Dean • Nurse Executive • Esq.	Executive Board • 1 CEO • 3 Nurse Executives (from funding hospitals) • 1 Nurse Executive (from contributing hospital) • 2 Schools of Nursing Deans • Ex officio attorney
13	Advisory Board	Advisory Board (28 members) • Hospitals/Healthcare Agencies • Educational Institutions • Nursing Organizations
14	Speakers' Bureau	Speakers' Bureau (200 active members) • Hospitals/Healthcare Agencies • Educational Institutions • Nursing Organizations • Nursing Community
15	2001-2002 Organizational Goals	Goals

Slide #	Narrative	Slide Content

16		Goals
		• To disseminate information about Registered Nursing as a dynamic profession to the following groups:
		    Elementary School Age
		    Middle School Age
		    High School Age
		    Adult Learners
		    Career Mobility Nurses

17	Focus on the traditional student and non-traditional student	Traditional Students • Elementary School Age • Middle School Age • High School Age Non-traditional Students • Adult Learners • Second Degree Students
18	LPN, ASN, BSN, MSN, DNSc, PhD	Career Mobility Nurses • LPN to RN • RN to BSN • RN to MSN • BSN to MSN • ND, DNSc, PhD

19	Four Career Roles Within Nursing
	Nursing
	• Roles overlap
	• Interdependent Clinician
	• Clinical Nurse
	• Advanced Practice Nurse
		CAREER ROLES
		1. Clinician including Advanced Practice Nurse
		  • Clinical Specialist
		  • Nurse Anesthetist
		  • Nurse Midwife
		  • Nurse Practitioner
		2. Educator
		3. Manager/Administrator
		4. Researcher

20	Hospital Settings	Hospital Settings
		  Critical Care
		  Emergency
		  Maternal/Child Care
		  Medical
		  Operating Room/Recovery Room
		  Pediatrics
		  Psychiatric/Mental Health
		  Surgical

Slide #	Narrative	Slide Content

21	Non-Hospital Settings	Non-Hospital Settings
		   Public/Community Health
		   Home Healthcare
		   Physician's Office
		   Health Maintenance
		      Organizations and
		      Managed Care
		      Companies
		   Insurance
		   Occupational Health
		   Research Centers

22	Non-Hospital Settings (continued)	Extended Care Facilities Clinics Hospices Community Schools and Settings Military Branches Independent Practice Schools of Nursing

23	In addition, some RNs combine two careers. Others have served as consultants to businesses, schools, and healthcare institutions. Some are combining the field of nursing and computer technology (Informatics Specialist).	COMBINING CAREERS in
		Nursing + Law
		      Business
		      Computer Technology
		      And more

24	Nursing Roles in Managed Care	Nursing Roles in Managed Care • Primary Care Provider • Case Manager • Triage Nurse • Utilization Nurse • Risk Manager • Provider Liaison • Benefits Interpreter • Evaluator
25	An integrated healthcare delivery system requires nurses to gain more education for expanding responsibilities	Integrated Healthcare System RN with increased responsibilities ⟵⟶ RN with increased education
26	RNs make up the largest number of health professionals. • Need for RNs will continue to increase to meet a variety of needs from prevention, to care for an…	RN Supply in U.S. 1983 1.1 million 1990 2.2 million > Doubled! 2000 2.6 million

Slide #	Narrative	Slide Content
27	Aging Population	Aging Poulation in U.S. 1998 34.4 million over 65 years 2030 70 million older persons
28	As healthcare changes require more nurses to shift roles into ambulatory care settings, 40% of nurses are employed outside of hospitals.	Healthcare Changes Majority of RNs in acute care →shift Majority of RNs in ambulatory care (40% occurred by 2000)
29	During the last decade, a shift to ambulatory care occurred	Shift to Ambulatory Care Between 1985-1992 – outpatient visits in short-stay hospitals grew by 50%

30	Where Patients Are – The Nurses Are
	Ambulatory Care
	Physician practice groups
	Clinics
	Health maintenance organizations
	Nurse managed clinics
	Surgery centers
	Birthing centers
	
	Hospitals
	Acute care
	  Medical surgical units
	  Intensive care
	  Operating rooms
	  Emergency rooms
	  Mental health
	  Family centers
	Transitional
	  Acute
	  Subacute
	Rehabilitation
	
	Extended Care/Nursing Homes
	Hospital affiliated
	Non-hospital affiliated
	Resident community facilities
	
	Home Care
	Home healthcare agencies
	Hospice
	
	Community/Public health
	Health departments
	Visiting nurse associations
	Substance abuse facilities
	Senior centers, shelters
	Schools, churches
	Day care centers
	Occupational health
	Health planning agencies
	Correctional facilities
		Where Patients Are – The Nurses Are
		• Ambulatory Care
		• Hospitals
		• Extended Care/Nursing Homes
		• Home Care
		• Community/Public Health

Slide #	Narrative	Slide Content
31	GOAL #2	GOAL To support nurses in educational career mobility and clinical practice to advance nursing careers
32	Nursing 2000's support of educational career mobility.	Support Career Mobility Nursing 2000 offers • LPN to RN Mobility Guide • RN Education Mobility Guide • Guide to Specialty Certification • Advanced Practice Seminar and Reference Materials • Re-Entry Seminar
33	Photo of APN panel at Seminar, *Regarding Advanced Practice Nursing*	Photo of APN Seminar panel.
34	GOAL #3	GOAL To impact the education of nurses through collaboration between nursing service and education.
35	Total number of basic RN programs remains constant. Associate degree programs are in the majority. Baccalaureate programs are increasing.	Slide of Pie of Number of Basic RN Programs
36	Nursing school enrollments are increasing after a six-year period of decline.	Graph of BSN, AD and diploma enrollments
37	Enrollments	Slide of Enrollment Statistics for BSN, MSN, DNSc enrollments
38	Enrollment of men continues to climb.	Slide of bar graph of enrollment of men
39	Collaboration of nurses from service and education to raise scholarship money for nursing students. Planning committee for the benefit, held annually in May.	Slide of Nursing 2000 Scholarship Benefit planning committee
40	Additional collaboration occurred during a seven-minute videotape titled *Nursing Today and Beyond 2000*. It has been distributed to all middle schools, high schools, public libraries, schools of nursing, and hospitals in the eight-county area.	Slide of planning committee member holding videotape
41	GOAL #4	GOAL To attract students into nursing who have demonstrated those potential academic abilities that will lead to a successful career in nursing
42	Map of Indiana High School Locations	Map of Indiana High School Locations

Slide #	Narrative	Slide Content
43	Eight-County Area Served	Eight-County Area Served
44	A. A Day in the Life of a Nurse Shadow Program – 520 high school seniors and juniors attend the program that is offered one day in the fall and one day in the spring.	A Day in the Life of a Nurse Shadow Program • High School Students • Spring and Fall • Formal Application Process • 68/68 High Schools Participate
45	A Day in the Life of a Nurse Shadow Program	Slide of students and RN preceptors during welcome
46	A Day in the Life of a Nurse Shadow Program	Three students in scrubs
47	A Day in the Life of a Nurse Shadow Program	In ICU – RN preceptor and student
48	A Day in the Life of a Nurse Shadow Program	Mother and daughter team
49	A Day in the Life of a Nurse Shadow Program	RN preceptor and student with scope
50	A Day in the Life of a Nurse Shadow Program	Eight students at Riverview Hospital with Nursing 2000 backpacks full of career materials
51	B. School Classroom Presentations	School Classroom Presentations • Roles and Specialties of Nursing • Compensation • Academic Preparation • Types of Nursing Programs
52	School Classroom Presentations	Photo of a classroom presentation
53	School Classroom Presentations	Photo of IPS elementary school children with coloring books
54	C. Career Days/Job Fairs/Displays	Career Day/Job Fairs/Displays • 1:1 or group counseling • Distribute Educational Materials
55	Large Display with Folders Out	Photo of Display Table
56	Small Display with Papers Out	Photo of Speakers' Bureau member and student
57	Doppler – sound attracts students to table	Photo of Speakers' Bureau member and 2 students at Lawrence Central High School
58	D. A Program for Counselors and Science Teachers Also talk to high school and college counselors at the Indiana Association for College Admission Counseling Annual Congress and Exhibitors Fair	"Nursing as a Career…A Program for Counselors and Science Teachers" • Panel Discussion • Optional Shadow Experience
59	Panel	Photo of panel
60	E. Counselor Newsletter – mailed to middle and high school counselors	Photo of Counselor Newsletter

Slide #	Narrative	Slide Content
61	F. Adult Learner Seminars	Slide Adult Learner Career Seminar • Current Healthcare Environment • The Diversity of a Nursing Career • Types of Nursing Programs [educator] • Financial Assistance [financial aid counselor] • Compensation & Benefits • Challenge & Rewards of a Nursing Career – Biographical Sketches
62	GOAL #5	Goal To reflect a positive image of nursing to the public
63	A. Community Events and Displays	Community events and displays • 1:1 interaction • Distribute nursing career materials
64	Photo at Greenwood Park Mall – counseling an RN	Photo at Greenwood Park Mall
65	Children's Museum – Women's History Month	Photo of volunteer and young visitor
66	Children's Museum – Nurses' Day	Photo of OR nurses' display of instruments at Children's Museum
67	Ruth Lilly Health Education Center	Photo of volunteer and display
68	B. Library Window Display	Photo – library window display
69	Rotate window displays to libraries around eight-county area	Map of library locations
70	C. Scholarship Benefit	Annual Fundraiser • Provide Nursing Scholarships • Distributed to Schools of Nursing
71	First fundraiser	Slide of invitation
72	Speaker – Kaye Lani Rae Rafko (1991)	Photo
73	Speaker – Karren Kowalski (1992)	Photo
74	Speaker – Melodie Chenevert (1993)	Photo
75	Speaker – Vernice Ferguson (1994)	Photo
76	Speaker – Sally Karioth (1995)	Photo
77	Speaker – JoEllen Koerner (1996)	Photo
78	Speaker – Beverly Malone (1997)	Photo
79	Speaker – Tim Porter O'Grady (1998)	Photo
80	Speaker – Katherine Vestal (1999)	Photo
81	Speaker - Anne Ryder (2000)	Photo
82	Speaker – Sharon Cox (2001)	Photo
83	Anne Ryder (as emcee)	Photo

Slide #	Narrative	Slide Content
84	Speaker - Jo Manion (2002)	Photo
85	Table at Benefit	Photo
86	Spirit of Philanthropy In grateful recognition of voluntary service and contributing that have significantly advanced the teaching, research, and public service missions of this urban partnership between Indiana University and Purdue University	Slide of certificate of recognition

Appendix F. References to A Day in the Life of a Nurse Shadow Program

Chapter 4

School and School of Nursing Programs
High School A Day in the Life of a Nurse Shadow Program

F.01   Budget Estimation of High School A Day in the Life of a Nurse Shadow Program

F.02   Announcement of A Day in the Life of a Nurse Shadow Program to High School Counselors and Teachers

F.03   Letter of Invitation/Instruction to the Counselors Inviting their Students to Participate

F.04   A Day in the Life of a Nurse Shadow Program Student Application

F.05   Confirmation Letter Sent to Wait List Students

F.06   Wait List Student Return Form

F.07   Orientation Plan for A Day in the Life of a Nurse Shadow Program Coordinators with Welcome Letter, Clinical Opportunities, and Agenda for the Day

F.08   Application Outcome – Letter to Counselors and Sample Reporting Roster

F.09   Application Outcome – Letter to Accepted Students

F.10   Application Outcome – Letter to Accepted Students Placed on Wait List

F.11   Application Outcome – Letter to Denied Students

F.12   Application Outcome – Letter to Students who Previously Participated

F.13   Confirmation Memo to A Day in the Life of a Nurse Shadow Program Coordinator – pre-program

F.14   Registered Nurse Mentor Letter

F.15   Patient Confidentiality Statement

F.16   Evaluation Form Completed by Students

F.17   Content List of Student Folder for A Day in the Life of a Nurse Shadow Program

Appendix F.01. Budget Estimation of High School A Day in the Life of a Nurse Shadow Program
(n = 265 Students)

A Day in the Life of a Nurse Shadow Program

Application packets to school counselors (Flyer announcement, applications, and envelopes)	$3.00
Application outcome letter to counselor and student roster	
Confirmation letter to A Day in the Life of a Nurse Shadow Program Coordinator – pre- and post-program with enclosures	2.00
Application outcome letter to student	1.00
Name tags for students	1.00
Folder for career materials	1.50
Career materials in folder	6.00
Gift for the high school student (i.e., duffel bag)	8.20
Gift for the nurse mentors, coordinators, and helpers	5.50
Postage to counselors × 2	~~1.01~~
Postage to students × 1	.42
	$29.63 per student

Include in general program budget:
- mileage allowed for travel to deliver materials to hospital coordinators
- thank you gift for hospital coordinators (based on 23 coordinators; post-evaluation)
- postage to coordinators × 2 (based on 23 coordinators)

Appendix F.02. Announcement of A Day in the Life of a Nurse Shadow Program to High School Counselors and Teachers

EXPLORE A CAREER IN REGISTERED NURSING

As a nurse, you can make a DIFFERENCE—both in your life and the lives of others.

Registered Nursing is one of the most CHALLENGING and REWARDING careers you can choose.

Attend our A Day in the Life of a Nurse shadow program and explore a career in Registered Nursing.

PROGRAM:	*A Day in the Life of a Nurse*
DATE:	WEDNESDAY, MARCH 20, 2002
FOR:	Junior and Senior High School Students (Sophomores considered as space allows)
WHERE:	Indianapolis Area Hospitals
OBJECTIVES:	1) Observe the role of a Registered Nurse in a clinical setting.
	2) Discuss the varied roles of a Registered Nurse.
	3) Obtain information on educational programs that lead to a degree in Nursing.

SEE YOUR HIGH SCHOOL COUNSELOR FOR AN
APPLICATION TO PARTICIPATE IN THE PROGRAM.

SPONSORED BY:

(Call 317-574-1325 or visit our Web site at www.nursing2000inc.org
for more information about Nursing as a career)

Appendix F.03. Letter of Invitation/Instruction to the Counselors Inviting their Students to Participate

January 14, 2002

Dear Counselor and Science Teacher:

March 20, 2002, is the date selected for our spring A Day in the Life of a Nurse shadow program. We would like to invite your students interested in a nursing career to participate. Student feedback remains extremely positive, as the overall fall program evaluation was a 3.8 on a 4.0 scale! We are pleased to continue this career exploration experience that introduces the high school student to the discipline of nursing. The demand for nursing services continues to increase and opportunities span 50 specialties in a variety of settings.

Copies of application forms are enclosed for your use. You will note we have a total of 22 clinical sites for the students' four selection choices. The application process remains the same as follows:

1) Please request students fully complete the application form including both parent (or guardian) and guidance counselor signatures.

2) Since the program is limited to the 260 most qualified students, please advise students' acceptance will be based on quality of written responses on the application and academic preparation (minimum of algebra, biology, and chemistry or counselor's recommendation).

3) Please mail applications directly to Nursing 2000 (either by the counselor or the student). We will need to receive the applications no later than **Friday, February 15, 2002,** to facilitate assignment of students to the hospitals and to provide timely notification back to the students and counselors.

4) Nursing 2000 will send letters to counselors and their students on Tuesday, February 26, 2002, notifying them of acceptance status and assigned hospitals.

We will continue to market the program to junior and senior students (sophomores will be considered as space allows) and have enclosed a flyer for posting on bulletin boards. In addition, we have received feedback from students that publicizing the program date during morning announcements is very helpful. Thank you for your assistance in sharing this career exploration opportunity.

January 14, 2002

Page Two

As in the past, we will also send a copy of this letter to science teachers; it is the students enrolled in science classes who are often taking the prerequisites for a health career. Thank you in advance for announcing this opportunity in your classes, as you deem appropriate.

We are excited to offer the 24th A Day in the Life of a Nurse shadow program on **March 20**. Please do not hesitate to call us if you have any questions or if we can assist you in any way.

Thank you for your ongoing support of A Day in the Life of a Nurse shadow program. We extend our best wishes for 2002!

Sincerely,

_____   _____
Executive Director   Program Facilitator
Nursing 2000   Nursing 2000

Enclosures: Applications
               Announcement for posting

Appendix F.04. A Day in the Life of a Nurse Shadow Program Student Application

PROMOTE EDUCATE ADVANCE

A DAY IN THE LIFE OF A NURSE SHADOW PROGRAM STUDENT APPLICATION

November 12, 2002
7:30 a.m.—3:30 p.m.

9302 North Meridian Street
Suite 365
Indianapolis, Indiana 46260
317-574-1325
Fax 317-573-0875
info@nursing2000inc.org
www.nursing2000inc.org

A Day in the Life of a Nurse shadow program is a 1:1 <u>observational</u> experience designed to introduce students to the role of today's professional nurse. Providing the student a unique opportunity to "shadow" a nurse in the clinical setting, the program assists students in the process of making a career decision. As the program is limited to the 260 most qualified students, acceptance will be based on written responses on the application, academic preparation (<u>minimum of algebra, biology, and chemistry</u> or counselor's recommendation) and parent or guardian signature on the application. Senior and junior students will be given first preference **(who have not participated before)**. Sophomores will be considered based on space availability.

Student Name: _____

Home Address: _____   Phone: _____

_____   E-mail Address: _____
      City   Zip Code

Parent/Legal Guardian
High School: _____   Name: _____

    Grade: Sophomore __ Junior __ Senior __   Parent/Legal Guardian Daytime Phone
Number: _____

Guidance Counselor's Name: _____

1) The curriculum for nursing is challenging, and most schools require students to have taken a college preparatory curriculum in high school. Please list all high school level science and math classes you *HAVE HAD*, *ARE CURRENTLY TAKING*, and *PLAN TO TAKE IN THE FUTURE*:
Freshman _____
Sophomore _____
Junior _____
Senior _____

2) Why do you want to participate in the Nursing 2000 A Day in the Life of a Nurse shadow program and what do you hope to learn about nursing?

3) What are your plans after high school graduation (next 4-5 years)?

4) Are you considering another health career besides nursing? __Yes __ No
If yes, please indicate your additional career interest: _____

5) The following hospitals are participating in this program:

Please identify your hospital preferences:
1st Choice: _____
2nd Choice: _____
3rd Choice: _____
4th Choice: _____

*BE SURE TO COMPLETE <u>ALL FOUR CHOICES</u>

    I, _____ (student's parent or guardian), hereby give my permission for (student participant; hereinafter "Student") to participate in A Day in the Life of a Nurse shadow program sponsored by Nursing 2000, Incorporated. I understand that Student's participation in A Day in the Life of a Nurse shadow program will allow the Student to shadow nurses within a local hospital. This experience is designed to be observational though may involve exposure to health risks such as contact with patients and body fluids. I further understand and support that the Student will be educated regarding patient confidentiality and that the Student will be asked to sign a patient confidentiality statement.

    In consideration for participation of the Student in the program and the education and information which the Student will receive by participating in A Day in the Life of a Nurse shadow program, I hereby release, indemnify, and hold harmless Nursing 2000, Incorporated, its employees, participating hospitals, officers, and agents from any and all liability arising out of or resulting from the Student's participation in A Day in the Life of a Nurse shadow program.

_____   _____
Signature of Parent or Legal   Date
Guardian of Student Participant

During A Day in the Life of a Nurse shadow program, the opportunity may arise for the student's photograph to be taken for Nursing 2000 or hospital publications, such as newsletters. I grant Nursing 2000 and the assigned hospital permission to photograph (student participant) _____ for informative and educational purposes.

_____   _____
Signature of Parent or Legal   Date
Guardian of Student Participant

Thank you very much for applying to A Day in the Life of a Nurse shadow program. Please have your guidance counselor approve and sign below. The completed application must be sent to Nursing 2000, 9302 North Meridian Street, Suite 365, Indianapolis, Indiana 46260, by either yourself <u>or</u> your counselor, and **MUST** be received by **Friday, February 15, 2002**, to be considered for the program.

STUDENTS WILL BE NOTIFIED OF THEIR PARTICIPATION ON February 26, 2002. ACCEPTANCE LETTERS WILL INCLUDE ASSSIGNED HOSPITAL AND ADDITIONAL PREPARATORY INFORMATION.

Guidance Counselor _____   Phone: _____
                          Signature

Comments:

Appendix F.05. Confirmation Letter Sent to Wait List Students

January 15, 2002

Dear   :

As you recall last spring, you were accepted into our fall A Day in the Life of a Nurse shadow program. We have selected **March 20, 2002**, as the date and are looking forward to your participation. Although we have your application on file, we need you to complete the enclosed confirmation form **with your counselor's signature** and return it to Nursing 2000 in the enclosed self-addressed, stamped envelope by **February 13, 2002**. IT IS ESSENTIAL YOU MAIL YOUR CONFIRMATION FORM BACK TO US IN ORDER TO INSURE YOUR PARTICIPATION. PLEASE UNDERSTAND THAT FAILURE TO RETURN YOUR CONFIRMATION BY <u>FEBRUARY 13, 2002</u>, WILL RESULT IN YOUR SPACE BEING ASSIGNED TO ANOTHER STUDENT. We have more students apply for the program than clinical spaces available; therefore, we have an obligation to see that each space is fully utilized. After your confirmation is received, Nursing 2000 will send a notification letter to you February 26, 2002, regarding your hospital assignment.

Thank you for your interest in exploring nursing as a career. We look forward to seeing you on March 20!

Sincerely,

_____   _____
Executive Director   Program Facilitator
Nursing 2000   Nursing 2000

Enclosure: Confirmation form

Appendix F.06. Wait List Student Return Form

A Day in the Life of a Nurse Shadow Program

March 20, 2002

Name: _____

Address: _____

_____

Home Phone: _____

Parent/Legal Guardian Name: _____

Parent/Legal Guardian's Daytime Phone Number: _____

Name of High School: _____

Please indicate your attendance by checking the appropriate box and signing below:

☐ I _____(signature) **will** be attending
   the March 20, 2002, A Day in the Life of a Nurse shadow program.

☐ I _____(signature) **will not** be able to
   attend the March 20, 2002, A Day in the Life of a Nurse shadow program.

_____
Counselor's Signature

**Please return the confirmation form by FEBRUARY 13, 2002, in the enclosed
self-addressed, stamped envelope. THANK YOU!**

Appendix F.07. Orientation Plan for A Day in the Life of a Nurse Shadow Program Coordinators with Welcome Letter, Clinical Opportunities, and Agenda for the Day

Orientation Plan and Program Materials for
A Day in the Life of a Nurse Shadow Program

Coordinator Orientation

Orientation to Program Materials
Welcome letter to coordinator
Phone list of coordinators
Number of student opportunities at clinical sites
Agenda for the day
Student application
Flyers announcing program sent to high schools
Letter to student—individualized to particular hospital
Patient confidentiality statement
Letter to nurse
Copy of most recent post-evaluation meeting minutes
Copy of most recent speakers' bureau newsletter
Future Focus in Nursing, a newsletter for high school and middle school counselors
Speakers' bureau bag and gifts

Discussion
Indemnification agreement
Observation-only experience
Student safety
Patient confidentiality
Number of students
Nurse mentors

Appendix F.07. Orientation Plan for A Day in the Life of a Nurse Shadow Program Coordinators—Welcome Letter

February 25, 2002

Dear A Day in the Life of a Nurse Shadow Program Coordinator:

Welcome to A Day in the Life of a Nurse Shadow Program Planning Committee! Nursing 2000 is very appreciative that you will be assuming the role of coordinator for (Individual) Hospital. As you know, A Day in the Life of a Nurse shadow program has been our most popular program and continues to receive extremely positive feedback from high school students and their counselors and parents. I am confident you will enjoy the students as much as they enjoy their participation at (Individual) Hospital.

I also wanted to share that since you are directly contributing to the overall program as a coordinator for A Day in the Life of a Nurse shadow program, you are "automatically" a member of Nursing 2000's speakers' bureau. Correspondence regarding A Day in the Life of a Nurse shadow program is sent in early spring and fall. Please call at anytime that we can be of assistance.

We are really looking forward to working together on this program.
Please call at anytime — we are at your service.

Sincerely,

_____   _____
Executive Director   Program Facilitator
Nursing 2000   Nursing 2000

Appendix F.07. Orientation Plan for A Day in the Life of a Nurse Shadow Program Coordinators—Clinical Opportunities

March 20, 2002

Hospital	# of Students Requesting	# of Students Scheduled	Total # of Cancellations/ "No Shows"	# of Students Participating in Program
Community Hospital East	20-25			
Community Hospital North	10			
Community Hospital South	8			
Hancock Memorial	9			
Hendricks Community	20			
IU/Riley (20 each)	40			
Johnson Memorial	7-8			
Major	6			
Methodist	30			
Rehabilitation Hospital	5			
Riverview	10			
St. Elizabeth Ann Seton	3			
St. Francis				
Beech Grove	15			
Indianapolis	10			
Mooresville	5			
St. Vincent—86th	25-30			
St. Vincent Carmel	8			
St. Vincent Children's Specialty	2			
VA	10			
Westview	4			
Wishard	14-16			
Women's Hospital	10			
Total Capacity =	271-284			

Appendix F.07. Orientation Plan for A Day in the Life of a Nurse Shadow Program Coordinators—Agenda for the Day

Nursing 2000—A Day in the Life of a Nurse
Shadow Program
Tuesday, November 12, 2002

__23__ HOSPITAL SITES PARTICIPATING (Hospital sites are listed)
__260__ NUMBER OF STUDENTS HOSPITALS ARE CAPABLE OF HANDLING

Mon. 9/9/02	Nursing 2000 to send letter to counselors inviting Jr. and Sr. students to participate (sophomores to be considered). [9 weeks before event] Will enclose flyers to counseling department for additional marketing
Fri. 10/11/02	Student Applications due to Nursing 2000 (4 weeks before event)
Mon. 10/28/02	Nursing 2000 to notify counselors of number and names of students
Tues. 10/29/02	Nursing 2000 to send letters to students with specific information and map to hospital (2 weeks before event)
Fri. 11/1/02	Nursing 2000 to deliver names of students (rosters) to hospitals with Day in the Life materials
Tues. 11/12/02	A Day in the Life of a Nurse shadow program event **PLEASE CALL NURSING 2000 (telephone number) WITH ANY "NO SHOWS" SO WE CAN NOTIFY HIGH SCHOOL COUNSELORS**
Fall Counselor Newsletter	Nursing 2000 to thank counselors for their support of the program <u>Also include evaluation summary</u>

PROGRAM:	7:30 a.m. - 3:30 p.m.
7:30 a.m.	**Park and meet in lobby** (designate escort)
7:45 - 8:45	**General introduction and welcome** (morning nourishment) An overview of nursing Divide into small groups: Tour of Hospital - overview of nursing areas, i.e., Peds, Med/Surg, Nursing, L & D, Critical Care (if applicable)
8:45 - 9:00	**Change into scrubs** (if applicable) - Secure belongings
9:00 - 2:00	**Assigned to Unit** 1 to 1 with RN; Lunch with assigned RN (provide lunch passes)
2:00 - 3:15	**Group reconvenes** - (drinks and chips)

- ♦ **Polaroid photograph** of student in scrubs with assigned RN or earlier in day if convenient
- ♦ Have student sign Patient Confidentiality Statement
- ♦ Nursing video (while everyone is getting settled)
- ♦ Post-Conference (go around room and everyone shares their experiences)
- ♦ Invite nurse the student shadowed, nursing managers, clinical specialists, directors of nursing (as you deem appropriate and available)
- ♦ Students complete evaluation form of the program
- ♦ Distribute packet: - Hospital information (include volunteer information)
    – Nursing 2000 (Generalized nursing info, schools, financial aid)
    – Giveaway by Nursing 2000 (duffel bag)

__3:15 - 3:30 p.m. Change from scrubs__ (if applicable)—End of Day!

Hospital Financial Considerations:	Nursing 2000 will provide:
• Parking	• Written correspondence and coordination of event
• Lunch (student and nurse being shadowed)	• Generalized nursing packet
• Morning nourishment and afternoon snack	• Student—career information packet, duffel bag, nurses gift
• **Polaroid picture** of student with RN	• Name tags for students

Appendix F.08. Application Outcome – Letter to Counselors and Sample Reporting Roster

February 25, 2002

Dear Counselor:

Thank you very much for your assistance in selecting qualified students for participation in A Day in the Life of a Nurse shadow program. We are very pleased with the response and have placed **262** students in the March 20, 2002, program.

Enclosed is a listing that indicates participation of all the students from your high school who applied for the March 20 A Day in the Life of a Nurse shadow program. Nursing 2000 will send letters to **all students** who applied to the program regarding their participation. Students accepted for the March 20 program will receive letters identifying their assigned hospital and providing them additional information to prepare for their experience. Additional students who met the criteria but for which there was not space will receive letters notifying them of their automatic acceptance for the fall 2002 program. Students who did not meet the criteria will also receive a letter indicating the reason. Student letters will be sent on **Wednesday, February 27.**

Thank you again for your support of the **24th** A Day in the Life of a Nurse shadow program. We will continue to work hard to provide an educational offering deserving of your time and students' time. We are open to suggestions at any time (phone number), and highly value your input. In addition, our Web site is accessible at (Web site) for ongoing career information.

Sincerely,

_____   _____
Executive Director   Program Facilitator
Nursing 2000   Nursing 2000

Appendix F.08. Application Outcome – Sample Reporting Roster

Nursing 2000
A Day in the Life of a Nurse Shadow Program

Name of High School

Accepted to the March 20, 2002, Program

Student Name:	Class:	Hospital Assigned To:
	Senior	
	Senior	
	Senior	
	Junior	
	Senior	
	Senior	

Accepted to the Fall 2002 Program

Student Name:	Class:
	Junior
	Junior

Not Accepted to the Program

Student Name:	Class:	Reason:
	Senior	Participated before
	Senior	Enrollment in or completion of algebra and chemistry
	Senior	Enrollment in or completion of chemistry

Appendix F.09. Application Outcome – Letter to Accepted Students

February 26, 2002

(first name), (last name)
(address)
(city), IN (zip)

Dear (first name):

We are looking forward to having you participate in our A Day in the Life of a Nurse shadow program on Wednesday, March 20, 2002, from 7:30 a.m. - 3:30 p.m. You have been assigned to <u>Name of Hospital</u> for your experience. **The following information is to assist you as you prepare for the day:**

1. **PLEASE <u>EAT</u> BREAKFAST BEFORE REPORTING TO THE HOSPITAL.** This is very important in preventing weakness or faintness in the clinical areas. Lunch passes will be provided by the hospital.
2. Parking is available, at no charge, in the parking garage. Please bring ticket inside.
3. You will meet <u>(Name), RN,</u> in the main lobby at 7:30 a.m.
4. Wear comfortable shoes (white athletic shoes are appropriate). You will have the opportunity to change into scrubs (hospital attire) before accompanying your assigned nurse. Your clothing will be secured during your experience on the unit (please do not bring valuables with you to the hospital).
5. Be apprised that each hospital may have specific policies regarding dress code. In addition, electronic devices such as cell phones <u>are</u> <u>prohibited</u> to use within the hospital due to potential interference with patient monitoring equipment. Please do not bring cell phones or pagers.

An <u>approximate</u> schedule for the day is as follows:

7:30 a.m.	Park and meet your hospital representative
7:45 - 8:45	General introduction and welcome
	Discussion of nursing as a career followed by a hospital tour
8:45 - 9:00	Change into scrubs (if applicable)—secure belongings
9:00 - 9:30	Meet your assigned RN
9:30 - 12:00	One to one observational time with your RN (Including lunch)
12:30 - 2:00	Observational time with RN on clinical unit
2:00 - 3:15	Post-Conference—share experiences from the day
	Distribution of career information
3:15 - 3:30	Change from scrubs (if applicable). End of Day!

If for any reason you are unable to participate, please notify us, as it is our responsibility to report attendance to the counselor and to inform the hospital. We do ask if you are ill and/or running a fever to notify us at (telephone number), for it is important not to expose our patients to potential illness. Also, if your extracurricular schedule requires you to leave early, please make prior arrangements through Nursing 2000, as leaving early is disruptive to the clinical site.

Students often request a specific clinical specialty in which they would like to spend the day. Due to the many varied requests and availability of the nursing staff, we are unable to meet individual preferences. However, we are confident a day spent directly observing your assigned nurse providing patient care will assist in your career exploration. We encourage you to take advantage of this 1:1 opportunity to ask questions. This is an exciting and challenging time to be considering nursing as a career. We look forward to seeing you on March 20!

Sincerely,

_____
Executive Director
Nursing 2000

_____
Program Facilitator
Nursing 2000

Appendix F.10. Application Outcome — Letter to Accepted Students Placed on Wait List

February 27, 2002

(First name), (Last Name)
(Address)
(City), IN (Zip)

Dear (First Name):

Thank you for your interest in the Nursing 2000 A Day in the Life of a Nurse shadow program. We are pleased to inform you that you have been accepted to participate in the **fall 2002** program. As a result of the large response to the March 20 program, a number of applicants were placed in the fall 2002 program. Because your application met all the criteria requested, we have automatically reserved a space for you in the fall 2002 program. Nursing 2000 will send you a letter of notification in September 2002 confirming the date and requesting your individual confirmation at that time.

This is an exciting and challenging time to be considering a career in nursing. We look forward to providing you an introduction to the role of a professional nurse in the fall of 2002! In the interim, please visit our Web site at _____ for career information.

Sincerely,

_____

Executive Director
Nursing 2000

_____

Program Facilitator
Nursing 2000

Appendix F.11. Application Outcome – Letter to Denied Students

February 27, 2002

(First name), (Last Name)
(Address)
(City), IN (Zip)

Dear (First Name):

We have received your application for Nursing 2000's A Day in the Life of a Nurse shadow program scheduled for March 20, 2002. It is with regret that we must share with you that your application was not accepted for the program on this date. Our minimum criteria for selection (as indicated on the application) included:

_____ Completion of, currently enrolled, or planned enrollment in algebra
_____ Completion of, currently enrolled, or planned enrollment in biology
_____ Completion of, currently enrolled, or planned enrollment in chemistry
_____ Completion of each section of the application
_____ Quality of written responses on the application
_____ Parent and/or guardian signature on the application
_____ Counselor's signature on the application

In addition, we are not able to accept applications with:

_____ No expressed interest in considering nursing as a potential career choice.

We have indicated the area(s) above that is applicable to your application.

Nursing 2000 conducts A Day in the Life of a Nurse shadow program in the spring and fall each year. We encourage you to apply for our fall 2002 program indicating your additional progress/plans toward the above selection criteria. In the interim, you can access our Web site at _____. The Nursing Organization Resource List offers additional Web site resources to access.

If we can be of any assistance to you regarding your pursuit of a nursing career, please let us know. We'd be happy to assist in any way possible and look forward to hearing from you in the fall!

Sincerely,

_____   _____
Executive Director   Program Facilitator
Nursing 2000   Nursing 2000

Appendix F.12. Application Outcome – Letter to Students who Previously Participated

February 27, 2002

(First name), (Last Name)
(Address)
(City), IN (Zip)

Dear (First Name):

Thank you for your continued interest in A Day in the Life of a Nurse shadow program. As a result of the response to the spring program, priority was given to those students who have not had the opportunity to participate. Due to your previous participation, I am sorry that we are unable to process your application for the spring 2002 program, as we had more students apply than available clinical positions.

We invite you to visit our Web site at _____ and additional nursing organizations listed on the Nursing Organization Resource List (on our Web site). Career information is evolving and updated frequently. In particular, note the National Student Nurses Association Web site at www.nsna.org. With the increased demand for health services, nursing offers an abundant diversity of career opportunities for individuals entering the profession. Please do not hesitate to call Nursing 2000 if we can provide any additional information regarding your interest in a nursing career.

Thank you again. Our best wishes for your future!

Sincerely,

_____   _____
Executive Director   Program Facilitator
Nursing 2000   Nursing 2000

Appendix F.13. Confirmation Memo to A Day in the Life of a Nurse Shadow Program Coordinator — Pre-Program

MEMORANDUM

TO: A Day in the Life of a Nurse Shadow Program Coordinators

FROM: _____, Executive Director, Nursing 2000

                 _____, Program Facilitator, Nursing 2000

SUBJECT: March 20 A Day in the Life of a Nurse Shadow Program Confirmation

DATE: January 31, 2002

March 20 is rapidly approaching for the spring A Day in the Life of a Nurse shadow program! The **agenda plan** is enclosed for your reference. We will deliver your A Day in the Life of a Nurse shadow program materials, **including your student rosters,** according to the following schedule:

Delivery, March 7 & 8		Per Mail, Arrival approximately March 13
CHE	St. Vincent-86th Street	Hancock
CHN	St. Vincent Carmel	Hendricks
CHS	St. Vincent Children's Speciality	Johnson Memorial
Clarian IU and Riley	VA Medical Center	Major
Clarian Methodist	Westview	Riverview
Rehab	Wishard	St. Francis Mooresville
St. Elizabeth Ann Seton	Women's Hospital	
St. Francis		
St. Francis Indianapolis		

We hope you will plan to use the Nursing 2000 **videotape,** "Nursing Today and Beyond 2000" in your pre- or post-conference. Your "shelf copy" was delivered to you in the past; however, please call Nursing 2000 if you need to receive another copy. We will put it with your A Day in the Life of a Nurse shadow program delivery materials.

Once again, a **guide sheet** is enclosed that can be included with the confirmation letter (or other communication) that each coordinator sends to the RN. If you recall, the A Day in the Life of a Nurse shadow program Committee recommended we include the guide sheet to emphasize patient confidentiality and "no direct hands-on care."

At our spring 2001 post-evaluation meeting, feedback indicated the **Patient Confidentiality Statement** continues to be a helpful tool to the Program. A copy is enclosed for you to duplicate and utilize in your pre- or post-conference. As the committee requested, the signed copies by the students are to be mailed to Nursing 2000 with the evaluation forms after the **March 20 program**.

Just a reminder that the post-evaluation meeting for 2001-2002 will be held on **Thursday, April 18, 2002, from 2:30 - 4:00 p.m., at the Nursing 2000 office.**

Thank you for your ongoing commitment to A Day in the Life of a Nurse shadow program. Your coordination, time, and effort have <u>directly</u> contributed to our 24th offering of A Day in the Life of a Nurse shadow program!!

Enclosures:
1. Agenda Plan (timeline)
2. RN letters (guide sheet) from Nursing 2000
3. Patient Confidentiality Statement

Appendix F.14. Registered Nurse Mentor Letter

March 2002

Dear Registered Nurse,

On behalf of Nursing 2000, thank you for your contribution to the March 20, 2002, A Day in the Life of a Nurse shadow program. **Your individual effort in providing a nursing observational experience assists high school students to make a more informed career choice about their future.** During the fall 2001 experience, one senior student stated, reflective of the total evaluations, "I can't believe how much this helped with my decision to become a nurse. Now I am sure this is what I really want to do."

Survey:

In July of 1998, an expanded research survey was sent to graduating high school seniors that participated in A Day in the Life of a Nurse shadow program. Highlights include:
- Majority stated career decision was made while a student was in high school.
- Impact of family members, nurses, and high school teachers/counselors was significant.
- Impact of observing a nurse "while caring" for family member or "while at work" was significant.
- **Eighty-four percent** stated A Day in the Life of a Nurse shadow program experience was influential in their career decision.

Our A Day in the Life of a Nurse shadow program 2001 evaluation survey sent to graduating high school seniors found 65% of respondents chose nursing as a career. An additional 24% selected health-related careers. **Thank you for the time you are giving to students.**

Demand for Nursing:

The rising complexity of acute care; advancing technology; and the delivery of healthcare across inpatient, outpatient, and community settings are factors contributing to the demand for RNs. In addition, a wave of RN retirements is expected to peak in the next decade. RNs are needed at all educational levels (ASN through Doctorate) to meet tomorrow's healthcare needs. Therefore, **your time spent with high school students who express an interest in healthcare is making a difference in meeting future nursing care needs.**

CNN/USA Today/Gallup Poll:

According to a CNN/USA Today/Gallup Poll, nurses rank second for their honesty and integrity. Firefighters displaced nurses this year in the number one rating following the September 11 tragedy. The military, police, pharmacists, medical doctors, and the clergy followed. A greater compliment could not be extended to our profession.

Student and Patient Safety:

In order to create a safe environment for patients and the students, it is important that each nurse:

- Stress **patient confidentiality** with the student. (You may need to emphasize throughout the day based on the student's maturity level.)
- Emphasize that it is an **observational experience only—no hands-on care.**
- Accompany student (you or your designee) at all times; if you are not able to accompany the student to lunch, contact A Day in the Life of a Nurse shadow program coordinator.

Application Criteria:

Nursing 2000 is frequently asked for the criteria used in student selection for A Day in the Life of a Nurse shadow program. The criteria include:

- algebra, biology, and chemistry
- counselor's approval and signature
- parent's approval and signature
- expressed interest in nursing as a potential career choice
- senior and junior students given first priority, sophomores as space allows

A Day in the Life of a Nurse shadow program provides college-bound traditional students—who are choosing from an abundance of increasing career options—the opportunity to explore nursing as a career choice. Due to the 11-year success of A Day in the Life of a Nurse shadow program, requests to duplicate the learning experience have been received from across the country. Thank you for making the experience possible and contributing to nursing!

Sincerely yours,

Executive Director
Nursing 2000

Program Facilitator
Nursing 2000

Appendix F.15. Patient Confidentiality Statement

A Day in the Life of a Nurse Shadow Program
at (Name of Hospital)

Patient Confidentiality

As evidenced by my signature below, I understand the importance of maintaining patient confidentiality. I shall not disclose any patient information—including name, diagnosis, and any other identifying information—learned through my participation in the A Day in the Life of a Nurse shadow program.

_____   _____

STUDENT   DATE

Appendix F.16. Evaluation Form Completed by Students

A DAY IN THE LIFE OF A NURSE
SHADOW PROGRAM
STUDENT EVALUATION
March 20, 2002

Participating Hospital: (Institution Name)

Thank you for attending A Day in the Life of a Nurse shadow program.
In order to evaluate and improve this program for future participants, we need
your assistance. Please take a few minutes to complete this evaluation and
provide us with an honest evaluation of the program. We hope you enjoyed
your participation in A Day in the Life of a Nurse shadow program.
THANK YOU for completing this evaluation.

EVALUATION

Please rate to what degree you agree with the following statements. (4 is high and 1 is low)

Please circle your response

<u>High = 4</u>   <u>Low = 1</u>

1. The information <u>sent</u> to me was adequate to prepare me   4   3   2   1
   for my experience in A Day in the Life of a Nurse
   shadow program.

2. This experience was helpful in increasing my knowledge   4   3   2   1
   of nursing in the hospital setting.

3. I enjoyed the opportunity to work directly with a nurse.   4   3   2   1

4. This experience was helpful to me in making a career   4   3   2   1
   decision.

5. I would recommend this experience to others who are   4   3   2   1
   interested in a career in nursing.

6. Overall, I would rate my day as being a positive   4   3   2   1
   experience.

COMMENTS (Regarding items #1 through #6):

7. From my experience, two characteristics that describe a nurse are:

_____

_____

_____

8. Suggestions for changes in the program or any additional comments:

_____

_____

_____

_____

9. How did you hear about this program?
Guidance Counselor _____ Teacher _____ Friend _____ Flyer Describing the Program _____
School Announcement _____   Other (please specify) _____

10. Please share the following information to assist in evaluating A Day in the Life of a Nurse shadow program.

Sophomore _____   Junior _____   Senior _____

_____ I plan to pursue nursing as a career.

_____ I plan to pursue another health career. Please indicate _____

_____ I do not plan to pursue a nursing or health career.

11. Name of high school:

_____

The following demographic information is optional; however, the following information would be most helpful in evaluation of the total Nursing 2000 program.

12. Gender   Female _____   Male _____

13. Racial/Ethnic Background
_____ African American   _____ Hispanic
_____ Asian American   _____ Native American
_____ Caucasian   _____ Other

THANK YOU FOR YOUR ASSISTANCE IN EVALUATING OUR PROGRAM! WE WILL USE IT TO PLAN FUTURE PROGRAMS.

OPTIONAL: NAME _____

Appendix F.17. Content List of Student Folder for A Day in the Life of a Nurse Shadow Program

Contents of Student Folder for
A Day in the Life of a Nurse Shadow Program

1. Welcome letter to the student

2. "A Career in Registered Nursing" handout

3. List of schools of nursing in Indiana

4. "Specialties in the Career of Registered Nursing" handout

5. Resource list of nursing organizations

6. List of hospitals in Marion County and seven surrounding counties (participating hospitals of Nursing 2000 are noted)

7. Volunteer opportunities in affiliated hospitals

8. Financial aid resource

9. School brochures from:
   Indiana University
   Ivy Tech State College
   Marian College
   University of Indianapolis

10. Student Financial Assistance Booklet from the U.S. Department of Education

11. Student Financial Assistance from Indiana Career and Postsecondary Advancement Center

Appendix G. Materials Relevant to Classroom Presentations

Chapter 4

School and School of Nursing Programs
Classroom Presentations

Appendix G.01. Budget Estimation of Classroom Presentations
(n = 2,100 Students)

Classroom Presentations

Folders for career materials	$1.40
Career materials in folder	2.00
Promotional item to attendee (i.e., pens, pencils)	.34
	$3.74 per attendee
Thank you gift for the counselors/teachers (based on 70 presentations)	2.00
Thank you gift for Nursing 2000 volunteers (based on 70 presentations)	2.00
Thank you letter to Nursing 2000 volunteers (based on 70 presentations)	1.00
	$5.00 per presentation

Include in general program budget:
- mileage for delivery of materials to Nursing 2000 volunteer by staff
- audiovisual development (slides, CD ROM, videos, etc.)

Appendix G.02. Scripted Classroom Presentation for High School/Middle School Slide Presentation

SCRIPTED CLASSROOM PRESENTATION
HIGH SCHOOL/MIDDLE SCHOOL SLIDE PRESENTATION

<u>Introduce Self</u>   Hi, I'm _____. I'm a registered nurse. I'm happy to be here today to talk to you about a career in registered nursing. Nursing is a career with unlimited opportunities – ranging from caring for the very old to the newborn, in settings from high intensity (emergency rooms, critical care areas, etc.) to health wellness and promotion (clinics, occupational health) and everything in between! For the men in the audience, I hope you won't discount my comments thinking nursing is for women only, as more men are entering nursing today because of job security, mobility, advancement opportunities, and competitive salaries. Average starting salaries in the Indianapolis area for registered nurses are about $32,000-$35,000 per year.

I'd like to share with you a little about my background. – education and work experience.

**Review packet of information distributed: 1) Nursing 2000 programs on inside of folder, 2) Career in nursing handout, 3) Schools of nursing in Indiana.

SLIDE PRESENTATION

Slide #	Narrative	Slide Content
1	Nursing 2000 – an organization that promotes careers in registered nursing through counseling, education, and public presentation.	Title Slide Nursing 2000
2	Do you have lots of questions about your life right now?	Lots of different size question marks
3	Do you wish that you could look into a crystal ball and find some answers? Like these points of light, your life can take many directions.	Shimmering crystal ball

Slide #	Narrative	Slide Content
4	How do you know the right choices for you? Let's explore some options in nursing, as well as examining the path in education that might help you to reach your goal.	Show a dirt road, possibly with a fork in the road
5	First of all: What is nursing? Many have defined nursing as being both an art and a science. In its most basic definition, nursing is the care of others. It involves a human side, the art of nursing, coupled with the science of nursing, which is the knowledge base for what is done. These two elements work together to help people reach their maximum function and quality of life. Some have referred to this as the "high-tech" and "high-touch" aspects of nursing.	Split slide: nurse with baby/critical care nurse with monitor
6	What do nurses do? This is not meant to be a lesson in anatomy! They care for patients 24 hours a day, 365 days a year (including weekends and holidays!) This fact has resulted in the American Nurses Association (ANA) calling nurses the "backbone of the healthcare system." It also results in a career with a lot of flexibility!	Schematics of two skeletons: 1 upright ("backbone") and 1 bending ("flexibility")
7	Nurses also work together with physicians and other members of the healthcare team. In addition, they —	Nurse and MD
8	— perform wound care and change dressings	Nurse changing dressing
9	— start and monitor intravenous (IV) therapy	Nurse filling drip chamber with IV fluids
10	— take vital signs (heart rate, blood pressure, respiratory rate, and temperature)	Nurse taking heart rate
11	— give injections	Nurse drawing up an injection
12	— and work with complex monitors and equipment	Nurse working in critical care setting
13	There is a lot of diversity! Nursing can be a very rewarding profession.	"At 10:26 AM, the nurse brought 57-year-old heart patient back to life." What did you accomplish this morning?
14	Nurses are present during important times in people's lives – times of extreme joy...	Mother and newborn
15	— and at times of extreme sadness	Child crying
16	Here we see nurses involved in a memorial service as part of a support group organization for women who have experienced the loss of a baby.	A gravesite scene

Slide #	Narrative	Slide Content
17	Nurses also fulfill a very important role of teaching. They participate in patient education…	Slide of nurse teaching patient with a tracheotomy
18	— as well as community education. (ENCARE = Emergency Nurses Cancel Alcohol-related Emergencies)	Article about the ENCARE presentations
19	Nurses bridge technology with caring…remember the definition of the art and science of nursing!	Photograph of nurse at bedside
20	You may be asking yourself: How do I know if a career in nursing may be right for me?	Question mark slide
21	Consider these questions: Do I enjoy working with people? What age group? Under what life conditions (i.e., healthy, needy, at risk, mentally ill, physically ill, disabled)? If you need some direction in this area, consider volunteer work or a summer job that might give you some experience in these areas…	Bullet points of the following questions: • Do I enjoy working with people? • What age groups? • Under what life conditions?
22	— or participate in Nursing 2000's A Day in the Life of a Nurse Shadow Program	Former group of participants
23	Additionally, nurses need physical stamina since much of their day may be spent standing or walking and emotional stamina to deal with the emergencies they may encounter on the job.	Nurse in a critical care unit
24	NURSING PRACTICE SETTINGS AND SPECIALTIES	Title slide
25	In the hospital, expanding healthcare technology requires increased nursing observation at the bedside.	Text slide
	Some of the specialties you find within the hospital are:	Neonatal intensive unit
26	• Critical Care – providing constant care to severely ill patients in highly specialized units. There are newborn, pediatric, and adult units.	
27	• Pediatric Nursing – providing nursing care to children. Nurses who work with children must have a specialized knowledge of growth and development.	Nurse with pediatric patient
28	• Maternal/Child Nursing – providing nursing care to moms, babies, and families during the entire birth process.	Birth family and nurse
29	• Mental Health Nursing – providing nursing care to patients experiencing emotional adjustments. Requires strong communication skills and understanding of human behavior.	Nurse with mental health patient

Slide #	Narrative	Slide Content
30	• Oncology Nursing – providing care to patients who are being treated for cancer. It may involve caring for both children and adults and working very closely with families.	Nurse with bone marrow transplant patient
31	• Medical Nursing – providing care to patients who often have a long-term illness. Some examples are problems of the kidney, lung, heart, or specific diseases such as diabetes and arthritis.	Nurse teaching patient glucose monitoring
32	• Surgical Nursing – providing care to patients who have experienced a surgical procedure (surgery). This may be in a hospital or outpatient center.	Nurse with patient after eye surgery
33	• Operating Room Nursing – providing care in the highly specialized, technical environment of surgery. The nurse works closely with the entire surgery team.	Nurse with operating room team
34	• Emergency Room – providing care to patients requiring immediate treatment (such as a heart attack) and who often have experienced trauma. Nurses who work in emergency rooms have to set priorities and make quick, life-saving decisions.	Emergency room team
35	• Rehabilitation – providing care to patients who have long-term disabilities and injuries. The patients are often young trauma victims or older individuals who have a debilitating experience.	Nurse assisting patient with walker
36	Non-hospital settings are predicted to employ 40% of all nurses. Some of the specialties you frequently see outside of the hospital setting are:	Text slide
37	• Public Health/Community Nursing – the nurse cares for patients and families of different ages in schools, clinics, and homes. Much emphasis is on prevention of illness.	"hands on care: public health service style"
38	• Home Health – the nurse cares for patients and families in their homes, often over an extended period of time. This is a growing area of nursing as patients are staying for shorter periods of time in the hospital. When they go home, they frequently need nursing care.	Nurse ringing doorbell
39	• Geriatric Nursing – the nurse works with the elderly. The need for nurses in this area is growing because people are living longer. The nurse works in clinics and runs nursing centers to help the aging population stay healthy.	Nurse with elderly patient

Slide #	Narrative	Slide Content
40	• Occupational Health Nursing – the nurse works with people in their employment settings. The nurse gives emergency care, performs health exams, and provides health teaching and counseling. Much emphasis is on prevention.	Employee with nurse
	Other – you will also find nurses working in clinics, physicians' offices, and (for some with master's and doctorate degrees) in their own independent practice.	
41	ROLES	Title slide
42	Generally, there are four career roles a nurse can choose. You can see from this slide, all the roles overlap and are interdependent with each other. However, it is important to know there are four careers within nursing!	Inter-related roles: Career paths
43	• Clinician • Educator • Manager/Administrator • Researcher	
44	• Clinical Specialist – a clinician with a master's degree or beyond who specializes in a specific area of care…such as we discussed earlier (critical care, pediatrics, maternal/child care, mental health, oncology, etc.). They work in all types of settings and provide direct care, develop nursing care procedures and ways to monitor the quality of nursing care, and can also be educators and researchers.	Consulting with other nurses
45	• Nurse Practitioner – a clinician prepared with a master's degree who provides basic healthcare for infants, children, and adults in settings ranging from community health centers, hospitals, schools, workplaces, and homes. They perform physical exams, diagnose and treat common illness, and counsel patients on health promotion. In many states, nurse practitioners have been granted legal authority to write prescriptions (prescribe medications).	Nurse performing ear exam
46	• Nurse-Midwife – a clinician who can provide prenatal and gynecological care to normal, healthy women; deliver babies in hospitals, private homes, or birthing centers; and provide follow-up care. Requires advanced education in an accredited certificate program.	Nurse midwife with family

Slide #	Narrative	Slide Content
47	• Registered Nurse Anesthetists – a clinician who gives anesthesia (drugs that put patients to sleep) for all types of surgery. Requires advanced education—usually a master's degree.	Nurse anesthetist
48	• Educator – a nurse with a minimum of a master's degree whose practice also includes teaching student nurses and practicing nurses. Educators include: – Clinical Instructor – teaches clinical skills to student nurses – College/University Professor – teaches and also does research; *we need more nurses prepared for these positions*; usually requires a doctoral degree – Staff Development Specialist – coordinates the continuing education for practicing nurses both in hospital and non-hospital settings	Educator with two students
49	• Manager/Administrator – coordinates the use of human, financial (budget), and technological resources (equipment) for patient care. Requires much collaboration with physicians, other managers, and administration. The manager is very much an advocate for the nursing staff to provide the resources they need to take care of the patients!	Manager collaborating with other team members
50	• Researcher – doctorally prepared nurse who uses statistical methodologies to discover or establish facts, principles, or relationships. Directly develops nursing's expanding knowledge base.	Nurse with computer
51	DIVERSITY As you can see, nursing's greatest strength is its diversity. Nurses can follow their personal and professional interests by working with any group of people, in any setting, at any time. There is no profession that offers as many different opportunities as does nursing.	Title slide
52	SALARY AND WORK ENVIRONMENT	Title slide
53	The average starting salary in the Indianapolis area is $35,000-$37,000 per year	Text slide
54	Advancement opportunities, compensation, and benefits are included.	Text slide

Slide #	Narrative	Slide Content

55	Many scheduling options are available that are compatible in meeting the personal needs of the nurse.
	1) day shift
	    evening shift
	    night shift
	2) 4 hours
	    8 hours
	    12 hours
		Text slide

56	What is nursing's future?	Crystal ball – What is nursing's future?
57	This is a time of great change in healthcare delivery. This is not unique to nursing! The focus of healthcare is changing from "illness and care to wellness and care." At the same time, both hospitals and outpatient settings are experiencing complex patient care demands that require RNs prepared with strong clinical judgment skills. But the effect that it is having on nursing is that fewer nurses will be employed by hospitals and more nurses will be employed in settings outside of the hospital, such as clinics, short stay surgery centers, health centers, hospices, homes, schools, and businesses. All of this is occurring at a time, according to the U.S. General Accounting Office, when the RN supply is projected to be 20% below requirements.	Split slide with nurse in a hospital setting/nurse in community health
58	However, advanced practice nurses (those with two to four years of graduate education, such as clinical specialists, nurse practitioners, nurse midwives, nurse anesthetists) will be increasing in demand to provide a full range of healthcare services to patients. More nurses with advanced practice degrees likely will be needed, as well as additional nursing faculty.	Advanced practice nurse with stethoscope listening to patient
59	What implications does this have for you if you are considering a career in nursing? More nurses will be needed with baccalaureate degrees (four years of education) to care for patients in all of these settings.	Nurse at graduation
60	Your opportunities are vast and diverse in nursing!	"The sky's the limit!" hot air balloon
61	EDUCATIONAL PREPARATION FOR A NURSING CAREER What about educational preparation for a career in nursing?	Title slide

Slide #	Narrative	Slide Content
62	Students who are thinking about nursing as a career should plan a college preparatory curriculum.	Text slide
63	*Recommended High School Subjects* English 4 years Math 2-4 years Algebra & Geometry Science 2-4 years Biology & Chemistry Social Studies 3-4 years Foreign Language 2 years —Emphasize taking all science and math courses available. Helps to prepare student for college level anatomy, physiology, chemistry, microbiology, genetics, psychology, etc.	Text slide
64	How do you decide which nursing program is right for you?	Text slide
65	TYPES OF NURSING PROGRAMS	Title slide
66	*Entry levels:* Associate Degree Diploma Program Bachelor Degree Graduates of all three programs are eligible to take state board examination and, upon successful completion, be licensed as a registered nurse— All are good programs but they <u>are</u> different— let me explain-	Text slide: Education Requirements
67	*Associate Degree Program* • Length of Program: usually two academic years • Academic Credentials: Associate of Science in Nursing, ASN • Setting: Technical Institute or College/University • Role Preparation: Prepares graduates competent to serve in entry level nursing positions and qualified to provide direct care to individuals and families with well-defined health needs in a variety of care settings. The ASN curriculum includes courses in the physical and behavioral sciences. • ASN graduates have a variety of career opportunities. They also have completed basic course requirements for entering an RN-BSN completion program.	Text slide: Associate Degree Program

Slide #	Narrative	Slide Content
68	*Bachelor Degree Program*	Text slide: Bachelor Degree Program

68 — *Bachelor Degree Program*
- Length of program: usually four academic years
- Academic Credentials: Bachelor of Science in Nursing, BSN
- Setting: College or University
- Role Preparation: Prepares graduates to provide direct and indirect nursing care to individuals, families, groups, and communities in a variety of settings that span the continuum of care. The BSN curriculum includes courses in the physical sciences, behavioral sciences, and humanities. Emphasis on communication, health education and promotion, leadership, and research is included. Clinical experiences occur in acute, chronic, and wellness settings.
- BSN graduates have greater career options and advancement opportunities in nursing. The Bachelor of Science in Nursing also serves as the foundation for graduate study.

Slide Content: Text slide: Bachelor Degree Program

---

69 — *Advanced Nursing Education Programs*
– Important to know these programs exist if you choose to advance your education for expanded career opportunities

Slide Content: Text slide: Advanced Nursing Education

---

70 — *Master's Degree Program*
- Length of Program: two to three years post-bachelor's degree full-time; four to six years part-time
- Academic Credentials: Master's Degree in Nursing, MSN
- Setting: College or University
- Role Preparation: Prepares graduates for advanced nursing roles, including clinical specialist, nurse practitioner, nurse anesthetist, nurse midwife, educator, and administrator.

Slide Content: Text slide: Master's Degree Program

---

71 — *Doctoral Degree Program*
- Length of Program: three years post-master's degree; five years post-bachelor's degree full-time; part-time study is available
- Academic Credentials: Doctor of Nursing, ND, DNSc, PhD
- Setting: College or University
- Role Preparation: Prepares graduates to be scholarly researchers. Graduates may become nurse researchers, university teachers, consultants, health policy analysts.

Slide Content: Text slide: Doctoral Degree Program

Slide #	Narrative	Slide Content
72	Will you make more money with one type of educational preparation over another? Probably not at the entry level. However, students have shown that over a lifetime, those with a BSN degree will earn more. Part of that is due to greater opportunities for advancement.	Text slide: BSN graduates have greater career options and advancement opportunities in nursing.
73	How do you find a college that is right for you?	Slide: "Finding the right college…"
74	Start with the basics, such as the type of program you have chosen, location of the college or university, and size. — There are pros and cons in regard to size, again depending upon your individual preference. Schools with small enrollments tend to offer a smaller student-faculty ratio, which results in more personal contact. Schools with larger enrollments may offer more facilities, for example, library resources. — Visit the campus, talk to current students and faculty.	Slide with bullet points of the following info: • What type of program have you chosen? • Where is the university located? • What is the size of the university and the school of nursing?
75	Which nursing program is the "best"? — Ask about what types of clinical experiences you will have. Do these fit with your career goals? — Ask if the school of nursing is nationally accredited. (This is important if you intend to go on to graduate school.) — Ask if the school of nursing has approval of the local State Board of Nursing. (This is important for graduates to be allowed to take the licensure exam.) — Go to the public library and browse through *Peterson's Guide to Nursing Programs*. Browse national nursing organizations' Web sites. Access via www.nursing2000inc.org, click on organization resource list. — Or write to the National League for Nursing at 61 Broadway, New York, NY 10006 or the American Association of Colleges of Nursing at One Dupont Circle, Suite 530, Washington, DC 20036-1120 to request a list of nursing schools in your area.	Slide with bullet points of the following info: • Ask about clinical sites • Ask about accreditation • Review *Peterson's Guide to Nursing Programs*

Slide #	Narrative	Slide Content

76	Additional points to consider:
	— Application to nursing school is frequently a two-step process: First, admission to the university. Second, admission to the school of nursing.
	— Be alert to deadlines for both application to the college/university/school of nursing.
	— Don't worry about costs as much at this point; do ask about financial aid.
		Slide with the following bullet points:
		• Two-step admission process
		  1) Admission to the university
		  2) Admission to the school of nursing
		• What are the admission criteria for clinicals?
		• What about financial aid?

77	Again, nursing's greatest strength is in its diversity. Nurses can follow their personal and professional interests by working with many groups of people, in many settings, at any time.	Janet Rodgers slide quote
78	A career in nursing offers lots of possibilities.	Tree slide: "Life is change, growth is optional."
79	Is nursing right for you? Only you can decide!	Crystal ball slide
80	Nursing 2000	Nursing 2000 slide

Reference

Peterson's Guide to Nursing Programs, www.petersons.com

Appendix H. Materials Relevant to School Counselor Newsletter

Chapter 4

School and School of Nursing Programs
School Counselor Newsletter

H.01 Budget Estimation of Counselor Teacher Program

H.02 Planning Meeting Outcomes – School Counselor Newsletter

H.03 Photograph Release Form

Appendix H.01. Budget Estimation of Counselor Teacher Program (n = 550 Counselors/Teachers)

Counselor Teacher Program

Exhibit at the Indiana Association of College Admissions Counseling Congress [annual fee of $225.00]	$ .45
(based on n = 500 counselor visitors)	
Folders	1.50
Career materials	2.00
Promotional item (pen plus item)	2.00
Newsletter publication—includes photographs for the newsletter (film and development)	1.30
(based on n = 550) 1.22 per newsletter	
× number of middle school and high school counselors	
× number of issues per year	
Postage for counselor mailings	
	.57
	$7.82 per counselor

Include in general program budget:
- mileage incurred for counselor newsletter interviews and photographs
- communication to volunteer editorial board

Appendix H.02. Planning Meeting Outcomes —
School Counselor Newsletter

Future Focus in Nursing
Planning Meeting Outcomes
2001/2002 Academic Year

Fall Issue	Winter Issue	Summer Issue

Entrepreneur, Attorney, Business Owner… All Nurses
 	
• Nurse Attorney
• CEO
• Homecare Business Owner
• Entrepreneur
 	
"Tell your story" approach for each interview
 	
Ongoing column: "The Power to Make a Difference" debuts
	Career Development
	
	Professional Development
	• Institute of Leadership
	• National meetings
	• Certifications
	
	Decision making in care giving
	• Clinical Decisions
	• Patient Advocacy
	
	Personal Development
	• Richness of environment
	• Diversity of people
	• Privilege to be involved with patients in private times
	
	Interviews with multiple RNs—"people on the street" approach
	• "What do you like/what keeps you going?"
	• "Recent decision you made that had a significant impact on your patient"
	
	Ongoing column: "The Power to Make a Difference"
		Do You Have What it Takes To Be A Nurse? (or Nursing Can Be For You)
		
		Profile assessment
		• Ivy Tech attribute testing
		• Tie in Nursing 2000 career decision making survey
		
		What's Important to You?
		• Tie in multigenerational values
		• Include key nursing career components:
		  o portability
		  o autonomy
		  o continual training
		  o schedule flexibility
		  o high tech and high touch
		
		Mentoring
		• Q&A of current traditional student nurses—diverse in selection
		• Who was your mentor?
		• How did your mentor influence your decision?
		
		Sidebar—Required characteristics
		
		Ongoing column: "The Power to Make a Difference"

Appendix H.03. Photograph Release Form

RELEASE FORM

I, _____ (or child's parent or legal guardian), hereby consent to the videotaping/photographing and use of my likeness (or likeness of my child, _____) by NURSING 2000, INC. (a not-for-profit organization) and _____.

Further, I grant NURSING 2000, INC. and _____ the right to use my name and voice for informative, educational, and promotional purposes.

I agree to hold harmless NURSING 2000, INC. and/or _____ and their employees, agents, licensees, and/or assigns from any and all liability, suit, or claims arising out of or resulting from photographing, recording, and/or illustration of my person (or my child) by NURSING 2000, INC. and _____.

_____
Print name
(including parent or legal guardian)

_____
Print name of child

_____
Signature
(including parent or legal guardian)

_____
Signature of child

_____
Date

_____
Date

I am over 18 years of age.
Yes _____   No_____

Appendix I. Materials Relevant to School Career Fairs

Chapter 4

School and School of Nursing Programs
Career Fairs

Appendix I.01. Budget Estimation of Career Fairs

School/Community Career Fairs

Career Materials (based on average of 75 visitors per event taking materials)	$1.30
Promotional item for attendee (i.e., pens, pencils)	.34
	$1.64 per attendee
Promotional item for counselors/teachers (based on 35 events)	$2.00
Promotional items for students (based on 35 events)	.22
Thank you gifts for volunteers (based on 35 events)	2.00
Thank you letters to volunteers (based on 35 events)	1.00
	$5.22 per event

Include in general program budget:
- mileage incurred to events
- mileage incurred for delivery of materials to Nursing 2000 volunteers
- event participation/exhibit fees
- organization's display board and drape for exhibits

Appendix I.02. A Career in Registered Nursing

A CAREER IN REGISTERED NURSING
...Nursing is in demand

9302 North Meridian Street
Suite 365
Indianapolis, Indiana 46260
317-574-1325
Fax 317-573-0875
info@nursing2000inc.org
www.nursing2000inc.

AN OVERVIEW—Present and Future

Exciting and rewarding career opportunities exist for men and women entering the profession. As healthcare access continues to be on the forefront of America's agenda, Nursing will be increasingly called upon to help provide a broader range of services due to a variety of factors.

- As **healthcare delivery shifts** from an illness focus to a health promotion focus, nurses will be providing care across the entire health continuum.
- As healthcare technology advances, more individuals will be living with **chronic conditions** that require nursing care.
- Hospitals and outpatient settings will have increasingly **complex patient care demands** that require RNs prepared with strong clinical judgment skills.
- Expanding **healthcare technology** and scientific breakthroughs will require increased patient care monitoring by RNs in diverse settings. Technology has enabled patients—from premature infants to elderly individuals with complex health problems—to survive who simply would not have done so a few years ago.
- The explosion of healthcare knowledge brings **specialization** to the nursing role. There are over 50 specialties in which RNs can become certified.
- A growing **complexity of environmental and social problems** creates an increased need for nursing services.
- As **life spans increase**, more health services will be needed. It is projected 12% of the U.S. population will be over age 85 by the year 2030. The population age 65 years and older will double between 2000 and 2030. In 1991, life expectancy at birth reached 75.5 years.

U.S. Department of Health & Human Services, 1996
American Nurses Association, 2000
U.S. General Accounting Office, Nursing Workforce, 2001

NURSING'S FOCUS

- Nurses care for individuals who are healthy and ill; of all ages and cultural backgrounds; and who have physical, emotional, psychological, intellectual, social, and spiritual needs.
- Nursing is a profession that combines physical science, social science, nursing theory, and technology in the care of others.
- Nurses provide complex patient care monitoring and evaluation.
- Nurses are the coordinators of patient care.
- Nurses provide patient education.
- Nurses apply research in practice.

NURSING'S PROFILE

- Nursing is the nation's largest healthcare profession with 2.7 million nurses. Currently, 2.2 million RNs are employed in nursing.
- The current RN workforce is aging. Retirements are expected to peak in the next decade adding to the demand for RNs.
- Nursing students account for 52% of all health profession students in the United States.
- Nurses comprise the largest single component of hospital staff, are the primary providers of hospital care, and deliver most of the nation's long-term care.
- While 59% of RNs are employed in hospitals, increasingly nurses are delivering care in a wide range of settings including home care, clinics, short-stay surgery centers, transitional care, rehabilitation, health centers, hospices, schools, and businesses.
- The demand for master's and doctorally prepared nurses for advanced practice, clinical specialties, teaching, and research continues to increase.
- Employment of registered nurses is expected to grow faster than the average through 2008. Nursing is 1 of the 10 occupations projected to have the largest number of new jobs.

http://stats.bls.gov/oco/ocos083.htm,14 July 2000
American Association of Colleges of Nursing, 2000
HRSA, Bureau of Health Professions, Division of Nursing, February 2001

CAREER PATHS—Individual nursing practice is determined by the career path selected and is dependent upon education, experience, work setting, and geographical location.

Clinician

   Clinical Staff Nurse—Provides scientific, psychological, and technological knowledge in the care of patients and families (average salary $35,000).

   Advanced Practice Nurse—Provides primary care and specialized advanced nursing services to patients and families. Includes clinical specialist, nurse practitioner, nurse midwife ($50,000-$76,000/yr+); nurse anesthetist (average salary $88,000).

Educator—Utilizes educational methodologies to present current information in patient care settings, universities, and communities ($40,000-$76,000/yr+). Positions may include instructor, professor, university or college administrator, chair, or dean.

Researcher—Utilizes statistical methodologies to discover or establish facts, principles or relationships ($50,000-$75,000/yr+).

Administrator—Coordinates the use of human, financial, and technological resources to provide patient care services. Positions may include facilitator, manager, director, chief nurse executive, or vice president. Salary is commensurate with scope of responsibility ($50,000-$120,000).

CAREER DIVERSITY—Nurses may follow their personal and professional interests by working with any group of people, in any setting, at any time. The settings in which nurses work are reflective of the specialties in nursing. There is no profession that offers as many opportunities for diversified roles as does nursing.

ROLES:
Clinician
   Clinical Staff Nurse
   Advanced Practice Nurse
      Clinical Specialist
      Nurse Practitioner
      Nurse Anesthetist
      Nurse Midwife
Educator
   Clinical Instructor
   College/University Professor
   Staff Development Specialist
   Patient Education Specialist
Manager/Administrator
Researcher

HOSPITAL SETTINGS:
   Critical Care
   Emergency
   Maternal/Child Care
   Medical: Cardiology, Diabetes,
      Gastroenterology, Gerontology,
      Nephrology, Neurology,
      Oncology, Pulmonary,
      Rehabilitation, Renal,
      Rheumatology, Urology
   Operating Room/Recovery Room
   Pediatrics
   Psychiatric/Mental Health
   Surgical: Burn, Cardiovascular,
      Ear/Nose/Throat,
      Gastroenterology, Orthopedics,
      Plastic/Reconstructive,
      Transplant

NON-HOSPITAL SETTINGS:
   Public/Community Health
   Mental Health Agencies
   Home Healthcare
   Physician's Office
   Insurance
   Occupational Health
   Research Centers
   Extended Care Facilities
   Clinics
   Outpatient Surgery Centers
   Hospices
   Community Schools, Day Care
      Centers
   Military Branches
   Independent Practice
   Schools of Nursing
   Senior Centers, Shelters,
      Churches

Note: In addition, some nurses have combined two careers (i.e., nurse attorney). Others have served as consultants to businesses, schools, and healthcare institutions. Some are combining the field of nursing and computer technology (informatics specialist).

JOB MARKET
- RN positions are open for new graduates and experienced nurses in a variety of settings and specialties.
- Increasing inpatient days and ambulatory care delivery demand RN expertise.
- Heightened recognition of the RN role leads to expanding opportunities.

SALARIES/WORK ENVIRONMENT—Salaries are competitive with other professions and attracting more men and women into nursing. In the central Indiana area, a new graduate starts out at approximately $35,000 per year. Nationally, the average annual earnings of RNs employed full time is $46,782. A **highly experienced registered nurse,** for example in a hospital setting, can earn $56,000 per year. The nurse who works evenings, nights, or weekends receives added compensation. Nurses choosing careers in advanced practice, administration, education, and research may earn more, depending on the amount of responsibility associated with their roles.

QUALIFICATIONS
- Knowledgeable, articulate, competent—caring and compassionate
- Problem-solver, critical thinker, decision maker
- Responsible, accountable, and adaptable

PHYSICAL AND PSYCHOLOGICAL DEMANDS
- Good health and stamina
- Excellent interpersonal skills
- Developed coping skills; ability to work well under pressure, and adaptable to change

WORKING CONDITIONS—Working conditions have changed significantly in recent years. A variety of scheduling options are offered that are compatible in meeting the personal needs of the nurse and are dependent on the role and setting.
- Flexible work schedules; health, education, and retirement benefits
- Progressive healthcare environments
- State-of-the-art technology
- Potential exposure to hazards, i.e., drugs, physical injuries, infectious diseases, environmental

HIGH SCHOOL COURSES REQUIRED BY MOST SCHOOLS OF NURSING

PREPARATION—Students who are thinking about nursing as a career should plan a college prep curriculum:

English—4 years   (verbal and written communication skills essential)

Math—2 to 4 years   (algebra necessary for success in chemistry and medication administration; geometry)

Science—2 to 4 years   (biology and chemistry essential; physics recommended; computer science)

Social Studies—3 to 4 years (psychology; sociology; history; government; economics are all recommended)

Foreign Language—2 years   (highly recommended: some variation among individual nursing schools)

Visit ***www.nursing2000inc.org*** for a listing of Indiana colleges and universities offering nursing degrees.

Visit ***www.nsna.org***, ***www.aacn.nche.edu***, or ***www.nln.org*** for a nationwide listing of colleges and universities offering nursing degrees.

ENTRY LEVEL NURSING PROGRAMS

TYPE OF PROGRAM	SETTING	LENGTH OF PROGRAM	ACADEMIC CREDENTIALS
Associate Degree Program	May be in Technical Institutes or College/University	Usually 2 academic years	Associate Degree (ASN, AD, or ADN)

Role Preparation: Prepares graduates competent to serve in entry level nursing positions and qualified to provide direct care to individuals and families with well-defined health needs in a variety of care settings. The ASN curriculum includes courses in the physical and behavioral sciences.

- *ASN graduates have a variety of career opportunities. They also have completed basic course requirements for entering an RN-BSN completion program.*

Baccalaureate Degree Program	College or University	Usually 4 academic years	Bachelor's Degree (BSN)

Role Preparation: Prepares graduates to provide direct and indirect nursing care to individuals, families, groups, and communities in a variety of settings that span the continuum of care. The BSN curriculum includes courses in the physical sciences, behavioral sciences, and humanities. Emphasis on communication, health education and promotion, leadership, and research is included. Clinical experiences occur in acute, chronic, and wellness settings.

- *BSN graduates have greater career options and advancement opportunities in nursing. The Bachelor of Science in Nursing also serves as the foundation for graduate study.*

Graduates of both programs are eligible to take the state board examination to become licensed as a registered nurse.

ADVANCED NURSING EDUCATION PROGRAMS

Master's Degree Program	College or University	2-3 years post Bachelor's Degree full-time; 4-6 years part-time	Master's Degree (MSN)

Role Preparation: Prepares graduates for advanced nursing roles, including clinical specialist, nurse practitioner, nurse anesthetist, nurse midwife, educator, and administrator.

Doctoral Degree Program	College or University	3 years post Master's Degree; 5 years post Bachelor's Degree full-time; part-time study is available.	Doctor of Nursing (ND, DNSc or PhD)

Role Preparation: Prepares graduates to be scholarly researchers. Graduates may become nurse researchers, university teachers, consultants, health policy analysts.

Appendix I.03. Specialties in the Career of Registered Nursing

9302 North Meridian Street, Suite 365
Indianapolis, Indiana 46260-1820
317-574-1325
info@nursing2000inc.org
www.nursing2000inc.org

Specialties in the Career of Registered Nursing

a resource for students and adults exploring the specialties in nursing

Nursing's Focus...

Nursing is a scientific profession directed toward caring for healthy and ill individuals who have physical, emotional, psychological, intellectual, social, and spiritual needs. The focus of the registered nurse (RN) is determined by the career path selected and is dependent upon the nurse's work setting, education, and experience. The career paths in nursing are clinician, educator, researcher, and administrator.

Many Options...

There are many options within the single career of nursing. Once you earn the title of RN, opportunities in several specialties are available. The diversity is extensive. For example, a registered nurse who cares for sick newborns and children may also plan a community health awareness project. In the emergency room, the RN can immediately administer intravenous medications to a patient whose heart has stopped and then a few hours later may be teaching high school students about alcohol-related emergencies. A diabetic specialist not only educates patients about nutrition, but also teaches students and newly employed nurses how to use the newest blood sugar monitoring equipment. A nurse manager works with a BSN nursing student in the morning and in the afternoon serves on a task group to make recommendations about expanding services to the elderly population. These are a few examples of many specialty roles available in nursing.

In Nursing School...

During clinical classes in nursing school, the nursing student has learning experiences in many of the specialties. Each level (associate, baccalaureate, master's, doctorate) of formal nursing education provides additional exposure to clinical areas. Following graduation, students usually have identified which clinical areas interest them the most.

*A Not-For-Profit Organization Committed to Promoting Careers in Registered Nursing through Counseling, Education, and Public Presentations

Specialty Certification...

Registered nurses gain their specialty knowledge through extensive clinical experience, self-study, staff development programs, and continuing education. Certification by examination is available to individuals who choose to specialize and provides formal recognition of the RN's expertise. Certification signifies personal growth and professional achievement and may contribute to career advancement.

Specialties and Subspecialties

Community Health

Community health nurses care for patients in a variety of settings, such as public health clinics, private practices, public and private health centers, hospices, homes, schools, and work settings. As healthcare shifts from inpatient (hospital and extended care facilities) to outpatient (ambulatory and home care), more registered nurses will be caring for patients in community settings. The approach of community nursing is holistic; that is, the nurse looks at the whole person and at the dynamics of the patient's interaction with his family and community.

Nursing certification is available in:
- Community Health Nursing
- Occupational Health Nursing
- School Nursing
- College Health Nursing

Medical

The profession of nursing is centered around maintaining and improving health, as well as providing care to people with impaired health. Knowledge about medical illnesses and their prevention is essential in outpatient and inpatient settings. Nurses may become certified in the subspecialties of:
- Cardiac (focusing on heart rehabilitation)
- Diabetes
- Gastroenterology (digestive tract)
- Infection Control
- Nephrology (kidney)
- Neuroscience (nervous system)
- Nutrition and Intravenous Therapy
- Oncology (cancer)
- Pain Management
- Rehabilitation
- Urology

Other medical subspecialties are:
- Allergy/Immunology
- Cardiovascular (heart and vessels)
- Metabolic Disorders
- Pulmonary (lungs)
- Rheumatology

Surgical

Nurses care for patients before and after operative procedures. Preparing the patient for surgery through education and physical means may be done before or during hospitalization.

Following surgery, a patient will require nursing care of varying intensities in critical care, a post-surgical unit, an office, and home settings. Nurses may choose to become certified in the following specialties:
- Medical-Surgical
- Orthopaedic (muscular – skeletal mobility)
- Enterostomal Therapy (intestinal surgery)
- Ophthalmic (eyes)
- Plastic and Reconstructive Surgery

Surgical nurses also care for patients with the following surgical conditions:
- Burn
- Cardiovascular (heart and vessels)
- Ear/Nose/Throat
- Gastroenterology (digestive tract)
- Gynecology (female reproductive system)
- Neurosurgical (nervous system)
- Thoracic (chest)
- Organ Transplant

Operating Room

Registered nurses in the operating room (OR) work with surgeons, anesthesiologists, other RNs, and staff. Operating rooms have both scrub and circulating nurses as members of the surgical team. The scrub nurse passes surgical instruments and assists the surgeon with the instrumentation portion of the surgical procedure. The circulating nurse is accountable for the patient's care while in the operating room and monitors patient safety, equipment, and supplies. Immediately following surgery, the patient is closely monitored by a registered nurse in the post-anesthesia room (PAR). RNs may be certified in:
- Perioperative Nursing
- Perianesthesia Nursing

Critical Care

Nurses care for patients in critical care unit or intensive care unit (ICU) settings where they interact with highly sophisticated life support and monitoring equipment. They apply knowledge from the other specialties while working side by side with physicians and other healthcare team members. Using nursing diagnosis, the RN coordinates information from many sources. Critical assessment and care of seriously ill patients also occur in the emergency room, in emergency centers, and in air and ground transportation vehicles. Nurses may become certified in:

- Flight Nursing
- Emergency Nursing
- Critical Care Nursing

Psychiatric/Mental Health

Mental health nurses care for children, adolescents, and adults with chemical dependency, acute and chronic mental illness, behavioral disorders, and Alzheimer's disease through assessment, monitoring, crisis intervention, counseling, pharmacological intervention, and education. Strong communication skills and an understanding of human behavior are primary tools in this specialty. Certification may be obtained in:

- Addictions Nursing
- Psychiatric and Mental Health Nursing

Maternal/Child

Registered nurses in this specialty care for women before, during, and after delivery (obstetrics); for newborn babies; and for all aspects of women's health (gynecology) from puberty through the post-menopausal age. Many certifications are available in maternal/child nursing:

- Inpatient Obstetrical Nurse
- High-Risk Obstetric Nurse
- Maternal Newborn Nurse
- Neonatal Intensive Care Nurse
- Low-Risk Neonatal Nurse
- Ambulatory Women's Healthcare Nurse
- Lactation Consultant

Pediatric

Pediatric nurses provide care to children with medical, surgical, and psychological illnesses. In addition to providing skilled bedside nursing care for the sick and injured, RNs teach young people and their parents about accident prevention and the promotion of good health, which will positively affect them at all ages of life. Certification is available in:

- General Pediatric Nursing

Gerontology

Many registered nurses study the medical, surgical, and psychological conditions of older adults and how age affects the mind and body and apply this knowledge to their nursing practice. The number of Americans over 65 years will grow 76% between 1986 and 2020. Expanded life expectancies will require more nurses to specialize in gerontology. Registered nurses may become certified as:

- Gerontological Nurses

Nursing Education

Registered nurses learn new skills, theories, treatment modalities, and other information by reading books, journals, and computerized documents written by nurses. RNs who specialize in education also present current information at hospitals, universities, community settings, and business-sponsored continuing education programs. Nurses need to be able to teach other nurses. Certification is available in:

- Nursing Continuing Education/Staff Development

Nursing Research

It is imperative that registered nurses expand their knowledge and contribute to the profession. Clinical nurses, administrators, and educators utilize the scientific process to research and develop more information. The rapidly changing technological advances and demanding proficiency in clinical and administrative areas require more nursing research. Baccalaureate degree programs include courses in research. Doctoral degree programs specifically prepare graduates to be scholarly researchers and add to the knowledge base in their specialty of clinical practice, administration, and education.

Nursing Administration

The registered nurse facilitates the clinical nursing team of RNs, licensed practical nurses, and other team members and coordinates the use of human, financial (budget), and technological (equipment) resources to deliver patient care. The manager collaborates with physicians, other managers, and administrators and works closely with the nursing staff to provide the resources needed for patient care. Experience and additional education are required in areas such as leadership theories, financial management, health policy, resource utilization, and information systems. Certification is available in:

- Nursing Administration
- Advanced Nursing Administration

Other Nursing Team Members

LPN – Licensed practical nurses (LPN) or licensed vocational nurses (LVN) attend state-approved programs offered by vocational and technical schools and colleges that are approximately one year in length. Graduates must pass a written state examination to become licensed as LPNs. Several LPN to RN mobility educational programs exist in Indiana for individuals desiring to further their education (refer to Nursing 2000's LPN to RN Mobility Guide).

CNA – Individuals seeking entry level positions as certified nursing assistants (CNA) attend an introductory course. The course, offered for several weeks in vocational and technical schools, includes classroom instruction and clinical experience. Graduates must pass a written state exam and a skills test to become certified.

Beyond RN

Certification Requirements...

The eligibility requirements for certification can be obtained from the American Nurses Credentialing Center and from specialty organizations (refer to Nursing 2000's Specialty Nursing Certification Guide for addresses).

"Certification is reserved for those nurses who have met requirements for clinical or functional practice in a specialized field, pursued education beyond basic nursing preparation, and received the endorsement of their peers. After meeting these criteria, nurses take certification examinations based on nationally recognized standards of nursing practice to demonstrate their knowledge, skills, and abilities within the defined specialty" (American Nurses Credentialing Center Generalist Board Certification Catalog). Following certification, credentials are added behind the RN initials such as CCRN (Certification in Critical Care Nursing).

Advanced Practice Nurses...

As healthcare becomes more accessible to all U.S. citizens and residents through healthcare reform, there will be an increased need for advanced practice nurses who provide primary care and advanced nursing services. Specialization and certification as an advanced practice nurse (nurse practitioner, clinical specialist, nurse midwife, or nurse anesthetist) usually require a master's degree or higher in nursing and state licensure. Specialty certification is also offered to advanced practice nurses.

In the specialty of Maternal/Child Nursing, a registered nurse may become certified as:
- Ob/Gyn Nurse Practitioners
- Neonatal Nurse Practitioners
- Nurse Midwives who deliver babies

Nurses may also become certified as:

- School Nurse Practitioners
- Adult Nurse Practitioners
- Family Nurse Practitioners
- Pediatric Nurse Practitioners
- Gerontological Nurse Practitioners

Clinical specialists may choose the specialties of:

- Community Health Nursing
- Medical-Surgical Nursing
- Adult Psychiatric Mental Health Nursing
- Child and Adolescent Psychiatric and Mental Health Nursing
- Gerontological Nursing

Another option in advanced practice for RNs is to become a:

- Certified registered nurse Anesthetist who administers anesthesia

---

The general and specific knowledge registered nurses have is extensive

---

References

American Nurses Credentialing Center. (n.d.). *American Nurses Credentialing Center.* Retrieved from http://www.nursingworld.org/ancc/

NLN *Guide to Undergraduate RN Education* (2nd ed.). (1994). New York, NY: National League for Nursing Press.

Appendix I.04. Indiana Schools of Nursing — Undergraduate Programs

UNDERGRADUATE NURSING PROGRAMS IN INDIANA

BACCALAUREATE DEGREE PROGRAMS

ANDERSON UNIVERSITY
Dean, School of Nursing
Anderson University
1100 East 5th
Anderson, Indiana 46012
(765) 641-4380 www.anderson.edu

*BALL STATE UNIVERSITY
Director, School of Nursing
Ball State University
2000 University Avenue
Muncie, Indiana 47306-0265
(765) 285-5571 www.bsu.edu

BETHEL COLLEGE
Dean of Nursing
Bethel College
1001 West McKinley Avenue
Mishawaka, Indiana 46565
(219) 257-3369
www.bethel-in.edu

GOSHEN COLLEGE
Director of Nursing
Department of Nursing
Goshen College
1700 South Main Street
Goshen, Indiana 46526
(219) 535-7370 www.goshen.edu

*INDIANA STATE UNIVERSITY
Dean, School of Nursing
Indiana State University
8th and Chestnut
Terre Haute, Indiana 47809
(812) 237-2316
www.indstate.edu

*Also offers Master's Program

*INDIANA UNIVERSITY
University Dean
IU School of Nursing
1111 Middle Drive
Indianapolis, Indiana 46202
(317) 274-2806
http://nursing.iupui.edu
[also offers doctoral program]

INDIANA UNIVERSITY, BLOOMINGTON
Dean of Nursing
IU Bloomington
Room 400, Sycamore Hall
Bloomington, Indiana 47405
(812) 855-1736
www.indiana.edu/iubnurse/

INDIANA UNIVERSITY EAST, RICHMOND
Dean of Nursing
Indiana University East
2325 Chester Boulevard
Richmond, Indiana 47374
(765) 973-8257
www.iue.indiana.edu

INDIANA UNIVERSITY, INDIANAPOLIS
Associate Dean, Undergraduate
Programs
Indiana University
1111 Middle Drive
Indianapolis, Indiana 46202
(317) 274-2806
http://nursing.iupui.edu
[required general education courses also available on Bloomington and Columbus campuses]

INDIANA UNIVERSITY, KOKOMO
Dean of Nursing
Indiana University Kokomo
2300 South Washington
PO Box 9003
Kokomo, Indiana 46904-9003
(765) 455-9384
www.iuk.edu

INDIANA UNIVERSITY NORTHWEST, GARY
Dean, Division of Nursing
Indiana University Northwest
3400 Broadway
Gary, Indiana 46408
(219) 980-6603
www.iun.edu

INDIANA UNIVERSITY, SOUTH BEND
Director of Recruitment and Retention
Division of Nursing and Health Professions
IU South Bend
1700 Mishawaka Avenue
Northside Hall 444
South Bend, Indiana 46634
(219) 237-4282
www.iusb.edu

INDIANA UNIVERSITY SOUTHEAST, NEW ALBANY
Dean, Division of Nursing
Life Sciences Building
4201 Grant Line Road
New Albany, Indiana 47150-6405
(812) 941-2340
www.ius.indiana.edu/nursing

INDIANA UNIVERSITY-PURDUE UNIVERSITY FORT WAYNE/PARKVIEW NURSING PROGRAM (RN to BSN Mobility)
Chair, School of Nursing
IU-PU Ft Wayne/Parkview Nursing Program
2101 Coliseum Boulevard East
Neff Hall B50V
Fort Wayne, Indiana 46805
(260) 481-6816
www.ipfw.edu/nursing/

*INDIANA WESLEYAN UNIVERSITY
Chair, Division of Nursing Education
Indiana Wesleyan University
4301 South Washington Street
Marion, Indiana 46953
(765) 677-2266
www.indwes.edu

MARIAN COLLEGE
Chair, Department of Nursing
Marian College
3200 Cold Spring Road
Indianapolis, Indiana 46222
(317) 955-6167 www.marian.edu

*PURDUE UNIVERSITY, CALUMET CAMPUS
(RN to BSN Mobility)
Head, Department of Nursing
Dean, Schools of Professional Programs
Purdue University Calumet Campus
Gyte Annex Room X138
2200 169th Street
Hammond, Indiana 46323-2094
(219) 989-2814
www.calumet.purdue.edu

PURDUE UNIVERSITY, W. LAFAYETTE
Head, School of Nursing
Associate Dean of Pharmacy, Nursing &
Health Sciences
Purdue University
1337 Johnson Hall of Nursing
West Lafayette, IN 47907-1337
(765) 494-4004
www.nursing.purdue.edu/

SAINT MARY'S COLLEGE
Chairperson, Nursing Department
Saint Mary's College
Notre Dame, Indiana 46556-5001
(219) 284-4680
www.saintmarys.edu

*Also offers Master's Program

UNIVERSITY OF EVANSVILLE
Department Chair, Nursing and Health Sciences
University of Evansville
1800 Lincoln Avenue
Evansville, Indiana 47722
(812) 479-2343
www.evansville.edu/nursing

*UNIVERSITY OF INDIANAPOLIS
Dean, School of Nursing
University of Indianapolis
1400 East Hanna Avenue
Indianapolis, Indiana 46227
(317) 788-3206
www.uindy.edu

*UNIVERSITY OF ST. FRANCIS
Chairperson, Department of Nursing
University of St. Francis
2701 Spring Street
Fort Wayne, Indiana 46808
(219) 434-3240
www.sfc.edu/nursing/

*UNIVERSITY OF SOUTHERN INDIANA
Dean, School of Nursing and Health Professions
University of Southern Indiana
8600 University Boulevard
Evansville, Indiana 47712
(812) 464-1708
http://health.usi.edu

*VALPARAISO UNIVERSITY
Dean, College of Nursing
Valparaiso University
Valparaiso, Indiana 46383
(219) 464-5289
www.valpo.edu

*Also offers Master's Program

ASSOCIATE DEGREE PROGRAMS

BETHEL COLLEGE
Dean of Nursing
Bethel College
1001 West McKinley Avenue
Mishawaka, IN 46565
(219) 257-3369
www.bethel-in.edu

INDIANA STATE UNIVERSITY
Dean, School of Nursing
Indiana State University
8th and Chestnut
Terre Haute, Indiana 47809
(812) 237-2316
www.instate.edu/nurs/

INDIANA UNIVERSITY, INDIANAPOLIS
Associate Dean, Undergraduate Program
Indiana University
1111 Middle Drive
Indianapolis, Indiana 46202
(317) 274-2806
www.nursing.iupui.edu/

[LPN to ASN Mobility available on Columbus campus]

INDIANA UNIVERSITY, KOKOMO
Dean of Nursing
Indiana University Kokomo
2300 South Washington
PO Box 9003
Kokomo, Indiana 46904-9003
(765) 455-9384
www.iuk.edu

INDIANA UNIVERSITY NORTHWEST, GARY
Associate Professor and Dean,
Division of Nursing
Indiana University Northwest
3400 Broadway
Gary, Indiana 46408
(219) 980-6603
www.iun.edu

INDIANA UNIVERSITY-PURDUE UNIVERSITY FORT WAYNE/ PARKVIEW NURSING PROGRAM

Chair, School of Nursing
Indiana University-Purdue University
Ft Wayne/Parkview Nursing Program
2101 Coliseum Boulevard East
Neff Hall B50V
Fort Wayne, Indiana 46805
(219) 481-6816
www.ipfw.edu/nursing/

MARIAN COLLEGE

Chair, Department of Nursing
Marian College
3200 Cold Spring Road
Indianapolis, Indiana 46222
(317) 955-6167
www.marian.edu

PURDUE UNIVERSITY CALUMET CAMPUS

Head, School of Nursing
Dean of Professional Programs
Purdue Univ. Calumet Campus
Gyte Annex Room X138
2200 169th Street
Hammond, Indiana 46323-2094
(219) 989-2813
www.calumet.purdue.edu

PURDUE UNIVERSITY, NORTH CENTRAL

Chairperson, School of Nursing
Purdue University North Central
1401 South US 421
Westville, Indiana 46391-9528
(219) 785-5226

UNIVERSITY OF INDIANAPOLIS

Dean, School of Nursing
University of Indianapolis
1400 East Hanna Avenue
Indianapolis, Indiana 46227
(317) 788-3206
www.uindy.edu

UNIVERSITY OF ST. FRANCIS

Chairperson, Department of Nursing
University of St. Francis
2701 Spring Street
Fort Wayne, Indiana 46808
(219) 434-3240
www.sfc.edu/nursing/

VINCENNES UNIVERSITY

Chairperson, Department of Nursing
Vincennes University
Vincennes, Indiana 47591
(812) 888-4243
www.vinu.edu

IVY TECH STATE COLLEGE

REGION 1
ASN Program Chair
1440 East 35th Avenue
Gary, Indiana 46409
(219) 981-1111

REGION 2
Associate Degree Program in Nursing
220 Dean Johnson Boulevard
South Bend, Indiana 46601
(219) 289-7001

REGION 4
Director of Nursing
3101 S. Creasy Lane
PO Box 6299
Lafayette, Indiana 47903
(765) 772-9192

REGION 8
Program Chair of Nursing
1 West 26th
PO Box 1763
Indianapolis, Indiana 46206-1763
(317) 921-4428
www.ivytech.edu

REGION 9
Nursing Chairperson
2325 Chester Boulevard
Richmond, Indiana 47374
(765) 983-3210 or (765) 966-2656

REGION 10
Nursing Program Chair
3116 Canterbury Court
Bloomington, Indiana 47401
(812) 332-1559

REGION 11
ASN Program Chair
Highway 62 and Ivy Tech Drive
Madison, Indiana 47250
(812) 265-2580

REGION 12
Division Chair of Nursing
3501 First Avenue
Evansville, Indiana 47710-3398
(812) 429-1496

REGION 13
Program Chair of Nursing
8204 Highway 311
Sellersburg, Indiana 47172
(812) 246-3301

HOSPITAL—DIPLOMA PROGRAM
ST. ELIZABETH HOSPITAL
Director, School of Nursing
St. Elizabeth Hospital
1508 Tippecanoe Street
Lafayette, Indiana 47904
(765) 423-6400
www.ste.org/newson/

Appendix I.05. Nursing Resource Organization List

ORGANIZATION RESOURCE LIST

American Association of Colleges of Nursing
One Dupont Circle
Suite 530
Washington, DC 20036-1120
202/463-6930
Fax: 202/785-8320
www.aacn.nche.edu

American Board of Nursing Specialties
4035 Running Springs
San Antonio, TX 78261
830/438-4897
www.nursingcertification.org

American Hospital Association
One North Franklin
Chicago, IL 60606
312/422-3000
www.aha.org

American Nurses Credentialing Center
600 Maryland Avenue SW
Suite 100 West
Washington, DC 20024-2571
800/284-CERT (2378)
Fax: 202/651-7004
www.nursingcenter.com

American Nurses Association
600 Maryland Avenue SW
Suite 100 West
Washington, DC 20024-2571
202/554-4444
http://www.nursingworld.org

American Organization of Nurse Executives
One North Franklin
Chicago, IL 60606
312/422-2800
www.aone.org

Chi Eta Phi Sorority, Inc.
National Headquarters
3029 13th Street NW
Washington, DC 20009
202/232-3858
www.chietaphi.com

Indiana Hospital and Health Association
One American Square
PO Box 82063
Indianapolis, IN 46282
317/633-4870
www.inhha.org

Indiana Organization of Nurse Executives
One American Square
PO Box 82063
Indianapolis, IN 46282
317/633-4870

Indiana State Board of Nursing
Health Professions Bureau
402 W. Washington Street
Suite 041
Indianapolis, IN 46204
317/232-2960
www.in.gov/hpb/

Indiana State Nurses Association
2915 N. High School Road
Indianapolis, IN 46224-2969
317/299-4575
Fax: 317/297-3525
www.indiananurses.org

National Black Nurses Association, Inc.
8630 Fenton St., Suite 330
Silver Springs, MD 20910-3803
301/589-3200
www.nbna.org

National League for Nursing
61 Broadway
New York, NY 10006
800/669-1656 or 800/669-9656 Ext. 472
http://www.nln.org

National Student Nurses Association
555 W. 57th Street
Suite 1327
New York, NY 10019
212/581-2211
www.nsna.org

Sigma Theta Tau International
550 W. North Street
Indianapolis, IN 46202
317/634-8171
Fax: 317/634-8188
www.nursingsociety.org

Academy of Medical-Surgical Nurses
PO Box 36266
Indianapolis, IN 46236

Indiana Association of Nurse Anesthetists
www.inana.org

Emergency Nurses Association
915 Lee Street
Des Plaines, IL 60016-6569
800/900-9659
www.ena.org

Indiana Deans and Directors
Director of Nursing
Department of Nursing
Goshen College
1700 S. Main St.
Goshen, IN 46526
219/535-7370

Indiana Nursing Staff Development Organization
Clinical Education, Community Hospital
1500 N. Ritter Ave.
Indianapolis, IN 46219

Career Resource: Nurses for a Healthier Tomorrow
www.nursesource.org

Career Resource: Discover Nursing
www.discovernursing.com

Career Resource: Nursing 2000
www.nursing2000inc.org

Appendix I.06. Volunteer Opportunities in Affiliated Hospitals

Volunteer Opportunities
at
Healthcare Agencies in Local Area

Program Name	Who Student Contacts	Prerequisite
Clarian Health Partners, Inc. Methodist Campus	Volunteer Coordinator (962-8758)	
IU Campus	Volunteer Coordinator (278-3776)	
Riley Campus	Volunteer Coordinator (274-8682)	
Community Hospital East	Volunteer Services (355-5503)	
Community Hospital North	Volunteer Services (841-5283)	
Community Hospital South	Volunteer Services (887-7145)	
Hancock Memorial Hospital	Volunteer Coordinator (317/462-0245)	
Hendricks Community Hospital	Volunteer Services (317/745-4451)	
Johnson Memorial Hospital	Volunteer Services (317/736-3300)	
Major Hospital	Volunteer Services (317/398-5334)	
Rehabilitation Hospital of Indiana	Volunteer Information (329-2233)	May be able to accommodate special interests
Riverview Hospital	Director of Volunteers (773-0760)	
St. Elizabeth Ann Seton Hospital of Central Indiana	Volunteer Services [ask for Social Services] (582-8500)	

Program Name	Who Student Contacts	Prerequisite
St. Francis Hospital and Health Centers	Volunteer Department (787-3311)	
St. Francis Beech Grove Campus **St. Francis Indianapolis Campus** **St. Francis Mooresville Campus**		
St. Vincent Hospitals and Health Services		
St. Vincent Hospital Indianapolis	Volunteer Services (338-2055)	
St. Vincent Carmel	Volunteer Services (582-7158)	
St. Vincent Children's Specialty Hospital	Volunteer Information (415-5500)	Must be at least 16. Requires orientation. Pairs volunteer to a child.
Westview Hospital	Volunteer Services (920-7390)	Offers a summer volunteer program for students in a variety of fields, such as nursing, pre-medicine, radiology, and physical therapy
Wishard Health Services	Department of Volunteer Services (639-6671)	
Women's Hospital of Indianapolis	Volunteer Services (875-5994)	

Appendix I.07. Financial Aid Information

PROMOTE EDUCATE ADVANCE

Financial Aid Information

OVERVIEW

9302 North Meridian Street
Suite 365
Indianapolis, Indiana 46260
317-574-1325
Fax 317-573-0875
info@nursing2000inc.org
www.nursing2000inc.org

A college education to earn an associate or baccalaureate degree in nursing at a state-supported or private college or university is a large financial investment. It requires saving money and investigating financial aid resources to supplement what the student and his/her family is expected to pay.

In order to receive financial aid, the student and family should follow the steps below. Study reference materials and applications that have more complete guidelines.

Step I. Write colleges/universities for general information and application materials.

Step II. Apply early to chosen school(s) for admission and housing.

Step III. Obtain, complete, and mail before the deadline the Free Application for Federal Student Aid (FAFSA—available from a high school or college counselor or by calling 1-800-4-FED-AID; www.fafsa.org) and other requested forms/applications, such as the Financial Aid PROFILE. The Financial Aid Form (FAF) processed by the College Scholarship Services (CSS) is the principal application form for students applying for financial aid in Indiana. Forms are available from your high school counselor, financial aid office of the college/university of your choice, or state scholarship/grant agencies. Respond quickly to any additional information requests. Financial aid is awarded for one year only; you must reapply each year with new forms.

Step IV. Review and reply to your financial aid award letter by the deadline. An analysis of a family's financial situation based upon a government-approved formula is used to calculate the Expected Family Contribution (EFC). The formula is...Total Cost of Attendance (fees, tuition, room, board, books, supplies, personal expenses, and transportation) Minus Expected Family Contribution (EFC) Equals Financial Need, which may be met with various types of financial aid from federal, state, institutional, and private sources of funding. Your Expected Family Contribution should be "roughly the same regardless of which college you attend." The students who don't appear to have financial need may receive scholarships or grants based on the student's academic performance, specific talent, or ability ("merit aid").

Step V. Consult with your high school guidance counselor for additional resources.

TYPES OF FINANCIAL AID

Type I. **SCHOLARSHIPS** (also known as GRANTS or GIFT AID) are gifts and do not have to be repaid. However, some scholarships may have qualifiers, or specified criteria, to meet designated requirements of the scholarships (i.e., assistance may be tied to a work commitment following graduation). Scholarships can also be based on academic achievement or financial need. Funds from a combination of sources and programs are usually called a "financial aid package" and range from a hundred to several thousand dollars.

Type II. **LOANS** (generally referred to as SELF-HELP AID) are borrowed monies, which must be repaid with interest.

Type III. **STUDENT EMPLOYMENT** (generally referred to as SELF-HELP AID) consists of work-study programs and jobs during the academic year. Students with at least one semester of clinical nursing experience may be eligible to work as a student nurse. Salaries range from $9.00-$12.00 per hour depending upon the healthcare agency/hospital.

Type IV. **TUITION REIMBURSEMENT** is often available to employees of healthcare agencies and other work settings working a certain minimum number of hours per pay period as an employee benefit and does not require repayment. Employment as a student nurse usually does not qualify the individual for tuition reimbursement.

Review all eligibility requirements and deadlines before applying. Examples of some requirements are residential location (i.e., county); a particular skill, interest, or background; enrollment in an accredited nursing program at a college/university within 1-2 years of high school graduation; commitment to work during or following the college education; and/or enrollment of at least half time.

FINANCIAL AID RESOURCES

1. NATIONAL

- American Association of Colleges of Nursing
  One Dupont Circle, Suite 530
  Washington, DC 20036-1120
  202/463-6930
  Fax: 202/785-8320   www.aacn.nche.edu

- National Student Nurses' Association
  555 W. 57th St.
  New York, NY 10019
  212/581-2211   www.nsna.org

- Military
  – Air Force: ROTC Scholarship Program
    9240 North Meridian Street, Suite 360
    Indianapolis, IN 46260   1-800-423-USAF; 317/580-7717
    www.airforce.com/nursing

  – Army: Nurse Advisor
    US Army ROTC Cadet Command
    Ft. Monroe, VA 25651-5000   1-800-USA-ROTC
    www.armyrotc.com

- National Black Nurses' Association, Inc.
  Fenton Street, Suite 330
  Silver Springs, MD 20910-3903
  310/589-3200 www.nbna.org

- National Society, Daughters of the American Revolution
  Office of the Committee NSDAR
  Administration Building
  1776 D Street, NW
  Washington, DC 20006-5392   202/879-3292
  www.dar.org/natsociety/edoutreach.html

- USA Funds
  1-888-2SALLIE or 1-888-272-5543

- Johnson and Johnson
  The Campaign for Nursing's Future
  www.discovernursing.com

- National Student Nurses' Foundation
  45 Main Street, Suite 606
  Brooklyn, NY 11201
  718/210-0705   www.nsna.org/foundation

  – Navy: NROTC Scholarship Program
    9152 Kent Avenue, Building 401, Suite 352
    Indianapolis, IN 46216   317/549-0701 ext. 135
    www.navy.com

- National League for Nursing 8630
  350 Hudson Street
  New York, NY 10014   1-800-669-1656
  1-800-669-1656 www.nln.org

- Nurses for a Healthier Tomorrow
  www.nursesource.org

- United Negro College Fund, Inc.
  8260 Willow Oaks Corporate Drive
  Fairfax, VA 22031
  703/205-3400 www.uncf.org

2. STATE

- Indiana Nurses Foundation
  2915 North High School Road
  Indianapolis, IN 46224-2969
  317/299-4575
  Fax: 317/297-3525 www.indiananurses.org
  Scholarships available for registered nurses advancing their education by pursuit of baccalaureate, master's, or doctoral degree.

- Indianapolis Urban League, Inc.
  777 Indiana Avenue
  Indianapolis, IN 46202
  317/693-7603
  Provides information about scholarships and financial aid

- Indiana College Placement and Assessment Center (ICPAC)
  Hotline (800/992-2076) sponsored by the Indiana Commission for Higher Education and the Indiana Secondary Market for Education Loans provides "The ICPAC Guide to Student Financial Aid" and more
  www.icpac.indiana.edu

- State Student Assistance Commission of Indiana (SSACI)
  150 West Market Street, Suite 500
  Indianapolis, IN 46204 317/232-2350
  The SSACI awards tuition scholarships and grants to eligible students who attend Indiana colleges.

3. LOCAL—In the eight-county central Indiana area, contact:

- Financial Aid Office of the college/university with nursing programs

  IUPUI
  317/274-4162
  www.iupui.edu/finaid/

  Marian College
  317/955-6040
  ww.marian.edu

  Ivy Tech State College
  317/921-4777
  www.ivytech.edu

  University of Indianapolis
  317/788-3217
  www.nursing.uindy.edu

- Community Lending Institutions (i.e., banks, private organizations)

- Health Care Institutions—Contact the following individual(s) in the Patient Care Services or the Human Resource Department

NOTE: - Scholarships and loans usually have academic and work commitment restrictions.
  - Range $250-$5,000 per year.
  - Student nurse employment *does not* usually qualify for tuition reimbursement.
  - **SUGGESTION:** Ask institution if preceptor and/or practicum programs are available and tied to subsequent employment.

CLARIAN HEALTH PARTNERS, INC.
Nurse Recruiters: 317/278-3552 or 317/278-7565   www.clarian.org
(Offers scholarships, tuition reimbursement, student nurse employment)

COMMUNITY HOSPITALS INDIANAPOLIS
Nurse Recruiters: 317/621-2329 or 317/621-7033   www.ehealthindiana.com
(Offers scholarships*, tuition reimbursement, student nurse employment)

LOCAL (continued)

· Health Care Institutions—Contact the following individual(s) in the Patient Care Services or the Human Resource Department

HANCOCK MEMORIAL HOSPITAL AND HEALTH SERVICES
Nurse Recruiter: 317/468-4510   www.hmhhs.org
(Offers scholarships, tuition reimbursement, student nurse employment)

HENDRICKS COMMUNITY HOSPITAL
Human Resources: 317/745-8633   www.hendrickshospital.org
(Offers scholarships, tuition reimbursement, student nurse employment)

JOHNSON MEMORIAL HOSPITAL
317/738-7856   www.johnsonmemorial.org
(Offers scholarships, loans, tuition reimbursement, student nurse employment)

MAJOR HOSPITAL
Nurse Recruiter: 317/392-321   www.majorhospital.com
(Offers scholarships, tuition assistance, student nurse employment)

THE REHABILITATION HOSPITAL OF INDIANA
Nurse Recruiters: 317/329-2233 or 317/329-2470   www.rhin.com
(Offers tuition reimbursement, student nurse employment)

RIVERVIEW HOSPITAL
Nurse Recruiters: 317/776-7455 or 317/770-7791   www.riverviewhospital.org
(Offers scholarships, tuition reimbursement, student nurse employment)

ST. ELIZABETH ANN SETON HOSPITAL OF CENTRAL INDIANA
Nurse Recruiters: 317/582-8470   www.stvincent.org
(Offers scholarships, tuition reimbursement, student nurse employment)

ST. FRANCIS HOSPITAL AND HEALTH CENTERS
Nurse Recruiters: 317/783-8588 or 317/783-8629   www.stfrancishospitals.org
(Offers scholarships, loans, tuition reimbursement, student nurse employment)

ST. VINCENT HOSPITALS AND HEALTH SERVICES
Nurse Recruiters: 317/338-2241 or 317/582-7384   www.stvincent.org
(Offers scholarships, tuition reimbursement, student nurse employment)

ST. VINCENT CHILDREN'S SPECIALTY HOSPITAL
Nurse Recruiters: 317/415-5538   www.stvincent.org
(Offers tuition reimbursement, student nurse employment)

WESTVIEW HOSPITAL
Director of Nursing: 317/924-6661 ext. 290 www.westviewhospital.org
(Offers tuition reimbursement, student nurse employment)

LOCAL (continued)

WISHARD HEALTH SERVICES

Nurse Recruiters: 317/630-6064 or 317/630-2419

www.wishard.edu

(Offers scholarships*, tuition reimbursement, student nurse employment)

WOMEN'S HOSPITAL OF INDIANAPOLIS

Nurse Recruiters: 317/554-6947 www.womenshospital.org

(Offers scholarships, tuition reimbursement, student nurse employment)

Needs to be student nurse employee or employee of institution.

· Other

Additional resources at the local, state, and national levels may be obtained in the financial aid section (Social Sciences Division) of your local public library. Plan to spend a few hours researching the materials. Most will be "reference" books and cannot be checked out.

Peterson's Education Center: Financial Planning Tools
http://petersons.com/finaid/default.asp
"The Student Guide," free from the Federal Student Aid Information Center,
PO Box 84, Washington, DC, 20044-0084
http://www.ed.gov/

Appendix I.08. Nursing is AMAZING! Middle School Handout

Nursing is Amazing!

CHALLENGE YOURSELF

Want to have fun at work?

Travel the USA

Do physical examinations

Do life saving research

Use computers to help others

Be part of the team

Be a nurse anesthetist in surgery

Help very ill children become healthy

Work with complex monitors and equipment

Nurses work in exciting places!

Helicopters

Military base in a foreign land

Hospital emergency rooms

Intensive care units

The White House

Cruise ships

Central Indiana
9302 North Meridian Street
Suite 365
Indianapolis, Indiana 46260
(317) 574-1325
FAX (317) 573-0875
info@nursing2000inc.org

Nursing 2000
PROMOTE EDUCATE ADVANCE

www.nursing2000inc.org

North Central Indiana
P.O. Box 250
LaPorte, Indiana 46350
(219) 326-2365
FAX (219) 325-5403
ncinfo@nursing2000inc.org

CHANGE LIVES

Want to make a difference in someone's life?

Give life saving medications

Help deliver a newborn baby

Work with a team of professionals who care

Care for the tiniest infant

to the oldest adult

Do CPR--Save a life

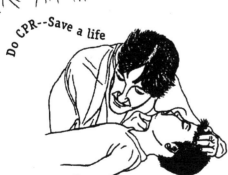

Teach people how to stay healthy

CHOOSE NURSING

Want to know the facts?

Largest healthcare profession

One million new nurses needed by 2010*

Increased education leads to increased salary

You can work when and where you want

You still have time for fun and friends

What should you do?

Start planning to go to college today

Math and science are top priorities

Don't forget English, social sciences and foreign language

Problem solving skills are essential

Take college prep courses

Develop skillful communication, caring, compassion

Learn technical skills to treat patients

You, too, can be a part of this exciting profession!

* Monthly Labor Review, U.S. Bureau of Labor Statistics

A CAREER TO LAST A LIFETIME

Illustrations by Laura Rodebaugh

Nursing 2000 is funded by:
- Clarian Health Partners, Inc.—Methodist • IU • Riley
- Community Health Network
- St. Francis Hospital and Health Centers
- St. Vincent Hospitals & Health Services
- Wishard Health Services

Contributions by:
- Hancock Memorial Hospital & Health Services
- Hendricks Community Hospital
- Johnson Memorial Hospital
- Major Hospital
- The Rehabilitation Hospital of Indiana
- Riverview Hospital
- St. Elizabeth Ann Seton Hospital of Central Indiana
- Westview Hospital
- Women's Hospital of Indianapolis

School of Nursing Affiliations:
- Indiana University
- Ivy Tech State College
- Marian College
- University of Indianapolis

Nursing 2000 North Central is funded by:
- Elkhart General Healthcare System
- LaPorte Regional Health Centers
- Memorial Hospital of South Bend
- St. Anthony Memorial Health Centers
- St. Joseph's Regional Medical Center

School of Nursing Affiliations:
- Bethel College
- Goshen College
- Indiana University Foundation
- Ivy Tech State College
- Purdue University

Appendix J. Materials Relevant to the Scholarship Benefit

Chapter 4

School and School of Nursing Programs
Scholarship Benefit Program

Appendix J.01. Budget Estimation of Scholarship Benefit

Program

Keynote Speaker

Honorarium ($1,500-$2,000)		$1,500.00
Hotel and meals		125.00
Travel		450.00
	Subtotal:	$2,075.00

Printing Costs

Invitations and Envelopes/Response Cards and Envelopes (1,800)		$1,450.00
Program Brochure for the evening (625)		2,050.00
Sponsorship/Ad Opportunities		600.00
Certificates for Recipients and Sponsors		100.00
Postage		500.00
Trophies/Frames/Table Stands		320.00
	Subtotal:	$5,020.00

Entertainment

Music - Harpist		$ 225.00
- Pianist		225.00
	Subtotal:	$ 450.00

Photographer

@ $50/hr × 4 1/2 hr + film + photos		$ 400.00
	Subtotal:	$ 400.00

Audiovisual

Lavaliere mic, microphone, easels, video camera, converter, 4 monitors, mixer, lights, tripod		$1,200.00
Tech hours		360.00
	Subtotal:	$1,560.00

Public Relations

Flyer announcements [pre-event] (1,000)		$ 500.00
Posters (Patron Room and Speaker)		90.00
Public Relations		750.00
	Subtotal:	$1,340.00
	Program Total:	$10,845.00

Facility
Dinners @ $21.75
  19.50% Service
  Beverage/Bar Set Up ($125 each)

Patron Reception
Beverage/Bar Fee ($1,400-$1,600)
  plus Set Up ($125 each)
  19.50% Service

Appendix J.02. 2002 Scholarship Benefit Timeline Overview

September - November 2001
Confirm speaker, facility
Begin soliciting volunteers for committees

December 2001
Invite honorary chair for scholarship
benefit
Development Committee—prepare
materials and update contact list

January 2002
Co-chair planning meeting – approve
budget and set direction for event
Update invitation list
Development Committee—corporate
sponsorship opportunities; mail
corporate sponsorship packets
Make initial contact with 2001 recipients
to invite them

February 2002
Development Committee follow-up calls
to corporate contacts
Order invitations and response cards by
February 8 in order to have by
March 8 to prepare for mailing
Nursing school (via rotation—U of I; IU;
Marian; Ivy Tech) to select 2001
recipient representative to make
comments—U of I
Publicity co-chairs meet with PR
consultant—week of February 11
Submit request for mayor's and governor's
proclamations per PR consultant

March 2002
Publicity co-chairs to have flyer ready by
March 8
Distribute flyer to advisory board members
the week of March 18 for posting and
marketing
Send letter to nursing organizations and
healthcare agencies to promote event
and sponsor tables
Send publicity announcement to nursing
organizations

Send publicity information to hospital
newsletters
Mail invitations week of March 18 &
March 25
Deliver to hospitals for distribution week
of March 25 to save postage
Send **two** invitations to speakers bureau
with flyer, etc.
Finalize and **format generic content**
for the written program at the March
co-chair planning meeting
Send invitations to former (cumulative)
recipients with cover letter

April 2002
Press release to newspapers and PSAs
Camera-ready artwork for program from
corporate and advertisers
Mail corporate sponsors their invitations
included in "package"
Collect photos of speakers, emcee,
recipient, honorary chairs

May 2002
Bring draft of written program to advisory
board meeting for review of sponsorship
accuracy, names, etc.
Order plaques and certificates (frames &
folders)
RSVP due for event on May 3, 2002
Finalize script week of May 13
Calls to corporate sponsors confirming
their representative to be recognized
from podium
Frame proclamations, prepare honorarium
to speaker, musicians, etc., gift for emcee.
**Written program to printer on May 8;
proof May 10**
**Send patron invitation letters on
May 10**
**Seating Committee meeting on
May 13 or May 15**
Compile list of corporate sponsors for
patron reception; convert to poster
format
May 17—Welcome Speaker to the Event!

Appendix J.03. Committee Co-Chairs and Responsibilities

NURSING 2000 - 12TH ANNUAL
2002 SCHOLARSHIP BENEFIT PLANNING COMMITTEE
AND
DEVELOPMENT COMMITTEE

Publicity Committee

Co-Chairpersons: _____ Phone: _____ E-mail: _____

_____ Phone: _____ E-mail: _____

Responsibilities: Coordinate publicity to heighten public awareness of the event and increase reservations in the community, hospitals, and universities. Develop promotional flyer (by March 8, 2002); promotional packet for Nursing 2000 volunteers (by March 22, 2002). Meet with public relations consultant for press release, PSAs, other promotional efforts the week of February 11, 2002. Submit requests for mayor's and governor's proclamations per PR consultant. Prepare photo list for any press that may attend.

Patron Reception Committee

Co-Chairpersons: _____ Phone: _____ E-mail: _____

_____ Phone: _____ E-mail: _____

Responsibilities: Coordinate format for patron reception, including selection of beverages and hors d'oeuvres and greeting and hosting guests. Obtain photographer and musician (harpist preferable) for reception. Determine order of events. Coordinate list of preferred photographs and designated times for the photographer.

Invitation/Program Committee

Co-Chairpersons: _____ Phone: _____ E-mail: _____

_____ Phone: _____ E-mail: _____

Responsibilities: Develop and coordinate all printed materials. Proof invitations and written program brochure. Order invitations by February 4, 2002. Finalize written program at May 3, 2002, advisory board meeting.

Dining/Decorations/Entertainment Committee

Co-Chairpersons: _____ Phone: _____ E-mail: _____

_____ Phone: _____ E-mail: _____

Committee Members: _____ Phone: _____ E-mail: _____

_____ Phone: _____ E-mail: _____

Responsibilities: Select menu for event and provide for appropriate decorations, including flowers, table centerpieces, signage, room set-up. Arrange for a master of ceremonies, background music, public address, lighting and audiovisual systems as needed. Coordinate format for portion of the evening including dedicated speeches, presentations, awards and recognition.

Registration Committee

Co-Chairpersons: _____ Phone: _____ E-mail: _____

_____ Phone: _____ E-mail: _____

<u>Responsibilities</u>: Coordinate volunteers the evening of the event to assist in registration and greeting process, including greeters to be available (seek two months ahead) to escort guests who need assistance in locating their tables. Obtain greeters for "special guest" recognition.

Seating Committee

Co-Chairpersons: _____ Phone: _____ E-mail: _____

_____ Phone: _____ E-mail: _____

<u>Responsibilities</u>: Coordinate one or two meetings the week of May 13 to determine table assignments and seating arrangements for all in attendance (patrons, corporate sponsors, guests, registrants, etc.)

Development Committee

Acting Chairperson: _____ Phone: _____ E-mail: _____

Committe Members: _____ Phone: _____ E-mail: _____

_____ Phone: _____ E-mail: _____

_____ Phone: _____ E-mail: _____

_____ Phone: _____ E-mail: _____

_____ Phone: _____ E-mail: _____

<u>Responsibilities</u>: Seek scholarship proceeds and/or support for scholarship event via identification and relationship building with patrons, sponsors, and contributors. Develop materials to support development activities.

Appendix J.04. Nursing 2000 Scholarship Benefit Sponsorship/Donation Categories

Supporting categories that appear in the program:

Corporate Sponsors

Corporations that give $500 or more as outlined in Sponsorship/Advertising Opportunities. Levels are: Diamond ($5,000), Platinum ($3,000), Gold ($1,500), Silver ($1,000), Bronze ($500).

Patron Table

Table reservation for 8 people ($720).

Sponsored Table

Table reservation for 8 people ($480).

Friend Sponsorship

Patron dinner reservations for two guests ($250).

Individual Patron

An individual who purchases a $90 reservation. The entire amount must be paid by that individual to be recognized in the program. An organization may buy a patron reservation and the organization will be recognized in the program.

Individual Contributors

Individual, agency, or organization that makes a monetary contribution directly to the scholarship fund.

Individual Sponsorships

Individual, agency, organization that sponsors a person/people to attend (less than a table). Often times, this is a student(s) or nurse(s) who is "sponsored."

In-Kind Donations

Business or individual who provides support by reducing fee for service or donation of a service.

RESERVATIONS

$60 . . . . sponsorship of one reservation
$90 . . . . sponsorship of one patron reservation
$30 . . . . sponsorship of one undergraduate nursing student
$480 . . . . sponsorship of one table reservation for 8 guests
$720 . . . . sponsorship of one patron table reservation for 8 guests (includes patron reception)

Appendix J.05. Scholarship Benefit Invitation

Reservation
May 17, 2002

I wish to:

☐ make ___ reservation(s) at $60.00 per person.

☐ make ___ reservation(s) at $30.00 per person.
(limited to students enrolled in first degree program)

☐ reserve ___ table(s) of 8 at $480.00 per table.

───────────── ◆ ─────────────

I wish to:

☐ make ___ patron reservation(s) at $90.00 per person.

☐ make ___ patron table(s) of 8 at $720.00 per table.

All patrons will receive an invitation to the patron reception and will be recognized in the program.

───────────── ◆ ─────────────

I wish to:

☐ sponsor ___ nursing student(s) at $30.00 per person.

☐ sponsor ___ individuals(s) at $60.00 per person.

☐ sponsor ___ individuals(s) at $90.00 per patron.

───────────── ◆ ─────────────

☐ Please accept my contribution of $_____ to the Nursing 2000 Scholarship Fund.

☐ I regret I cannot attend. Please accept my contribution of $_____ to the Nursing 2000 Scholarship Fund.

Please print names on back of card

Name _____
(If patron, please print your name the way you would like it to appear in the program.)

Address _____

_____ Phone _____

Organization/Affiliation _____

Guests will be seated at tables of 8. Please list names of individuals to be seated at your table

1. _____   5. _____

2. _____   6. _____

3. _____   7. _____

4. _____   8. _____

This serves as your reservation: no tickets are issued. Please respond by May 3, 2002. Reservations are limited.

Make checks payable to: Nursing 2000

For your tax information, all but $27.00 may be eligible for a charitable contribution.

Appendix K. Materials Relevant to the Adult Learner Career Seminar

Chapter 5

Community Programs
Adult Learner Career Seminar

Appendix K.01. Budget Estimation of Adult Learner Career Seminar (n = 40 Attendees)

Adult Learner Career Seminar

Flyer announcement to libraries, hospital newsletters, and community settings	$ 2.00
Advertisement in newspaper and on Web site (average $800)	20.00
Facility rental (i.e., library community room, on average $40)	1.00
Confirmation letters to attendees	1.00
Folders for career materials	1.50
Career materials in folder	2.00
Promotional item to attendees (i.e., pens)	.75
Refreshments	1.00
Thank you gift for Nursing 2000 volunteers/presenters	2.00
Thank you letter to Nursing 2000 volunteers/presenters	1.00
	$32.25 per attendee

Include in general program budget:
- mileage incurred to conduct seminar
- audiovisual development (slides, CD ROM, videos, etc.)

Appendix K.02. Promotional Flyer

ARE YOU CONSIDERING BECOMING A REGISTERED NURSE?

If so, attend ONE of the FREE seminars, "Nursing as a Career for the 21st Century."

Take the opportunity to learn more about:
- the richness and diversity of a nursing career now and in the future
- personal perspectives of registered nurses from our community
- educational programs that lead to a degree in nursing
- financial assistance

Date	Date
Time	Time
Facility	Facility
Address	Address
Directions to facility	Directions to facility

SPONSORED BY:

Nursing
2000
PROMOTE   EDUCATE   ADVANCE

(Call Nursing 2000 for more information; reservations NOT needed.)

*A Not-for-Profit Organization Committed to Promoting Careers in Registered Nursing Through Counseling, Education, and Public Presentations

Appendix K.03. Adult Learner Career Seminar Agenda

NURSING CAREER SEMINAR FOR ADULT LEARNERS

WARREN LIBRARY
9701 East 21st Street
Indianapolis, IN 46229

A G E N D A

12:30 – 12:40 p.m.	Welcome and Introduction _____, RN
12:40 – 12:55 p.m.	The Richness and Diversity of a Nursing Career Now and in the Future _____, RN
12:55 – 1:10 p.m.	Educational Programs that Lead to the First Degree in Nursing _____, RN
1:10 – 1:30 p.m.	Financial Assistance _____
1:30 – 2:00 p.m.	Personal Perspectives of registered nurses from our Community _____, RN _____, RN _____, RN (Moderator)
2:00 p.m.	Adjournment

Appendix K.04. Adult Learner Career Seminar Script

Adult Learner Career Seminar Presentation
"Nursing as a Career for the 21st Century"

Topic: The Diversity of a Nursing Career Now and in the Future

Presenter: Nursing 2000 Executive Director, Program Facilitator or
              Speaker's Bureau Volunteer

Time: 20 Minutes

INTRODUCTION

Welcome to one of the Adult Learner Career Seminars presented by
Nursing 2000. I am _____ and I am a registered nurse
(RN for short). I obtained a degree in nursing, then passed the nursing
boards to become registered. Before our speakers and I present information about a career as a registered nurse, I would like to discuss the material in the folder.

1. (Left inside of folder) Nursing 2000 is a not-for-profit education
    organization...
2. Agenda
3. Evaluation of this Adult Learner Career Seminar
4. Welcome letter from the Executive Director
5. White sheet—A Career in Registered Nursing—that summarizes
    much of the materials we will present today
6. Yellow sheet—professional nursing programs in Indiana
7. Area hospitals—* indicates funding/supporting hospitals of
    Nursing 2000
8. Resource list of Nursing Organizations
9. Green sheet – Financial Assistance
10. Several pamphlets

SLIDE VISUAL	SLIDE #	NARRATIVE
Nursing 2000	1	Nursing 2000
2.7 million are Nurses	2	There are 2.7 million registered nurses in the United States.
The Job Situation	3	The supply of RNs has doubled in the last decade. There has been a shift from inpatient to ambulatory care. Forty percent of nurses are working in settings outside hospitals.
Photo of paper clips of classified ads	4	These classified ads from the *Indianapolis Star* indicate hospital needs, but more ads will come from clinics, offices, extended care facilities, home healthcare businesses, ambulatory care centers, and businesses.
Factors Affecting the Demand for Nurses	5	I will identify four factors that affect the demand for nurses.
Patient Acuity	6	The first demand is patient acuity. This means how sick a patient is. Patients who are sicker require more RNs to care for them.
Photo of 2 neonatal intensive care nurses caring for infant	7	There are times when two registered nurses care for one patient in intensive care units. Slide shows premature infant in neonatal ICU.
High technology/medical advances	8	High technology and medical advances also influence the demand for nurses. This requires some RNs to maintain sophisticated equipment and provide education and emotional support to patients and families.
Photo of Cardiac Cath Lab	9	This shows some large equipment in the Cardiac Catheterization Lab.
Length of hospital stay	10	A third demand is length of hospital stay.
Shift to Ambulatory Care	11	Between 1985 and 1992, outpatient visits in short-stay hospitals grew by 50%.

SLIDE VISUAL	SLIDE #	NARRATIVE
Length of hospital stay has shortened.	12	While patients' severity of illness has risen, they are discharged more quickly from the hospital.
		Elderly population consumes a disproportionate amount of hospital services. People over 65 represent only 12% of the hospital population but account for 41% of the hospital days.
		The length of hospital stay increases with age.
Aging Population	13	The fourth factor affecting the demand for nurses is the aging population.
Graph of Aging Population	14	As life spans increase, more health services will be needed. It is projected 12% of the U.S. population will be over age 85 by the year 2030. The population age 65 years and older will double between 2000 and 2030. In 1991, life expectancy at birth reached 75.5 years.
Nursing	15	NURSING
Nursing can be defined...	16	Nursing can be defined as the diagnosis and treatment of human responses to actual or potential health problems.
Nurses care for people...	17	Nurses care for people all along the health-illness continuum from healthy to critically ill.
Photo of nurse with pediatric patient	18	• in the patient's everyday struggle to stay healthy
Photo of critical care patient	19	• as well as during severe illness
Nurses are present...	20	Nurses are present at the most critical times in a person's life.
Photo of mother and baby	21	• times of extreme joy – baby 1 hour old
Photo of family member and nurse in chapel	22	• and at times of extreme sadness – when someone has died

SLIDE VISUAL	SLIDE #	NARRATIVE
Nurses care for patients 24 hours…	23	Nurses care for patients 24 hours a day and carry out a plan of care for each patient.
Photo of nurse and MD	24	• they consult with physicians and other healthcare team members
Photo of nurse changing head dressing	25	• they perform a variety of complicated skills like: – changing dressings
Photo of nurse taking B/P	26	– taking blood pressures
Photo of nurse drawing up injection	27	– giving injections
Photo of nurse with monitor	28	– working with complex monitors and equipment
Photo of nurse teaching patient and wife	29	• they also teach patients and families about their health condition
Photo of nurse giving support	30	• and they provide psychological support to patients and families
Nursing is applying…	31	Nursing is applying scientific, psychological, and technological knowledge in the care of patients.
Nursing practice settings & specialties	32	NURSING PRACTICE SETTINGS AND SPECIALTIES
In the hospital…	33	In the hospital, expanding medical technology requires increased nursing observation at the bedside.
Photo of Neonatal Intensive Care Unit	34	Some of the specialties you find within the hospital are: • Critical Care Nursing – providing constant care to severely ill patients in highly specialized units. There are newborn, pediatric, and adult units.
Photo of nurse with pediatric patient in traction	35	• Pediatric Nursing – providing nursing care to children. Nurses who work with children must have a specialized knowledge of growth and development.

SLIDE VISUAL	SLIDE #	NARRATIVE
Photo of birth family and nurse	36	• Maternal/Child Nursing – providing nursing care to moms, babies, and families during the entire birth process.
Photo of nurse with psychiatric patient	37	• Mental Health Nursing – providing nursing care to patients experiencing emotional adjustments. Requires strong communication skills and understanding of human behavior.
Photo of nurse with bone marrow transplant patient	38	• Oncology Nursing – providing care to patients who are being treated for cancer. It may involve caring for both children and adults and working very closely with families.
Photo of nurse teaching patient glucose monitoring	39	• Medical Nursing – providing care to patients who often have a long-term illness. Some examples are problems of the kidney, lung, heart, or specific diseases such as diabetes and arthritis.
Photo of nurse with patient after eye surgery	40	• Surgical Nursing – providing care to patients who have experienced a surgical procedure (surgery). This may be in a hospital or an outpatient center.
Photo of nurse with operating room team	41	• Operating Room Nursing – providing care in the highly specialized, technical environment of surgery. The nurse works closely with the entire surgery team.
Photo of Emergency Room team	42	• Emergency Room Nursing – providing care to patients requiring immediate treatment (such as a heart attack) and who often have experienced trauma. Nurses who work in emergency rooms have to set priorities and make quick, life-saving decisions.
Photo of nurse assisting patient with walker	43	• Rehabilitation Nursing – providing care to patients who have long-term disabilities and injuries. The patients are often young trauma victims or older individuals who have debilitating experiences.

SLIDE VISUAL	SLIDE #	NARRATIVE
In non-hospital settings...	44	Some of the specialties you frequently see outside of the hospital setting are:
Photo of nurse ringing doorbell	45	• Public Health/Community Nursing – the nurse cares for patients and families of different ages in schools, clinics, and homes. Much emphasis is on prevention of illness.
	46	• Home Health Nursing – the nurse cares for patients and families in their homes often over an extended period of time. This is a growing area of nursing, as patients are staying for shorter periods of time in the hospital. When they go home, they frequently need nursing care.
Photo of nurse with elderly patient	47	• Geriatric Nursing – the nurse works with the elderly. The need for nurses in this area is growing because people are living longer. The nurse not only works with the 10% of the elderly population in nursing homes, but she works in clinics and runs nursing centers to help the aging population stay healthy!
Photo of employee with nurse	48	• Occupational Health Nursing – the nurse works with people in their employment settings. The nurse gives emergency care, performs health exams, and provides health teaching and counseling. Much emphasis is on prevention.
		Other – you will also find nurses working in clinics, physicians' offices, and (for some with master's and doctoral degrees) in their own independent practices.
Roles	49	ROLES

SLIDE VISUAL	SLIDE #	NARRATIVE
Career paths...	50	Generally, there are four roles a nurse can choose. You can see from the roles on this slide, all the roles overlap and are interdependent with each other. However, it is important to know there are <u>four careers within nursing!</u> • Clinician • Educator • Manager/Administrator • Researcher
Clinician...	51	**Clinician** – a clinical nurse who provides the direct care to the patient. The majority of nurses are clinicians. 1) Clinical Nurse – a clinician includes the brand new nurse and very experienced nurse. You see clinical nurses at hospitals, clinics, extended care facilities, ambulatory care centers...anywhere that nursing care is provided. The slides we just showed you were of clinical nurses. 2) Advanced Practice Nurse – a nurse prepared at the master's or doctoral degree with advanced knowledge of a clinical specialty.
Photo of Clinical Specialist consulting with other nurses	52	• Clinical Specialist – a clinician with a master's degree or beyond who specializes in a specific area of care...such as we discussed earlier (critical care, pediatrics, maternal/child care, mental health, oncology, etc.). They work in all types of settings and provide direct care, develop nursing care procedures and ways to monitor the quality of nursing care, and can also be educators and researchers.

SLIDE VISUAL	SLIDE #	NARRATIVE
Photo of Nurse Practitioner performing ear exam	53	• Nurse Practitioner – a clinician prepared with a master's degree who provides basic healthcare for infants, children, and adults in settings ranging from community health centers, hospitals, schools, workplaces, and homes. They perform physical exams, diagnose and treat common illness, and counsel patients on health promotion. In the majority of states, including Indiana, nurse practitioners have been granted legal authority to write prescriptions (prescribe medications).
Photo of Nurse Midwife and pregnant woman	54	• Nurse-Midwife – a clinician who can provide prenatal and gynecological care to normal healthy women; deliver babies in hospitals, private homes, or birthing centers; and provide follow-up care. Requires advanced education in an accredited certificate program.
Photo of Nurse Anesthetists with ambu bag	55	• Registered Nurse Anesthetist – a clinician who gives anesthesia (drugs that put patients to sleep for surgery) for all types of surgery. Requires master's degree.
Number of active registered nurses/Number of specialist and primary care physicians	56	Advanced practice nurses can work with physicians to help meet primary healthcare needs.
Nursing Centers	57	Advanced practice nurses provide outpatient health services to the general public via nursing centers. These centers rely on nurses to diagnose and treat patients, as well as focus on health promotion.

SLIDE VISUAL	*SLIDE #*	*NARRATIVE*
Photo of educator with 2 students	58	Another pathway – **Educator** – a nurse with a minimum of a master's degree whose practice also includes teaching student nurses and practicing nurses. Educators include: • Clinical Instructor – teaches clinical skills to student nurses • College/University Professor – teaches and also does research; we need more nurses prepared for these positions; usually requires a doctorate degree • Staff Development Specialist – coordinates the continuing education for practicing nurses both in hospital and non-hospital settings
Photo of Manager/Administrator collaborating with other team members	59	The third pathway – **Manager/ Administrator** – coordinates the use of human, financial (budget), and technological resources (equipment) for patient care. Requires much collaboration with physicians, other managers, and administration. The manager is very much an advocate for the nursing staff to provide the resources they need to take care of the patients!
Photo of researcher at computer	60	Fourth type of career – **Researcher** – doctorally prepared nurse who uses statistical methodologies to discover or establish facts, principles, or relationships. Directly develops nursing's expanding knowledge base.
Demand for MSN and DNSc	61	The demand for master's and doctorally prepared nurses for advanced practice, clinical specialties, teaching, and research is increasing.
Diversity	62	DIVERSITY As you can see, nursing's greatest strength is its diversity. Nurses can follow their personal and professional interests by working with any group of people, in any setting, at any time. There is no profession that offers as many different opportunities as does nursing.

SLIDE VISUAL	SLIDE #	NARRATIVE
Salary and work environment	63	SALARY AND WORK ENVIRONMENT
Average starting salary...	64	The average starting salary in the Indianapolis area is $35,000-$37,000 per year. 1) varies across country 2) ranges into mid $40s 3) increases with years and experience 4) often higher salaries for higher degrees
Advancement...	65	Advancement opportunities, compensation, and benefits are included.
Compensation and benefit packages...	66	Compensation and benefit packages: – competitive salaries – flexible work schedules – health & dental insurance – advancement opportunities – high level of mobility
Flexibility	67	Many scheduling options are available that are compatible in meeting the personal needs of the nurse. 1) day shift 　evening shift 　night shift 2) 4 hours 　8 hours 　12 hours
Quote from Janet A. Rodgers, RN, PhD, FAAN	68	"It's clear more and more first-time students, as well as adult career-changers, are turning to the largest health profession for career security and personal fulfillment at a time when healthcare's daily impact on Americans has become so tremendously dominant."

Appendix K.05. Script of Panel Questions

Adult Learner Career Seminar Presentation
"Nursing as a Career for the 21st Century"

Topic: Personal Perspectives of registered nurses from our Community

Presenters: Interactive Panel comprised of 2-3 Speakers' Bureau Members and a Moderator

Time: 25 minutes

Questions: Asked of each panel member by moderator.

1. How did you get interested in nursing?

2. What type of nursing education program did you attend?

3. In reflecting back on your nursing career, what concerns did you have prior to entering nursing?

4. What support systems were helpful to you during nursing school?

5. In what areas of nursing have you worked? (clinical areas and roles)

6. Is there a particular patient (client) situation that stands out in your mind that you'd like to share.

7. What changes have you seen in the workplace and what changes do you anticipate for nursing in the future?

8. Can you give us an idea of the different hours you have worked in your nursing career? How does this fit with your "life-style balance"?

9. What is the degree of flexibility available to nurses in the current workplace? (i.e., schedules, full time/part time, job sharing, etc.)

10. What are some non-traditional options to learning? (computerized self-teaching programs with access code fee, auditing classes)

11. How do you keep up-to-date with your nursing knowledge and what avenues are available for career development in your institution?

12. What advice do you have for someone beginning his/her career in nursing?

13. What facet of your career or experiences are you the proudest of?

Appendix K.06. Contents of Adult Learner Career Seminar Folder

Contents of
Adult Learner Career Seminar Folder

1. Agenda

2. "A Career in Registered Nursing" handout

3. List of schools of nursing in Indiana

4. List of area hospitals

5. Resource list of nursing organizations

6. Financial aid resource

7. School brochures from:
   Indiana University School of Nursing
   Ivy Tech State College
   Marian College
   University of Indianapolis

8. Evaluation tool

Appendix K.07. Adult Learner Career Seminar Evaluation Form

ADULT LEARNER CAREER SEMINAR
Date
Location
Time

EVALUATION

Thank you for attending our Adult Learner Career Seminar. Your assistance in evaluating today's seminar is very much appreciated.

Please rate how well the following objectives were met. (4 is high and 1 is low)

OBJECTIVES/CONTENT	Please circle your response High = 4		Low = 1	
1. Discuss the diversity of a nursing career, the job situation, and compensation. "The Job Situation, Diversity, and Compensation" Comments:	4	3	2	1
2. Share nursing career biographical sketches. "Biographical Sketches" Comments:	4	3	2	1
3. Describe educational programs that lead to understanding the differences in nursing programs, i.e., associate degree vs. baccalaureate degree. "Educational Options" Comments:	4	3	2	1
4. Present financial assistance available to me. "Financial Assistance" Comments:	4	3	2	1

EFFECTIVENESS

Please circle your response
High = 4   Low = 1

1. Overall, I would rate the seminar as being helpful.   4   3   2   1

   Comments:

2. I gained a greater understanding of a career in nursing   4   3   2   1
   from this seminar.

   Comments:

3. I would recommend this seminar to others.   4   3   2   1

   Comments:

4. The information shared in this seminar will be helpful   4   3   2   1
   to me in making a decision to pursue nursing as a career.

   Comments:

5. I am considering a career in registered nursing.   4   3   2   1

   Comments:

Thank you for your time spent in evaluating our program! Your feedback will be used in planning future Nursing 2000 seminars.

Appendix L. Materials Relevant to the Adult Learner A Day in the Life of a Nurse Shadow Program

Chapter 5

Community Programs
Adult Learner A Day in the Life of a Nurse Shadow Program

Appendix L.01. Budget Estimation of Adult Learner A Day in the Life of a Nurse Shadow Program (n = 48 Attendees)

Adult Learner Shadow Program

Folder for career materials	$1.50
Career materials in folder	6.00
Gift for adult attendee	8.20
Gift for nurse mentor and coordinator	5.50
	$21.20 per attendee

Include in general program budget:
- mileage or postage to deliver materials to hospital coordinator

Appendix L.02. Welcome Letter

Date

Dear Shadow Participant:

Welcome to the adult learner A Day in the Life of a Nurse shadow program sponsored by Nursing 2000! Nursing 2000 is a not-for-profit organization created to promote careers in registered nursing through counseling, education, and public presentations. Representatives of Nursing 2000 are practicing registered nurses from hospitals, universities, and professional nursing organizations, all working concertedly to inform you of the opportunities available in the career of nursing.

Nursing today is a challenging and rewarding career. Nurses can follow their personal and professional interests by working with various groups of people in a variety of settings at different times. As the focus of healthcare delivery moves from a curative to preventive focus, the nurse's role is spanning many settings and expanding in responsibilities. Nurses will be providing care across the health continuum – in the hospital, transitional care, the home, and the community.

We are pleased you chose to spend your day "shadowing" a registered nurse to learn about a career in registered nursing. We hope the experience and enclosed materials will be helpful to you. If you have any questions or require additional information, please feel free to contact Nursing 2000 via e-mail at _____ or phone at _____. Thank you very much for your participation in the adult learner A Day in the Life of a Nurse shadow program.

Sincerely,

_____
Executive Director
Nursing 2000

Appendix L.03. Release Form for Adult Learner Shadowing Experience

Release Form

Adult Learner Shadow Experience with RN

I, _____, understand that a "shadowing" experience with a nurse in a local hospital is designed to be observational though may involve exposure to health risks, such as contact with patients and body fluids.

In consideration for participation in the program and the education and information I will receive by participating in the adult learner shadow experience, I hereby release, indemnify, and hold harmless Nursing 2000, Incorporated, its employees, participating hospitals, officers, and agents from any and all liability arising out of or resulting from my participation in the adult learner shadow experience.

_____   _____
Signature   Date

Appendix L.04. Confidentiality Statement

Adult Learner Shadow Experience with RN

Patient Confidentiality Statement

Participating Hospital: _____

As evidenced by my signature below, I understand the importance of maintaining patient confidentiality. I shall not disclose any patient information—including name, diagnosis, and any other identifying information—learned through my participation in the adult learner shadow program.

_____   _____
Signature   Date

Appendix L.05. Adult Learner Shadow Evaluation Form

 ADULT LEARNER SHADOW EXPERIENCE

Participating Hospital: _____

Participant Name: _____

Address: _____

Phone Number: _____

....

EVALUATION

In order to evaluate the "shadow" experience for future participants, we need your assistance. Please rate to what degree you agree with the following statements. (4 is high and 1 is low)

Please circle your response

EFFECTIVENESS   High = 4   Low = 1

1. The "shadow" experience was helpful in increasing my knowledge of nursing in the hospital setting.   4   3   2   1

2. I enjoyed the opportunity to directly observe the role of the nurse.   4   3   2   1

3. This experience will be helpful to me in making a decision to pursue nursing as a career.   4   3   2   1

4. From my experience, two characteristics that describe the role of the professional nurse are:

    Comments: _____

    _____

5. As you explored the role of the professional nurse today, what observation/experience was most helpful to you?

    Comments: _____

    _____

6. Additional comments: _____

    _____

Thank you very much for your feedback! It will be used in future planning.

Appendix L.06. Content List of Folder Materials for Adult Learner A Day in the Life of a Nurse Shadow Program

Contents of Folder for
Adult Learner Shadow Experience

1. Welcome letter to the participant

2. "A Career in Registered Nursing" handout

3. List of schools of nursing in Indiana

4. "Specialties in the Career of Registered Nursing" handout

5. Resource list of nursing organizations

6. Volunteer opportunities in affiliated hospitals

7. Financial aid resource

8. School brochures from:
    Indiana University
    Ivy Tech State College
    Marian College
    University of Indianapolis

9. Student Financial Assistance Booklet from the U.S. Department of Education

10. Student Financial Assistance from Indiana Career and Postsecondary Advancement Center

Appendix M. Materials Relevant to Community Presentations

Chapter 5

Community Programs
Community Presentations
"Nursing Now—A First Look at Nursing as a Career"

M.01 Budget Estimation of Community Presentations

M.02 Promotional Flyer

M.03 Seminar Agenda

M.04 Contents of a Sample Community Presentation, "Nursing Now— A First Look at Nursing as a Career" Seminar Folder

M.05 Script of Panel Questions

M.06 Evaluation Form Completed by Attendees

Appendix M.01. Budget Estimation of Community Presentations (n = 85 Attendees)

"Nursing Now—A First Look at Nursing as a Career"

Flyer announcement to adult learners, previous A Day in the Life of a Nurse participants, and parents/guardians	$2.00
Advertisement in newspaper and Web site (average $800)	9.40
Facility rental (average $150)	1.75
Confirmation letters to attendees	1.00
Folders for career materials	1.50
Career materials in folder	2.00
Promotional item to attendees (i.e., pens)	.75
Refreshments	1.00
Thank you gifts for Nursing 2000 volunteers/presenters	2.00
Thank you gifts for school of nursing exhibitors	2.00
Thank you letters to Nursing 2000 volunteers	1.00
	$24.40 per attendee

Include in general program budget:
- mileage incurred to conduct the event
- audiovisual development (slides, CD ROM, video, etc.)
- postage for mailings

Nursing Now

A First Look at Nursing as a Career

Nursing 2000 is pleased to present an informational seminar for individuals who are considering a career in registered nursing.

Seminar Program:

- Nursing as a Career to Make a Difference
- Opportunities, Rewards, and Advancements in Nursing
- Perspectives from Practicing Nurses
- Academic and Life Experience Preparation Needed to Enter Nursing

Date and Location:

- Date and Time
- Location and Address

Registration is required. To register, contact Nursing 2000 by phone or e-mail.

Sponsored by Nursing 2000, a not-for-profit organization committed to promoting careers in registered nursing through counseling, education, and public presentations.

PROMOTE   EDUCATE   ADVANCE

Appendix M.03. Seminar Agenda

Nursing Now

A First Look at Nursing as a Career

Location
Date
Time

Seminar Agenda

6:00 – 6:05 p.m.	**Introduction—**_____, MSN, RN
6:10 – 6:20 p.m.	**Nursing as a Career to Make a Difference** View *Nursing Today and Beyond 2000*
6:20 – 6:30 p.m.	**Opportunities, Rewards, Advancements in Nursing** Response to video and overview of resource materials
	The Evolving Demand for Nursing Facts about the registered nurse shortage
6:30 – 7:15 p.m.	**Perspectives from RNs in Practice** _____, BSN, RN, panel moderator _____, MSN, RN _____, BSEd, ASN, RN _____, BSN, MSN, CNS _____, PhD, BSN, RN
7:15 – 7:30 p.m.	**Academic and Life Experience Preparation Needed** _____, MSN, RN, CS, FNP
7:30 p.m.	**Post-Seminar – School of Nursing Representatives Available for Individual Questions** Indiana University, _____, BA Ivy Tech State College, _____, MSN, RN Marian College, _____, BSN, RN University of Indianapolis, _____, EdD, RN

Appendix M.04. Contents of a Sample Community Presentation, "Nursing Now—A First Look at Nursing as a Career" Seminar Folder

Contents of Folder for "Nursing Now—A First Look at Nursing as a Career"

1. Agenda

2. "A Career in Registered Nursing" handout

3. Facts/Evolving Demand/Profile handout

4. Advanced Roles in Nursing handout

5. List of schools of nursing in Indiana

6. Financial aid resource

7. List of hospital nurse recruiters

8. Volunteer opportunities in affiliated hospitals

9. Resource list of nursing organizations

10. Brochure, Nursing the Ultimate Adventure

11. Evaluation tool

Appendix M.05. Script of Panel Questions

Introduction of the panel – incorporate name, degree, current position, place of employment

Clinical Nurse Role—Traditional

1. How long have you been a nurse?
2. When did you first become interested in nursing?
3. What would you tell high school students who are considering nursing?
4. How did you select your nursing program...I presume when you were a senior...?
5. What was the most significant adjustment for you from high school to college?
6. From your perspective, what does nursing uniquely offer?
7. Is nursing what you thought it would be?
8. What is most rewarding to you in providing patient care?
9. Is there anything else you would like to share with individuals considering nursing?

Clinical Nurse Role—Non-traditional

1. We understand that nursing is a second career (third?) for you? When did you first become interested in nursing?
2. In what way has nursing complemented (built upon) your prior career or work experience?
3. What type of nursing education program did you attend?
4. As a non-traditional nursing student, what was your most challenging experience (clinically, academically, or both)?
5. What concerns did you have prior to entering nursing?
6. Can you share with us the different hours you have worked in your nursing career? How does this fit with your "life-style balance"?
7. From your perspective, what is the degree of flexibility available to nurses in the current workplace?
8. How do you keep up-to-date with your nursing knowledge and competent with your nursing skills?

Advanced Practice Nurse

1. What is your current role? Describe some of the responsibilities…

2. What is the educational background required to be an advanced practice nurse? Touch upon the four advanced practice roles for us and your selection of clinical nurse specialist.

3. What were your experiences as a clinical nurse that led you to pursue an advanced practice role?

4. What is the most challenging aspect of your current role as a clinical nurse specialist?

5. What has been one of your most rewarding experiences as a clinical nurse specialist?

Expanded Career Nurse

1. Describe the career path you have chosen in nursing.

2. How do you draw upon your nursing background in your role as administrator and, secondly, as researcher?

3. What advice would you give to individuals considering a research career in nursing as a part of their future? How can they begin to prepare themselves **now**…as they are beginning their nursing program?

4. In your current role as associate dean, you were quoted: "The challenge in today's marketplace is to be prepared to reach beyond what you think you should be doing as a nurse to what you could be doing as a nurse." Please expand.

5. Where do you see nursing going in the future?

Ending Questions – target to all – one response if possible

1. What support systems were in place when you were enrolled in your nursing program? (Educators may also want to speak to this.)

2. Is nursing what you thought it would be?

3. Do you have a particular patient experience that you would like to share that epitomizes nursing to you?

4. Is there anything else you would like to share with individuals considering nursing as a career?

Appendix M.06. Evaluation Form Completed by Attendees

| **Nursing Now** |
| A First Look at Nursing as a Career |

Location
Date
Time

EVALUATION

Thank you for attending **"Nursing Now—A First Look at Nursing as a Career."** Your assistance in evaluating today's seminar is very much appreciated.

Please rate how well the following objectives and corresponding content were met. (4 is high and 1 is low)

Please circle your response

OBJECTIVES/CONTENT	High = 4		Low = 1	
1. Discuss the challenges, rewards, and opportunities in nursing as a profession that make a difference.	4	3	2	1
2. Interact with registered nurses representing diverse roles in nursing.	4	3	2	1
3. Describe academic and life experience preparation that are assets to enter a school of nursing.	4	3	2	1

EFFECTIVENESS

1. The speakers were well informed on the topic.	4	3	2	1
2. The opportunity for learner participation was adequate.	4	3	2	1
3. The content of the seminar was organized in a logical sequence.	4	3	2	1
4. The quality of learning resources (audiovisuals, handouts, etc.) facilitated my learning.	4	3	2	1
5. The information shared in this seminar will be helpful to me in making a career decision.	4	3	2	1
6. I would recommend this seminar to others who are interested in a nursing career.	4	3	2	1

ADDITIONAL COMMENTS:

Appendix N. Materials Relevant to Public Library Displays

Chapter 5

Community Programs
Public Library Displays

Appendix N.01. Budget Estimation of Public Library Displays

Budget Estimation of
Public Library Displays (3 per year)

Library Displays

Confirmation letter to Nursing 2000 volunteer	$3.00
Thank you gift for Nursing 2000 volunteer	6.00
Career materials and display items	6.00
"Nursing is AMAZING" poster	3.00
Assorted nursing textbooks/journals (average per year $180)	60.00
Photographs of practicing nurses	30.00
Other display items (i.e., stethoscope, equipment)	30.00
	$138.00 per 3 library displays

Include in general program budget:
- mileage for delivery and display set-up and retrieval at library by Nursing 2000 staff
- organization's display board and drape used for exhibits

Appendix N.02. Library Display Planning Log

Library Display
Planning Log

Library Name: _____

Address: _____

Contact person: _____ Telephone number: _____

Date of contact: _____ Scheduled dates of display: _____

Description/dimensions of display area: _____

Schedule display set-up:
- Date of set-up _____
- Volunteer: _____
- Telephone/E-mail: _____
- Materials delivered: _____

Schedule display takedown:
- Date of takedown: _____
- Volunteer: _____
- Telephone/E-mail: _____
- Materials picked up: _____

Prepare materials:
- Nursing 2000 display board _____
- Career information:
  Elementary _____
  Middle school _____
  High school _____
  Adult learners/career changers _____
  LPN and RN Mobility _____
- "Nursing is Amazing" poster _____
- Assorted nursing textbooks/journals _____

- Program announcements as appropriate:
  A Day in the Life of a Nurse _____
  Scholarship Benefit_____
  "Nursing Now" _____
  "Spotlight on Re-Entry" _____
  "Nurses' Celebration Saturday" ___
  Other: _____
- Special supplies:
  "Winnie the Pooh" _____
  Stethoscope _____
  Assorted colorful items with
  Nursing 2000 logo _____

Appendix O. Materials Relevant to Community Career and Health Fairs

Chapter 5

Community Programs
Community Career and Health Fairs

O.01   Budget Estimation of Community Career and Health Fairs

O.02   RN Mobility Guide

O.03   Graduate Programs of Nursing in Indiana

O.04   LPN-RN Mobility Guide

O.05   Content List of Materials to Take to Health Career Fairs

Appendix 0.01. Budget Estimation of Community Career and Health Fairs

Budget Estimation of
Community Career and Health Fairs
(per year)

Community Career and Health Fairs

Flyer announcements to elementary principals, school nurses, other age-based audiences	$ 300.00
Age-based career materials – pre-school through adult	1,500.00
Educational/career mobility materials	500.00
Promotional item for attendee • elementary (i.e., erasers, rulers) • middle school and high school (i.e., pencils)	360.00
Entertainment (i.e., clown for Nurses Celebration Saturday at The Children's Museum	270.00
Thank you gifts for volunteers	500.00
	$3,430.00

Include in general program budget:
- mileage to plan and conduct each event
- organization's display board and drape used for exhibits
- event participation and exhibit fees (usually nominal)
- postage for mailings

Appendix 0.02. RN Mobility Guide

9302 North Meridian Street
Suite 365
Indianapolis, Indiana 46260
317-574-1325
Fax 317-573-0875
info@nursing2000inc.org
www.nursing2000inc.org

RN Educational
Mobility Guide...BSN, MSN, PhD

August 2002   a resource for the RN exploring educational mobility

Assets You Bring
- Nursing experience and clinical practice on which to build
- Motivation for personal and professional growth
- Ability to apply previously learned skills in an educational setting
- Experience in collaboration with other RNs to bring clinical perspective to the learning environment
- Ability to exchange ideas with peers

Benefits To You
- Further development of your nursing career
- Potential for additional career options and advancement opportunities
- Expansion of clinical knowledge areas of community health, health promotion, leadership, and research
- Development of advanced communication skills in interactions with patients, families, and healthcare professionals and systems
- Opportunities for greater self-development to broaden your nursing focus

Support Systems
- Nursing colleagues, fellow students, faculty, advisors, and family
- Flexible scheduling to accommodate working RNs
- Potential tuition assistance from employer—talk with your human resource department

Selecting Your Educational Mobility Program
1. Make a career plan with goals and timelines.
2. Identify the schools of nursing that offer RN mobility programs that fit your needs.
3. Make an appointment with an academic advisor; have a copy of transcript to discuss what course work will apply.
4. Determine cost – include tuition, books and fees, travel expenses, child care, reduced work, etc.
5. Explore financial assistance options (including tuition reimbursement from your employer).
6. Integrate class schedule with work/personal life.
7. Submit application; if prior degree is from same university, determine if you need to re-apply.

Questions To Ask Your Academic Advisor When Applying To RN Mobility Program
- Is a specific advisor assigned to RN mobility students?
- Which credits will transfer from my previous educational preparation?
- How long do I have to complete the program?
- Can I attend part-time? If yes, how long before I go full-time?
- How long will it take to complete the program as a part-time or full-time student?
- How flexible are class options? Are on-site, on-line, evening, weekend, and/or summer classes available?
- Are there advanced placement options for clinical courses?
- What financial assistance is available?

Educational Degree Mobility

Baccalaureate degree program
The BSN program prepares graduates to provide direct nursing care to patients, families, and groups in a variety of settings that span the continuum of care, including content in leadership, community health, and research.

Master's degree program
The MSN program prepares graduates for advanced specialized practice roles, administration, and teaching.

Doctoral degree program
The DNSc program prepares graduates to be scholarly researchers, university teachers, consultants, administrators, and practitioners.

Career Options

Clinical Practice

Clinical nurse
This nurse clinician provides direct care to patients.

Advanced practice nurse
This nurse clinician has a master's or doctorate degree with advanced knowledge in a clinical specialty, such as, but not limited to, clinical specialist, nurse practitioner, nurse midwife, and nurse anesthetist.

Additional Opportunities for Nurses with Advanced Degrees

Manager/Administrator
A nurse who coordinates the use of human, financial, and technological resources for patient care.

Educator
A nurse who has a minimum of a master's degree whose practice includes teaching student nurses, mentoring current nurses, and educating patients in the community.

Researcher
A doctorally prepared nurse who utilizes research methodologies to develop and advance nursing science. This nurse directly develops nursing's expanding knowledge base, while contributing to a quality healthcare system through research.

Programs in Indiana Offering RN-BSN Mobility

Anderson University
Dean, School of Nursing
Anderson University
1100 East 5th
Anderson, IN 46012
(765) 641-4380
www.anderson.edu

Ball State University
Director, School of Nursing
Ball State University
2000 University Avenue
Muncie, IN 47306-0265
(765) 285-5571
www.bsu.edu

Bethel College
Dean of Nursing
Bethel College
1001 West McKinley Avenue
Mishawaka, IN 46565
(574) 257-3369
www.bethel-in.edu

Goshen College
Director of Nursing
Goshen College
1700 South Main Street
Goshen, IN 46526
(574) 535-7370
www.goshen.edu

Indiana State University
Dean, School of Nursing
Indiana State University
749 Chestnut
Terre Haute, IN 47809
(812) 237-2316
www.indstate.edu/nurs

Indiana University
Office of Educational Services
IU School of Nursing
1111 Middle Drive, NU 122
Indianapolis, IN 46202-5107
(317) 274-2806
http://nursing.iupui.edu

Indiana University East
Dean of Nursing
Indiana University East
2325 Chester Boulevard
Richmond, IN 47374
1-800-959-3278
www.iue.indiana.edu

Indiana University Kokomo
Dean of Nursing
Indiana University Kokomo
2300 South Washington
Kokomo, IN 46904-9003
(765) 455-9384
www.iuk.edu

Indiana University Northwest
Dean, Division of Nursing
Indiana University Northwest
3400 Broadway
Gary, IN 46408
1-888-YOUR-IUN
www.iun.edu

Indiana University South Bend
Dean, Division of Nursing and
Health Professions
Indiana University South Bend
1700 Mishawaka Avenue
Northside Hall 444
South Bend, IN 46634
(219) 237-4282
www.iusb.edu

**Indiana University Southeast,
New Albany**
Dean, Division of Nursing
Indiana University Southeast
Life Sciences Building
4201 Grant Line Road
New Albany, IN 47150
(812) 941-2340
www.ius.indiana.edu/nursing/

**Indiana University-Purdue University Fort Wayne/
Parkview Nursing Program**

Chair, School of Nursing
IU-PU Fort Wayne/Parkview
Nursing Program
2101 Coliseum Blvd East
Neff Hall B50V
Fort Wayne, IN 46805
260-481-6816
www.ipfw.edu

Indiana Wesleyan University
Chair, Division of Nursing
Education
Indiana Wesleyan University
4201 South Washington St
Marion, IN 46953
(765) 677-2269
www.indwes.edu

Marian College
Chair, Department of Nursing
Marian College
3200 Cold Spring Road
Indianapolis, IN 46222
1-800-772-7264
www.marian.edu

**Purdue University,
West Lafayette**
Head, School of Nursing
Purdue University
1337 Johnson Hall of Nursing
West Lafayette, IN 47907-1337
(765) 494-4004
www.nursing.purdue.edu

Purdue University Calumet
Head, Department of Nursing
Purdue University Calumet
Gyte Annex Room X138
2200 169th Street
Hammond, IN 46323-2094
(219) 989-2814
http://nursing.calumet.purdue.edu

Saint Mary's College
Chair, Nursing Department
Saint Mary's College
Notre Dame, IN 46556-5001
(574) 284-4000
www.saintmarys.edu

University of St. Francis
Chair, Department of Nursing
University of St. Francis
2701 Spring Street
Fort Wayne, IN 46808
1-800-729-4732
www.sf.edu

University of Indianapolis
Dean, School of Nursing
University of Indianapolis
1400 East Hanna Avenue
Indianapolis, IN 46227
1-800-232-8634
http://nursing.uindy.edu

University of Southern Indiana
Dean, School of Nursing
University of Southern Indiana
8600 University Boulevard
Evansville, IN 47712
(812) 464-8600
http://health.usi.edu/

Valparaiso University
Dean, College of Nursing
Valparaiso University
Valparaiso, IN 46383
(219) 464-5289
www.valpo.edu/nursing

Additional Programs in Indiana That Offer BSN Degree

Indiana University, Bloomington
Dean of Nursing
Room 437 Sycamore Hall
Bloomington, IN 47405
(812) 855-1736
www.indiana.edu/iubnurse/

Saint Mary's College
Chair, Nursing Department
Saint Mary's College
Notre Dame, IN 46556-5001
(574) 284-4000
www.saintmarys.edu

University of Evansville
Department Chair, Nursing
University of Evansville
1800 Lincoln Avenue
Evansville, IN 47722
(812) 479-2343
http://nursing.evansville.edu

Programs in Indiana Offering RN-MSN Mobility

Ball State University
Director, School of Nursing
Ball State University
2000 University Avenue
Muncie, IN 47306-0265
(765) 285-5571
www.bsu.edu

Indiana University
Office of Educational Services
IU School of Nursing
1111 Middle Drive, NU 122
Indianapolis, IN 46202
(317) 274-2806
http://nursing.iupui.edu

**Purdue University
Calumet Campus**
Chair, Department of Nursing
Purdue University Calumet
Gyte Annex Room X138
2200 169th Street
Hammond, IN 46323-2094
(219) 989-2814
http://nursing.calumet.purdue.edu

University of Southern Indiana
Dean, School of Nursing
University of Southern Indiana
8600 University Boulevard
Evansville, IN 47712
(812) 464-8600
http://health.usi.edu

University of St. Francis
Chair, Department of Nursing
University of St. Francis
2701 Spring Street
Fort Wayne, IN 46808
1-800-729-4732
www.sf.edu/nursing/

Additional Programs in Indiana That Offer MSN Degree

Indiana State University
Dean, School of Nursing
Indiana State University
749 Chestnut
Terre Haute, IN 47809
(812) 237-2316
www.indstate.edu/nurs

Indiana University Kokomo
Dean of Nursing
Indiana University Kokomo
2300 South Washington
PO Box 9003
Kokomo, IN 46904-9003
(765) 455-9384
www.iuk.edu/academics/nursing/

Indiana University-Purdue University
Fort Wayne/Parkview Nursing Program
Chair, School of Nursing
IU-PU Fort Wayne/Parkview Nursing Program
2101 Coliseum Boulevard East
Neff Hall B50V
Fort Wayne, IN 46805
(260) 481-6816
www.ipfw.edu

Indiana University-South Bend
Dean of Nursing
Indiana University-South Bend
School of Nursing
1700 Mishawaka Avenue
Northside Hall 444
South Bend, IN 46634
(219) 237-4282
www.iusb.edu/nursing

Indiana Wesleyan University
Chair, Division of Nursing Education
Indiana Wesleyan University
4201 South Washington Street
Marion, IN 46953
(765) 677-2269
www.indwes.edu

Purdue University, West Lafayette
Head, School of Nursing
Purdue University
1337 Johnson Hall of Nursing
West Lafayette, IN 47907-1337
(765) 494-4004
www.nursing.purdue.edu

University of St. Francis
Chairperson, Department of Nursing
University of St. Francis
2701 Spring Street
Fort Wayne, IN 46808
1-800-729-4732
www.sf.edu/nursing/

University of Indianapolis
Dean, School of Nursing
University of Indianapolis
1400 East Hanna Avenue
Indianapolis, IN 46227
1-800-232-8634
http://nursing.uindy.edu

University of Southern Indiana
Dean, School of Nursing
University of Southern Indiana
8600 University Boulevard
Evansville, IN 47712
(812) 464-8600
http://health.usi.edu

Valparaiso University
Dean, College of Nursing
Valparaiso University
Valparaiso, IN 46383
(219) 464-5289
www.valpo.edu/nursing/

PhD Program in Indiana

Indiana University
Office of Educational Services
IU School of Nursing
1111 Middle Drive, NU 122
Indianapolis, IN 46202
(317) 274-2806
http://nursing.iupui.edu

Additional Resources

For a publicized listing of programs in the U.S., contact:

American Association of Colleges of Nursing
One Dupont Circle
Suite 530
Washington, DC 20036-1120
(202) 463-6930
www.aacn.nche.edu

Appendix 0.03. Graduate Programs of Nursing in Indiana

Programs in Indiana Offering the Master's Degree in Nursing

UNIVERSITY/ CONTACT	AREA OF GRADUATE STUDY	UNIVERSITY/ CONTACT	AREA OF GRADUATE STUDY
Ball State University Director, School of Nursing 2000 University Avenue Muncie, IN 47306 (765) 285-5771 www.bsu.edu/nursing	• Adult/Family Nurse Practitioner (Post-master's certificate available) • Nursing Educator (Post-master's certificate available) • Nursing Leadership • Nursing Service Administration	**Indiana State University** Dean, School of Nursing 749 Chestnut Terre Haute, IN 47809 (812) 237-2316 www.indstate.edu/nurs/	• Adult Health Nursing • Community Health Nursing • Family Nurse Practitioner Program (Students also select a functional role specialization of nurse educator or administrator-manger)
Indiana University Associate Dean, Graduate Program IU School of Nursing Office of Educational Services 1111 Middle Drive, NU 122 Indianapolis, IN 46202-5107 (317) 274-2806 http://nursing.iupui.edu/	• Clinical Nurse Specialist: ◆Adult Health including: Critical/Acute Care Oncology Chronic Illness/ Disability Health Promotion ◆Child/Adolescent Psychiatric/Mental Health Nursing ◆Adult Psychiatric/ Mental Health Nursing ◆Community Health Nursing ◆Pediatric Clinical Nurse Specialist • Nursing Administration • Nurse Practitioner: ◆Acute Care Adult Nurse Practitioner ◆Adult Nurse Practitioner ◆Family Nurse Practitioner ◆Neonatal Nurse Practitioner ◆Pediatric Nurse Practitioner ◆Women's Health Nurse Practitioner **Dual Degree Options with:** • Health Administration (SPEA) • Public Affairs • Public Health • Philanthropy	**Indiana University, Kokomo** Dean of Nursing 2300 South Washington PO Box 9003 Kokomo, IN 46904-9003 (765) 455-9384 http://www.iuk.edu/ ACADEMICS/nursing/	• Community Health

UNIVERSITY/ CONTACT	AREA OF GRADUATE STUDY	UNIVERSITY/ CONTACT	AREA OF GRADUATE STUDY
Indiana University, South Bend Dean of Nursing 1700 Mishawaka Ave. Northside Hall 444 South Bend, IN 46634 (219) 237-4282 www.iusb.edu/nursing	• Adult Clinical Specialist ♦ Critical/Acute Care Oncology ♦ Chronic Illness/ Disability ♦ Health Promotion	**Indiana University-Purdue University Fort Wayne** Chair, School of Nursing 2101 Coliseum Blvd E Fort Wayne, IN 46805 (260) 481-6816 www.ipfw.edu/nursing/	• Nursing Administration • Family Nurse Practitioner • Clinical Nurse Specialist
Indiana Wesleyan University Chair, Division of Nursing Indiana Wesleyan University 4201 South Washington Marion, IN 46953 (765) 677-2266 www.indwes.edu/APS/disted/ DPI/MBS	• Community Health Nurse Practitioner • Primary Care Nurse Practitioner **Dual Major Option:** • Community Health/ Primary Care Nursing **Post-Master's Degree Certification Program in:** • Adult, Family, Primary Care, Gerontologic Nurse Practitioner	**Purdue University, West Lafayette** Head, School of Nursing 1337 Johnson Hall of Nursing West Lafayette, IN 47907-1337 (765) 494-4004 www.nursing.purdue.edu/	• Clinical Nurse Specialist • Family Nurse Practitioner
Purdue University-Calumet Head, School of Professional Programs 2200 169th Street Hammond, IN 46323-2094 (219) 989-2814 http://nursing.calumet.purdue.edu	• Clinical Nurse Specialist • Family Nurse Practitioner	**University of St. Francis** Chairperson, Dept of Nursing 2701 Spring Street Fort Wayne, IN 46808 (260) 434-3240 www.sf.edu/nursing	• Family Nurse Practitioner • Nursing in Health Systems
University of Indianapolis Coordinator, MSN Program School of Nursing 1400 East Hanna Avenue Indianapolis, IN 46227 (317) 788-3206 http://nursing.uindy.edu/	• Family Nurse Practitioner • Nursing Administration • Gerontological Nurse Practitioner • Nursing Education • Midwifery **Dual Degree Option:** • Master of Science in Nursing/Master of Business Administration	**University of Southern Indiana** Program Director, Graduate Nursing 8600 University Boulevard Evansville, IN 47712 (812) 465-1154 www.usi.edu	• Family Nurse Practitioner • Clinical Nurse Specialist • Acute Care Nurse Practitioner • Nursing Management and Leadership • Nursing Education
Valparaiso University Dean, College of Nursing Valparaiso, IN 46383 (219) 464-5289 www.valpo.edu	• Advanced Professional Nursing with concentration in: ♦ Adult Health ♦ Women's and Children's Health • Post-master's: ♦ Family Nurse Practitioner		

Appendix 0.04. LPN-RN Mobility Guide

9302 North Meridian Street
Suite 365
Indianapolis, Indiana 46260
317-574-1325
Fax 317-573-0875
info@nursing2000inc.org
www.nursing2000inc.org

LPN-RN Mobility Guide

August 2002 | a resource for the LPN exploring educational mobility

Assets You Bring
- Nursing education on which to build
- Motivation for personal and professional growth
- Personal and professional experience to apply in interactions with patients and families

Benefits to You
- Personal and professional advancement leading to more responsibility and accountability
- Choice of employment opportunities anywhere in the U.S.
- Increased opportunities for collaboration with nursing and other healthcare professionals
- Expanded clinical knowledge
- Stronger communication skills in interactions with patients, families, and colleagues
- Improved critical thinking skills

Support Systems
- Nursing colleagues, fellow students, faculty, advisors, and family
- Flexible scheduling to accommodate working RNs
- Potential tuition assistance from employer—talk with your human resource department

Selecting Your Educational Mobility Program
1. Make a career plan with goals and timelines.
2. Identify the schools of nursing that offer RN mobility programs that fit your needs.
3. Make an appointment with an academic advisor; have a copy of transcript to discuss what course work will apply.
4. Determine cost – include tuition, books and fees, travel expenses, child care, reduced work, etc.
5. Explore financial assistance options (including tuition reimbursement from your employer).
6. Integrate class schedule with work/personal life.
7. Submit application; if prior degree is from same university, determine if you need to re-apply.

Admission requirements
- High school diploma or Graduate Equivalency Exam (GED)
- Transcript(s) from all colleges or universities previously attended
- Copy of LPN license
- Other requirements, such as grade point average, required by each school

Support systems

- Nursing faculty, academic advisors, and peers in the classroom
- Tutorial assistance in a variety of subjects, including English, math, and the sciences, is usually available
- Sessions on test-taking, time management, and study skills are often offered
- Can take classes at own pace – whether one, two, three, or more courses each semester
- Tuition assistance or reimbursement available through your employer

Length of program

- Determined by each school, based on total number of credit hours required
- Depends on whether you are a part-time or full-time student
- Classroom = 1 credit for 1 hour of content per week
- Clinical = 1 credit hour for 3 hours of clinical contact per week
- Seminar/lab = 1 credit for 2/3 hours of content per week
- Associate degree (two-year) and bachelor degree (four-year) options are available

ASN Degree Option (usual equivalent – 60/64 credit hours)

Clinical focus – ASN programs prepare graduates who are competent to serve in entry-level nursing positions and qualified to provide direct care to patients and families with health needs in a variety of care settings.

Classroom focus – Colleges require courses in communication, writing skills, humanities, social sciences, physical sciences, and behavioral sciences.

BSN Degree Option (usual equivalent – 120/124 credit hours)

Clinical focus – BSN programs prepare graduates to provide direct nursing care to patients, families, and groups in a variety of settings that span the continuum of care, including content in leadership, community health and research.

Classroom focus – Colleges require courses in communication, humanities, social sciences, physical sciences, and behavioral sciences. The emphasis is on communication, health education, community health, leadership, and research.

General Considerations

- Graduates of both programs are eligible to take state board examination and, upon successful completion, be licensed as a registered nurse (RN).
- BSN graduates have increased opportunities for career advancement and managerial/leadership roles. They have completed course requirements to enter graduate programs (MSN or PhD degree).
- ASN graduates have a variety of career opportunities. They have also completed basic course requirements for entering an RN-BSN or, in some cases, RN-MSN completion program.

Programs in Indiana Offering LPN-ASN Option

Indiana University Northwest, Gary
Dean, Division of Nursing
3400 Broadway
Gary, IN 46408
1-888-YOUR-IUN
www.iun.edu/nurse

Indiana University – Columbus
LPN to ASN Coordinator
Indiana University/Purdue University
   Columbus
4601 Central Ave
Columbus, IN 47203
(812) 348-7250
http://www.columbus.iupui.edu/
   program/nursing/

Indiana University, Kokomo
Dean of Nursing
2300 South Washington
PO Box 9003
Kokomo, IN 46904-9003
(765) 455-9384
www.iuk.edu/academics/nursing

Indiana University – Purdue University
Fort Wayne/Parkview Nursing Program
Chairperson, School of Nursing
2101 Coliseum Blvd. East
Fort Wayne, IN 46805
(260) 481-6816
www.ipfw.edu/nursing

Ivy Tech State College
ASN Program Chair
1440 East 35th Avenue
Gary, IN 46409
(219) 981-1111 ext. 282

Ivy Tech State College
ASN Program Chair
1538 West Sample St.
South Bend, IN 46619
(219) 289-7001 ext. 269
www.ivytech.edu

Ivy Tech State College
ASN Program Director
3101 S Creasy Lane
PO Box 6299
Lafayette, IN 47903
(765) 772-9192
http://www.laf.ivy.tec.in.us/degree_
   programs/health/nursing.htm

Ivy Tech State College
ASN Program Chair
1 West 26th
PO Box 1763
Indianapolis, IN 46208
(317) 927-7177
http://www.ivytech.edu

Ivy Tech State College
ASN Program Chair
2325 Chester Boulevard
Richmond, IN 47374
(765) 983-3210 or (765) 966-2656
http://www.ivytech.edu/richmond/
   programs/asn.html

Ivy Tech State College
ASN Program Chair
3116 Canterbury Court
Bloomington, IN 47401
(812) 332-1559
http://168.91.42.5/ivytech/asn/GenInfo.htm

Ivy Tech State College
ASN Program Chair
Highway 62 and Ivy Tech Drive
Madison, IN 47250
(812) 265-2580
http://www.ivytech.edu/madison

Ivy Tech State College
ASN Program Chair
3501 First Avenue
Evansville, IN 47710
(812) 429-1496
http://www.ivytech.edu/evansville

Programs in Indiana Offering LPN-ASN Option – continued

Ivy Tech State College
ASN Program Chair
8204 Highway 311
Sellersburg, IN 47172
(812) 246-3301
http://www.ivytech.edu/sellersburg/
    Degrees/Nursing.html

Ivy Tech State College
ASN Program Director
4301 South Crown Road
Muncie, IN 47302
http://www.ivytech.edu/Muncie

Marian College
Prof & Chair, Dept. of Nursing
3200 Cold Spring Road
Indianapolis, IN 46222
1-800-772-7264 or 317-955-6130
www.marian.edu/departmentsandmajors/
    nursing.html

University of Indianapolis
Dean, School of Nursing
1400 E. Hanna Avenue
Indianapolis, IN 46227
1-800-232-8634 http://nursing.uindy.edu

University of St. Francis
Chairperson, Department of Nursing
University of St. Francis
2701 Spring Street
Fort Wayne, IN 46808
1-800-729-4732
www.sf.edu/nursing

Programs in Indiana Offering Advanced Placement Options

Anderson University
Chairperson, Dept. of Nursing
Anderson, IN 46012
(765) 641-4380
www.anderson.edu

Ball State University
Director, School of Nursing
2000 University Avenue
Muncie, IN 47306
(765) 285-5571
www.bsu.edu/nursing

Bethel College
Dean of Nursing
1001 West McKinley Avenue
Mishawaka, IN 46545
(219) 237-2316
www.bethel-in.edu/acadb/undgps/nursing/

Indiana State University
Dean, School of Nursing
749 Chestnut
Terre Haute, IN 47809
(812) 237-2316
www.indstate.edu/nurs

Indiana University Purdue University, Indianapolis
4601 Central Ave
Columbus, IN 47203
(812) 348-7250
http://nursing.iupui.edu/ (Course offered
    from the IUPUI-Columbus campus)

Indiana University, Kokomo
Dean of Nursing
2300 South Washington
PO Box 9003
Kokomo, IN 46904-9003 (765) 455-9384
www.iuk.edu/academics/nursing

Programs in Indiana Offering Advanced Placement Options

Indiana University Northwest, Gary
Dean, Division of Nursing
Indiana University Northwest
3400 Broadway
Gary, IN 46408
1-888-YOUR-IUN
http://www.iun.edu/~nurse/

**Indiana University – Purdue University
Fort Wayne/Parkview Nursing Program**
Chairperson, School of Nursing
2101 Coliseum Blvd. East
Fort Wayne, IN 46805
(260) 481-6816
www.ipfw.edu/nursing

Ivy Tech State College
1 West 26th
PO Box 1763
Indianapolis, IN 46208
(317) 927-7177
www.ivytech.edu

Marian College
Chair, Department of Nursing
3200 Cold Spring Road
Indianapolis, IN 46222
1-800-772-7264 or 317-955-6130
www.marian.edu/departmentsandmajors/
   bsn.html

Purdue University, Calumet Campus
Head, Department of Nursing
Dean, Schools of Professional Programs
Purdue University Calumet Campus
Gyte Annex Room X138
2200 169th Street
Hammond, IN 46323-2094
(219) 989-2814
www.calumet.purdue.edu/public/nursing/

Purdue University, West Lafayette
Head, School of Nursing
Associate Dean of Pharmacy, Nursing
   & Health Sciences
1337 Johnson Hall of Nursing
West Lafayette, IN 47907-1337
(765) 494-4004
www.nursing.purdue.edu/

Purdue University, North Central
Chairperson
Purdue University North Central
1401 South US 421
Westville, IN 46391-9528
(219) 872-0527
www.purduenc.edu/nu/

St. Elizabeth Hospital
Director, School of Nursing
St. Elizabeth Hospital
1508 Tipecanoe Street
Lafayette, IN 47904
www.ste.org/newson/

University of Indianapolis
Dean, School of Nursing
1400 E Hanna Avenue
Indianapolis, IN 46227
1-800-232-8634
http://nursing.uindy.edu

Vincennes University
Chairperson, Department of Nursing
Vincennes, IN 47591
(812) 888-4406
www.vinu.edu

† A Not-For-Profit Organization Committed to Promoting Careers in Registered Nursing through Counseling, Education, and Public Presentations

Appendix 0.05. Content List of Materials to Take to Health Career Fairs

Materials to Take to Health Career Fairs

1. "A Career in Registered Nursing" handout
2. "Specialties in the Career of Registered Nursing" handout
3. List of schools of nursing in Indiana—undergraduate programs
4. Resource list of nursing organizations
5. Volunteer opportunities in affiliated hospitals
6. Financial aid resource
7. RN mobility guide
8. Graduate programs of nursing in Indiana
9. LPN mobility guide

Appendix P. Materials Relevant to Career and Educational Counseling

Chapter 6

Career Advancement Programs
Career and Educational Counseling

P.01   Budget Estimation of Career and Educational Counseling

P.02   List of Career and Educational Counseling Materials and Web site

Appendix P.01. Budget Estimation of Career and Educational Counseling (per year – design, reformatting, updating cost factored in individual programs)

Career and Educational Counseling

Career material handouts:

"A Career in Registered Nursing"	$250.00
"A Career in Registered Nursing" for middle school audience	62.50
Financial Assistance	230.00
Schools of Nursing in Indiana	182.50
Specialties in the Career of Registered Nursing	150.00
Post Registered Nursing – Certification Guide	575.00
Nursing Resource Organization List	62.50
RN Educational Mobility Guide	190.00
LPN-RN Mobility Guide	190.00
Advanced Nursing Practice Resource List	62.50
Web site development and maintenance	1,080.00
Advertisement/listing in yellow pages of telephone directory	588.00
	$3,623.00

Include in general program budget:
- postage for mailings

Appendix P.02. List of Career and Educational Counseling Materials and Web site

List of Career and Educational Counseling Materials and Web site

Career Counseling

1. "A Career in Registered Nursing" handout

2. "Specialties in the Career of Registered Nursing" handout

3. List of schools of nursing in Indiana – undergraduate programs

4. Resource list of nursing organizations

5. Volunteer opportunities in affiliated hospitals

6. Financial aid resource

Educational Mobility Counseling

1. LPN-RN mobility guide

2. RN mobility guide

3. Graduate programs of nursing in Indiana

Web site

www.nursing2000inc.org

Appendix Q. Materials Relevant to Re-Entry into Nursing Seminar

Chapter 6

Career Advancement Programs
Re-Entry into Nursing Seminar
"Spotlight on Re-Entry: A Program for Inactive Registered Nurses"

Appendix Q.01. Budget Estimation of Re-Entry into Nursing Seminar (n = 50 Attendees)

Re-Entry into Nursing Seminar

Announcement flyer to target audiences (i.e., libraries, hospital newsletters)	$200.00
Newspaper advertisement and Web site	800.00
Facility rental fee (i.e., library)	50.00
Letter of invitation to RNs who have expressed interest × 100	200.00
Folder for materials @ $1.50 × 50	75.00
Career materials in folder × 50	100.00
Promotional item for attendees × 50	100.00
Thank you gifts for volunteers/presenters × 10	50.00
Thank you letters for volunteers/presenters	10.00
Survey development and distribution post-one year	180.00
Refreshments	50.00
	$1,815.00 per seminar

Include in general program budget:
- mileage incurred to conduct the seminar
- audiovisual development (slides, CD ROM, video, etc.)
- postage for mailings

Appendix Q.02. Promotional Flyer

Spotlight on Re-Entry:
A Program for Inactive Registered Nurses

Nursing 2000 is pleased to present an informational seminar for registered nurses who have not practiced for five or more years and are interested in returning to work.

Seminar Program:

- The Changing Healthcare Environment
- Roles and Responsibilities of RNs
- RN Refresher Course Opportunities
- Shared Experiences from Returning RNs
- Accessing Opportunities for Employment

Date and Location:

- Date
- Time
- Location

The seminar is free, but registration is required. To register, contact Nursing 2000 by phone at (317) _____, by fax (317) _____, or by e-mail _____.

Sponsored by Nursing 2000, a not-for-profit organization committed to promoting careers in registered nursing.

PROMOTE   EDUCATE   ADVANCE

Appendix Q.03. Letter of Invitation to Inactive Registered Nurses

Date

Name
Address
City, State, Zip Code

Dear <Name>:

Nursing 2000 would like to invite you to attend "Spotlight on Re-Entry: A Program for Inactive Registered Nurses." This informational seminar will be directed at RNs who have not clinically practiced for five or more years and are interested in re-entering the workforce. Content will include the changing healthcare environment, roles and responsibilities of registered nurses, and accessing opportunities for employment. Representatives of the current RN refresher programs that are available in the Indianapolis area will present refresher course opportunities. In addition, practicing RNs who completed refresher programs as part of their successful transition back into the workforce will share their experiences.

The seminar is scheduled as follows:

Date	Time	Location

If you are considering returning to clinical practice, we encourage you to attend this informational seminar. There is no fee, but registration is required. To register or to get additional information, please call Nursing 2000 at _____ or e-mail _____. We hope to see you at the seminar!

Sincerely,

_____, BSN, RN
Program Facilitator
Nursing 2000

Appendix Q.04. Seminar Agenda

SPOTLIGHT ON RE-ENTRY:
A Program for Inactive Registered Nurses

Location
Address

Date
Time

Program Agenda

6:00 - 6:05 p.m.   Welcome and Overview
- _____, RN

6:05 - 6:15 p.m.   Nursing's Role in a Changing Healthcare Environment
- _____, RN

6:15 – 6:45 p.m.   Panel of Returning RNs
- _____, RN
- _____, RN
- _____, RN

6:45 - 7:15 p.m.   RN Refresher Course Descriptions and Opportunities
- _____, RN—(Name of Institution)
- _____, RN—(Name of Institution)
- _____, RN—(Name of Institution)

7:15 - 7:30 p.m.   Accessing Opportunities for Employment
- _____, RN—Indiana Association of Healthcare
  Recruiters

7:30 p.m.   Evaluation and Adjournment

Appendix Q.05. Seminar Evaluation Form for "Spotlight on Re-Entry: A Program for Inactive Registered Nurses"

SPOTLIGHT ON RE-ENTRY:
A Program for Inactive Registered Nurses

NURSING 2000

LOCATION

TIME

DATE

E V A L U A T I O N

Thank you for attending "SPOTLIGHT ON RE-ENTRY: A Program for Inactive Registered Nurses." Your assistance in evaluating today's seminar is very much appreciated.

Please rate how well the following objectives and corresponding content were met.
(4 is high and 1 is low)

OBJECTIVES/CONTENT	High = 4		Low = 1	
1. Discuss nursing's role in a changing healthcare environment.	4	3	2	1
2. Interact with RN(s) who have experienced re-entry into nursing practice.	4	3	2	1
3. Define RN refresher course opportunities available in area healthcare agencies.	4	3	2	1

EFFECTIVENESS				
1. The speakers were well informed on the topic.	4	3	2	1
2. The opportunity for learner participation was adequate.	4	3	2	1
3. The content of the seminar was organized in a logical sequence.	4	3	2	1
4. The quality of learning resources (audiovisuals, handouts, etc.) facilitated my learning.	4	3	2	1
5. The information shared in this seminar will be helpful to me in making a decision to re-enter nursing practice.	4	3	2	1

APPLICATION:

1. My purpose in attending this seminar was to:

_____

_____

_____

_____

2. How did you hear about this program?

- Newspaper advertisement
- Hospital newsletter
- Nursing 2000 Web site

- Flyer posted in library
- Referral from whom _____

ADDITIONAL COMMENTS ARE WELCOMED!

Appendix R. Materials Relevant to Advanced Practice Nursing Seminar

Chapter 6

Career Advancement Programs
Advanced Nursing Practice Seminar

R.01   Budget Estimation of Advanced Practice Nursing Seminar

R.02   Promotional Flyer

R.03   Seminar Agenda

R.04   Advanced Practice Resource List

R.05   Evaluation Form for Advanced Practice Nursing Seminar

Appendix R.01. Budget Estimation of Advanced Practice Nursing Seminar

Expenses

Printing Costs

Flyer	$268.00
Advertisement – newspapers (major 800; local 250)	1,050.00
Folders/Handouts/Duplication	624.00

Audiovisual	$200.00

Facility

Room (seating 75-100) classroom and display tables	$200.00

Food

Continental breakfast, refreshment and nourishment break	<u>$600.00</u>

Gratuity

	$2,942.00

Registration Fee

$15 for participants

Exhibitor Fees @ $4.00 each × 4

Include in general program budget:
- mileage incurred to conduct the seminar
- audiovisual development (slides, CD ROM, video, etc.)
- postage for mailings

Appendix R.02. Promotional Flyer

ADVANCED ROLES IN NURSING...
OPPORTUNITIES AND CHALLENGES

Nursing 2000 and the Indiana League for Nursing are pleased to present an informational seminar for registered nurses to facilitate a collegial exchange regarding advanced roles in nursing. The purpose of the seminar is to provide career mobility information and support referral among registered nurses. An overview of advanced roles in nursing and opportunities in evolving healthcare delivery will be provided. Emphasis will be given to differentiating among advanced roles by discussing expectations and responsibilities. Representatives from graduate nursing schools will be available throughout the morning to share information regarding specific programs. Break-out sessions will provide individual contact with nurses in advanced roles.

DATE
Time
Location ◆ Address ◆ Phone

PROGRAM

8:00-8:15 a.m.	**Registration and Continental Breakfast**
8:15-8:30 a.m.	Welcome - _____, RN, EdD
8:30-9:15 a.m.	**Advanced Roles and Opportunities for Nursing - 2000**
	and Beyond - _____, RN, MS
9:15-9:45 a.m.	**Graduate Education Programs and Expectations -** _____, RN, PhD
9:45-10:05 a.m.	**Break and Graduate Nursing School Exhibits**
10:05-11:30 a.m.	**Differentiating Among Advanced Roles in Nursing**
	Panel Presentation:
	_____, RN, DNSc, FAAN, Presenter and Moderator
	_____, RN, CS, ANP, Nurse Practitioner
	_____, RN, MSN, CCRN, Clinical Nurse Specialist
	_____, RN, MSN, CS, Psychiatric/Mental Health Clinical Nurse Specialist
	_____, RN, PhD, Community Health Nurse (Advanced)
	_____, RN, MSN, Nurse Manager/Administrator
11:30-11:35 a.m.	**Written Evaluation**
	Graduate Nursing School Exhibits remain available throughout Break-out Sessions
11:35-12:00 noon	**Interactive Break-out Sessions**
	Choose one of the following: Nurse Practitioner; Clinical Nurse Specialist; Nurse Anesthetist; Nurse Midwife; Nurse Administrator; Nurse Educator; Community Health Nurse (Advanced); Doctorally Prepared Roles and Research

Detach and return

Reservations are required and seating is limited. A $20 registration fee is required to partially defray the cost of the seminar. Seminar faculty volunteer their time. To register, please fill out this form, include a check made payable to Nursing 2000, and mail by **(Date)** to: Nursing 2000
9302 North Meridian Street, Suite 365
Indianapolis, Indiana 46260-1820

Name _____

Name of Business/Organization _____

Position _____

Home Address _____

City _____ State _____ Zip _____

Home Phone ( ) _____ Business Phone ( ) _____

This written reservation confirms your attendance. Thank you for enrolling!

I plan to attend the following break-out session:

☐ Nurse Practitioner   ☐ Nurse Educator
☐ Clinical Specialist   ☐ Community Health
☐ Nurse Anesthetist   Nurse (Advanced)
☐ Nurse Midwife   ☐ Doctorally Prepared
☐ Nurse Administrator   Roles and Research
                         ☐ Undecided

LEARNING OBJECTIVES: Following this seminar, the participant should be able to:

1. Analyze the impact of the evolving healthcare environment on career opportunities in nursing.
2. Discuss advanced roles in nursing practice—nurse practitioner, clinical nurse specialist, nurse anesthetist, nurse midwife, nurse administrator, nurse educator, community health nurse (advanced).
3. Differentiate role expectations and responsibilities among advanced roles in nursing.
4. Discuss educational and nursing practice requirements to enter an advanced nursing practice program in Indiana.

PLANNING COMMITTEE:

_____, RN, MS   _____, RN, MSN, ANP

_____, RN, PhD   _____, RN, MSN

_____, RN, DNSc, FAAN   _____, RN, EdD

_____, RN, MSN, MS   _____, RN, BSN

_____, RN, MSN

LOCATION: Address

DIRECTIONS:

MAP

Nursing 2000 is a not-for-profit organization committed to promoting careers in registered nursing through counseling, education, and public presentations. Questions? Call Nursing 2000 at (317) _____.

ADVANCED ROLES IN NURSING...
OPPORTUNITIES AND CHALLENGES

Co-sponsored by Nursing 2000 and Indiana League for Nursing

Appendix R.03. Seminar Agenda

ADVANCED ROLES IN NURSING...
OPPORTUNITIES AND CHALLENGES

Nursing 2000 and the Indiana League for Nursing are pleased to present an informational seminar for registered nurses to facilitate a collegial exchange regarding advanced roles in nursing. The purpose of the seminar is to provide career mobility information and support referral among registered nurses. An overview of advanced roles in nursing and opportunities in evolving healthcare delivery will be provided. Emphasis will be given to differentiating among advanced roles by discussing expectations and responsibilities. Representatives from graduate nursing schools will be available throughout the morning to share information regarding specific programs. Break-out sessions will provide individual contact with nurses in advanced roles.

DATE
Time
Location ♦ Address ♦ Phone

PROGRAM/AGENDA

8:00-8:15 a.m.	**Registration and Continental Breakfast**
8:15-8:30 a.m.	**Welcome**
	_____, RN, EdD
8:30-9:15 a.m.	**Advanced Roles and Opportunities for Nursing - 2000 and Beyond**
	_____, RN, MS
9:15-9:45 a.m.	**Graduate Education Programs and Expectations**
	_____, RN, PhD
9:45-10:05 a.m.	**Break and Graduate Nursing School Exhibits**
10:05-11:30 a.m.	**Differentiating Among Advanced Roles in Nursing**
	Panel Presentation
	_____, RN, DNSc, FAAN, Presenter and Moderator
	_____, RN, CS, ANP, Nurse Practitioner
	_____, RN, MSN, CCRN, Clinical Nurse Specialist
	_____, RN, MSN, CS, Psychiatric/Mental Health Clinical Nurse Specialist
	_____, RN, PhD, Community Health Nurse (Advanced)
	_____, RN, MSN, Nurse Manager/Administrator
11:30-11:35 a.m.	**Written Evaluation**
	Graduate Nursing School Exhibits remain available throughout Break-out Sessions.
11:35-12:00 noon	**Interactive Break-out Sessions**
	Choose one of the following: Nurse Practitioner; Clinical Nurse Specialist; Nurse Anesthetist; Nurse Midwife; Nurse Administrator; Nurse Educator; Community Health Nurse (Advanced); Doctorally Prepared Roles and Research.

(next page)

LEARNING OBJECTIVE

Following this seminar, the participant should be able to:

1. Analyze the impact of the evolving healthcare environment on career opportunities in nursing.

2. Discuss advanced roles in nursing practice—nurse practitioner, clinical nurse specialist, nurse anesthetist, nurse midwife, nurse administrator, nurse educator, community health nurse (advanced).

3. Differentiate role expectations and responsibilities among advanced roles in nursing.

4. Discuss educational and nursing practice requirements to enter an advanced nursing practice program in Indiana.

PLANNING COMMITTEE

_____, RN, MS	_____, RN, MSN, MS	_____, RN, EdD
_____, RN, PhD	_____, RN, MSN	_____, RN, MSN
_____, RN, DNSc, FAAN	_____, RN, MSN, ANP	_____, RN, BSN

Appendix R.04. Advanced Practice Resource List

State and National Nursing Organizations
Advanced Practice Nursing Resource List

Note: The following is a <u>partial list</u> of national and state organizations that may be contacted to receive information about advanced practice nursing roles. The complete Directory of Nursing Organizations is available in the *American Journal of Nursing* and on Internet access http://www.nursingcenter.com

American Academy of Nurse Practitioners
National Administrative Office
PO Box 12846
Austin, TX 78711
512/442-4262
Fax: 512/442-6469
E-mail: admin@aanp.org

American Assembly for Men in Nursing
11 Cornell Road
Latham, NY 12110-1499
518/782-9400 Ext. 346
E-mail: aamn@aamn.org

American Association of Colleges of Nursing
One Dupont Circle NW, Suite 530
Washington, DC 20036-1120
202/463-6930
Fax: 202/785-8320
E-mail: webmaster@aacn.nche.edu
www.aacn.org

American Association of Nurse Anesthetists
222 South Prospect Avenue
Park Ridge, IL 60068-4001
847/692-7050
www.aana.com

American Board of Nursing Specialties
600 Maryland Avenue SW
Suite 100 West
Washington, DC 20024-2571
202/554-2054
Fax: 202/651-7004

American College of Nurse-Midwives
818 Connecticut Avenue NW, Suite 900
Washington, DC 20006
202/728-9860
Fax: 202/728-9897

American College of Nurse Practitioners
1111 19th Street NW, Suite 404
Washington, DC 20036
202/659-2190
Fax: 202/659-2191
E-mail: acnp@acnpweb.org

American Nurses Association
600 Maryland Avenue SW, Suite 100 West
Washington, DC 20024-2571
1-800-274-4ANA (4262)
Fax: 202/737-0575
www.nursingworld.org

American Nurses Credentialing Center
600 Maryland Avenue SW
Suite 100 West
Washington, DC 20024-2571
1-800-284-CERT (2378)
Fax: 202/651-7004
www.nursingcenter.com

American Organization of Nurse Executives
One North Franklin
Chicago, IL 60606
312/422-2800
Fax: 312/422-4503
www.aone.org

Association of Women's Health, Obstetric, and Neonatal Nurses
2000 L Street NW, Suite 740
Washington, DC 20036
1-800-673-8499
Fax: 202/728-0575
www.awhonn.org

Coalition of Advanced Practice Nurses of
Indiana
101 West Ohio Street, #1717
Indianapolis, IN 46204
317/229-3267
Fax: 317/684-3663

Indiana Organization of Nurse Executives
One American Square
PO Box 82063
Indianapolis, IN 46282
317/633-4870
www.aone.org (click Local Groups)

Indiana State Board of Nursing Health
Professions Bureau
402 West Washington Street, Room 041
Indianapolis, IN 46204
317/232-1105
www.state.in.us/

Indiana State Nurses Association
2915 North High School Road
Indianapolis, IN 46224
317/299-4575 Fax: 317/297-3525
www.indiananurses.org

International Society for Psychiatric-
Mental Health Nurses
ISPN National Office
1211 Locust Street
Philadelphia, PA 19107
800/826-2950 Fax: 215/545-8107

The National Alliance of Nurse Practitioners
325 Pennsylvania Avenue SE
Washington, DC 20003-1100
202/675-6350

National Association of Clinical Nurse
Specialists
3969 Green Street
Harrisburg, PA 17110
717/234-6799
www.nacns.org

National Association of Nurse Practitioners in
Reproductive Health
500 Capitol Court NE
Washington, DC 20002
202/408-7025 Fax: 202/408-0902
E-mail: nanprh@nurse.org

National Association of Pediatric Nurse
Associates and Practitioners
1101 Kings Highway North, Suite 206
Cherry Hill, NJ 08034-1912
1-877-662-7627 Fax: 856/667-7187
E-mail: info@napnap.org

National League for Nursing
61 Broadway
New York, NY 10006
1-800-669-1656 www.nln.org

National Organization of Nurse
Practitioner Faculties
1522 K Street NW, #702
Washington, DC 20005
202/289-8044 Fax: 202/289-8046
E-mail: nonpf@nonpf.org

Nurse Practitioner Associates for
Continuing Education
5 Militia Drive
Lexington, MA 02173
617/861-0270 Fax: 617/861-0279

Nursing 2000
9302 North Meridian Street, Suite 365
Indianapolis, IN 46260-1820
317/574-1325 Fax: 317/573-0875
E-mail: info@nursing2000inc.org
www.nursing2000inc.org

Sigma Theta Tau International
550 West North Street
Indianapolis, IN 46202
317/634-8171 Fax: 317/634-8188
E-mail: stti@stti.iupui.edu
www.nursingsociety.org

Web site Resources
"Expected Competencies of Associate,
Baccalaureate and Advanced Prepared Nurse
Providers" as adopted by the Indiana Deans and
Directors and the Indiana Organization of Nurse
Executives retrieveable at www.nursing2000inc.org

Colleagues in Caring Project
www.aacn.nche.edu

Nurses for a Healthier Tomorrow
www.nursesource.org

Appendix R.05. Evaluation Form for Advanced Practice Nursing Seminar

NURSING 2000

ADVANCED ROLES IN NURSING...
OPPORTUNITIES AND CHALLENGES

DATE

EVALUATION

Thank you for attending "Advanced Roles in Nursing...Opportunities and Challenges." Your assistance in evaluating today's seminar is very much appreciated.

Please rate how well the following objectives and corresponding content were met. (4 is high and 1 is low)

OBJECTIVES/CONTENT	High = 4		Low = 1	
1. Analyze the impact of the evolving healthcare environment on career opportunities in nursing.	4	3	2	1
2. Discuss advanced roles in nursing practice— nurse practitioner, clinical specialist, nurse midwife, nurse anesthetist, nurse administrator, nurse educator, community health nurse (advanced).	4	3	2	1
3. Differentiate role expectations and responsibilities among advanced roles in nursing.	4	3	2	1
4. Discuss educational and nursing practice requirements to enter an advanced nursing practice program in Indiana.	4	3	2	1

EFFECTIVENESS				
1. The speakers were well informed on the topic.	4	3	2	1
2. The speakers' presentation style facilitated my learning.	4	3	2	1
3. The opportunity for learner participation was adequate.	4	3	2	1
4. The content of the conference was organized in a logical sequence.	4	3	2	1
5. The teaching/learning methods were appropriate for the content.	4	3	2	1
6. The quality of learning resources (audiovisuals, handouts, etc.) facilitated my learning.	4	3	2	1

APPLICATION:

1. My purpose in attending this seminar was to:

    ☐ gain information to promote support and referral among registered nurses

    ☐ obtain career mobility information

2. I am interested in pursuing an advanced role in nursing:

    ☐ clinical specialist   ☐ community health nurse (advanced)

    ☐ nurse anesthetist   ☐ nurse administrator

    ☐ nurse midwife   ☐ nurse educator

    ☐ nurse practitioner

3. Today, I am planning to attend one of the following "How to Become..." break-out sessions:

    ☐ clinical specialist   ☐ community health nurse (advanced)

    ☐ nurse anesthetist   ☐ nurse administrator

    ☐ nurse midwife   ☐ nurse educator

    ☐ nurse practitioner

4. Other career information/programs that you would like to see offered in the future:

    _____:

    _____:

    _____:

    _____

COMMENTS: (Specific comments/suggestions, i.e., content, speakers, program are welcomed!)

Appendix S: Current Goals and Strategic Initiatives

Mission: Nursing 2000 promotes and supports careers in registered nursing as a concerted effort to meet future nursing resources.

GOALS	PROGRAM, SERVICE, AND OUTREACH		
	STRATEGIES	IMPLEMENTATION	COMPLETION %
DISSEMINATE INFORMATION ABOUT REGISTERED NURSING AS A DYNAMIC PROFESSION TO THE FOLLOWING GROUPS:	*Implement Phase II of Helene Fuld Trust Grant as Nursing 2000 – North Central as a pilot to promote nursing as a career adapted to a regional area.	January–September 2002	0%
	*Incorporate Nursing 2000–North Central project into Web site.	February 2002	0%
ELEMENTARY SCHOOL AGE MIDDLE SCHOOL AGE HIGH SCHOOL AGE ADULT LEARNERS CAREER MOBILITY NURSES	Offer seminar, "First Look at Nursing as a Career," to the community for traditional students and adult learners. Invite A Day in the Life of a Nurse previous participants and their parents.	February 2002	50%
	• *Incorporate a panel of experts presenting traditional and advanced nursing roles.	October 2002	50%
	• *Target displaced college students and workers and second career individuals.		
	Provide presentations and displays that span elementary, middle and high schools, and community events.	September 2001	30%
	Communicate with parents as a follow-up to A Day in the Life of a Nurse program.	July 2002	50%
	Expand nursing's visibility via library displays.	Ongoing	50%

Goal	Action	Target Date	% Complete
SUPPORT NURSES IN EDUCATIONAL CAREER MOBILITY AND CLINICAL PRACTICE TO ADVANCE NURSING CAREERS.	Facilitate program to support RNs as they "re-enter" nursing – "Spotlight on Re-Entry." *Evaluate effectiveness via three-year cumulative survey.	August 2002	50%
	Communicate BSN, MSN, and advanced role preparation necessary to prepare nurses for future workplace demands.	Ongoing	
IMPACT THE EDUCATION OF NURSES THROUGH COLLABORATION BETWEEN NURSING SERVICE AND EDUCATION.	*Facilitate a Statewide Nursing Workforce Summit to initiate a systematic planning approach to address the demand for registered nurses.	September 2001	20%
	*Participate in the development of an action plan for the Indiana Nursing Workforce Committee.	January 2002	50%
	*Implement RN generic exit survey tool based on retention factors identified at focus meetings.	September 2001	20%
	*Facilitate seminar that supports nurse leaders in management roles.	Fall 2002	0%
	Monitor nursing school enrollments, graduations, and employment opportunities in relation to future resources.	Ongoing	

*New Initiative

Continued

Appendix S: Current Goals and Strategic Initiatives—cont'd

PROGRAM, SERVICE, AND OUTREACH

GOALS	STRATEGIES	IMPLEMENTATION	COMPLETION %
RECRUIT A DIVERSE STUDENT BODY REFLECTIVE OF THE REGIONAL POPULATION.	Link students considering a nursing career to nurse mentors in partnership with Eta Chi Chapter, Chi Eta Phi Sorority, Inc., nursing organization whose membership represents many cultures and diverse backgrounds.	August 2002	30%
	Promote diversity throughout audiovisuals, publications, and presentations of Nursing 2000 and speakers' bureau.	Ongoing	
ATTRACT STUDENTS INTO NURSING WHO HAVE DEMONSTRATED THOSE POTENTIAL ACADEMIC ABILITIES THAT WILL LEAD TO A SUCCESSFUL CAREER IN REGISTERED NURSING.	Offer a second "Day in the Life of a Nurse" shadow experience to selected senior students who attended as sophomores or juniors in high school. Conduct survey post-graduation to assess career decisions.	November 2001 and March 2002	50%
	Expand corporate sponsorship in support of the Nursing 2000 scholarship program to en-list scholarship recipients as ambassadors for nursing.	May 2002	50%
REFLECT A POSITIVE IMAGE OF NURSING TO THE PUBLIC	*Implement Phase I of Helene Fuld Trust Grant to develop guide for use in duplicat-ing Nursing 2000 model in North Central Indiana.	November 2002	30%
	Provide consultation to nursing consortiums interested in the Nursing 2000 model.	As requested	

REFLECT A POSITIVE IMAGE OF NURSING TO THE PUBLIC (continued)		
Participate in RWJ Colleagues in Caring Project as an independently funded site to enhance exchange of nursing career materials, methodologies, and nursing workforce development.	Ongoing	
Strengthen reciprocal links with hospitals, schools of nursing, nursing organizations, and **external** organizations to promote career information on Nursing 2000's Web site.	March 2002	80%
Distribute poster project to middle/high school counselors and media centers to reach student population.	January 2002	50%
Expand statewide event, "Nurses' Celebration Saturday," at The Children's Museum with Indiana nursing organizations, Indiana schools of nursing, and affiliated nursing organizations.	May 2002	20%

*New Initiative

INDEX

Executive director
    of collaborative, 47-48
    and Colleagues in Caring program, 131
    of Nursing 2000, 124, 154
Exit tool, RN, 132

F

Faculty, nursing, 29. *See also* Nursing school
        programs
Fairs
    budget for, 211
    career, 51, 56, 95-98
    community, 85-86, 95-98
    educational, 11
    health, 51, 95-98
    materials for, 210
    public, 138
    school career, 71-74
Financial aid
    information on, 100-101, 232
    resources for, 233-236
    types of, 232-233
Financial management, assessment of, 140
Flexibility, in nursing, 261
Focus group project, 20, 131-132
Folder materials. *See* Packet information
the Forum, of Nursing 2000, Inc., 6, 7
Helene Fuld Health Trust, 135, 141
Full-time equivalents (FTE) scale, 12, 148
Funding
    developing plan for, 41
    fundraising, 140
    grants, 135-136
Future Focus in Nursing (newsletter), 67, 69-71

G

General Accounting Office (GAO), U.S., 25
Geriatric nursing, 257
Gerontology, as nursing specialty, 220
Goals, 1, 8
    assessment of, 139
    of collaborative, 39
    implementation of, 8-9
    of mission, 45
    of Nursing 2000, 147, 320-323
    of Nursing Workforce Summit, 134
Governance, assessment of, 139
Governmental agencies, xvii
Government allocations, 43. *See also* Funding
Grants, 43, 135-136. *See also* Funding
Grossman, D. G., 111
A Guide to Nursing in Indiana, 135
Gushuliak, T., 111

H

Handouts. *See also* Packet, information
    for career counseling, 100-101 (*See also* Packet,
        information)
    for middle school, 237-239
Health and Human Services (HHS), Dept. of, 25
Healthcare, use of term, 2-3
Healthcare agencies, volunteer opportunities with,
        230-231
Health Care Financial Administration, 25
Healthcare system, 10
    external assessment of, 25
    integrated, 160
    internal assessment of, 25-26
    and nursing collaboration, 24
    and promotion of nursing, 11
Health fairs, 51. *See also* Career fairs
    budget for, 285
    community, 85, 95-96
    development of, 97
    materials for, 284, 299
    program implementation for, 98
    volunteers at, 51
High schools
    career fairs at, 72, 73
    newsletter in, 69-71, 118, 163, 206-209
    preparation for nursing in, 214
    Shadow a Nurse program in, 56-66, 88-89, 91-92,
        113, 169-170
    slide presentation for, 195
Home health nursing, 257
Hospitals, xvii
    as clinical setting, 159
    in Nursing 2000, 157
Housing, for Nursing 2000, 45

I

Indiana Association of College Admission Counselor
        Conference, 67
Indiana Association of Healthcare Recruiters, 104
Indiana Association of Homes and Services for the
        Aging, 133
Indiana Health Care Association, 133
Indiana Hospital and Health Association, 133
Indiana League for Nursing, 48
Indiana Organization of Nurse Executives, 48, 133
Indiana State Board of Nursing, 107, 133
Indiana State Nurses Association, 48, 133
Indiana University School of Nursing, 113
Information
    for Adult Learner Career seminar, 262
    for Adult Learner Shadow a Nurse program, 272
    at community presentations, 91
    for "Day in the Life of a Nurse" program, 192

N

O

Occupational health nursing, 257
Oncology nursing, 256
Operating room nursing
  description, 256
  as specialty, 218
Organization, collaborative
  bylaws for, 46-47
  determining leadership of, 39
  financial management for, 53
  funding for, 40
  goals of, 39
  governance of, 40
  incorporation of, 46
  information support services for, 52
  legal assistance for, 52-53
  managing, 47
  marketing of, 53-54
  mission statement of, 38
  technical support for, 52
Organizational Self-Assessment Checklist, 138
Organizations
  non-profit, 143
  professional, 143, 158
Orientation program. *See also* Volunteers
  for volunteer editorial board members, 70
  for volunteers, 50

P

Packet, information
  for Adult Learner Career seminar, 262
  for Adult Learner Shadow a Nurse program, 272
  at community presentations, 91
  for "Day in the Life of a Nurse" program, 192
  for Nursing Now seminar, 277
  for Re-entry into Nursing seminar, 104
Patient confidentiality, in "A Day in the Life of a Nurse" program, 189. *See also* Confidentiality statement
Patient education, 197
Patients, settings for, 161
Patron reception committee, for scholarship benefit, 78
Pediatric nursing
  description, 255
  as specialty, 219
Photograph release form, 209
Pilot project, assessment of, 141-143
Planning
  assessment of, 141
  for funding, 41
  long-range, 41-42
Polls, nurses in, 34, 188

Population demographics. *See also* Market forces
  aging population, 161
  and nursing recruitment, 33
Post-conference, in Shadow a Nurse program, 60
Poster project, Nursing 2000's, 103, 131
PowerPoint
  for classroom presentations, 66
  using, 86
Practice, nursing
  "essence" of, 26
  internal assessment of, 27-28
Preceptors, in Shadow a Nurse program, 59-60
Press release, for Shadow a Nurse program, 60
Professional organizations
  and Nursing 2000, 143, 158
  resource list for, 228-229
Program logic model, 20-21
Programming, timetable for, 14, 15t-16t
Programs. *See also specific programs*
  assessment of, 139
  cost of, 149
Promotional flyers, 250
  for Advanced Practice Nursing seminar, 312-313
  for Nursing Now seminar, 275
  for Re-Entry into Nursing seminar, 305
Psychiatric care, as nursing specialty, 219
Public fairs, 138. *See also* Fairs
Public health/community nursing, 257
Publicity
  for community programs, 90-91
  promotional flyers, 250, 275, 305, 312-313
  for scholarship benefit, 78
Public library displays, 85
  budget for, 282
  materials for, 281
  planning log for, 283
Public relations, for Shadow a Nurse program, 60
Public trust, for nursing, 34

Q

Quality of work life, 131

R

Recruitment, nursing
  and "baby boomers," 34
  changes in, 27
Re-Entry into Nursing seminar, 99, 104-105, 307
  budget for, 304
  evaluation form for, 308-309
  letter of invitation to, 306
  materials for, 105, 303
  promotional flyer for, 305
Registered nurse anesthetists, 200, 222, 259

Other Books Available from
Sigma Theta Tau International

📖 *The Adventurous Years: Leaders in Action 1973-1999,* Henderson, 1998.

📖 *As We See Ourselves: Jewish Women in Nursing,* Benson, 2001.

📖 *Cadet Nurse Stories: The Call for and Response of Women During World War II,* Perry and Robinson, 2001.

📖 *Collaboration for the Promotion of Nursing,* Briggs, Merk and Mitchell, 2003.

📖 *The Communication of Caring in Nursing,* Knowlden, 1998.

📖 *Creating Responsive Solutions to Healthcare Change,* McCullough, 2001.

📖 *Gerontological Nursing Issues for the 21st Century,* Gueldner and Poon, 1999.

📖 *The HeART of Nursing: Expressions of Creative Art in Nursing,* Wendler, 2002.

📖 *Immigrant Women and Their Health: An Olive Paper,* Ibrahim Meleis, Lipson, Muecke and Smith, 1998.

📖 *The Language of Nursing Theory and Metatheory,* King and Fawcett, 1997.

📖 *Making a Difference: Stories from the Point of Care,* Hudacek, 2000.

📖 *The Neuman Systems Model and Nursing Education: Teaching Strategies and Outcomes,* Lowry, 1998.

📖 *Nurses' Moral Practice: Investing and Discounting Self,* Kelly, 2000.

📖 *Nursing and Philanthropy: An Energizing Metaphor for the 21st Century,* McBride, 2000.

📖 *The Roy Adaptation Model-Based Research: 25 Years of Contributions to Nursing Science,* Boston Based Adaptation Research in Nursing Society, 1999.

📖 *Stories of Family Caregiving: Reconsideration of Theory, Literature, and Life*, Poirier and Ayres, 2002.

📖 *Virginia Avenel Henderson: Signature for Nursing,* Hermann, 1997.

**Call toll-free 1.888.634.7575 (U.S and Canada) or
+800.634.7575.1 (International), or visit our Web site at
www.nursingsociety.org/publications for more information.**